POEMS FOR ASSEMBLIES

POEMS

FOR

ASSEMBLIES

Chosen by

T. G. DAFFERN

Headmaster-Warden, South Hunsley Secondary School

BASIL BLACKWELL · OXFORD

First published in 1963

Printed in Great Britain for BASIL BLACKWELL & MOTT, LTD.
by A. R. MOWBRAY & Co. LIMITED in the City of Oxford
and bound at the KEMP HALL BINDERY

Let there be singing and the strings of singing,
Let there be ease and light and captivation,
A lure of sound and not a slow dark stumble,
A lure of thought, and not rebuff in thinking,
A jewel of thought to set in God's high altar,
A banner of wit to fly on Wisdom's steeple,
A hammer of flame to plague the soul's abasement.
Let there be light till all the stars seem snowing.

Counsels to a Young Poet
HERBERT PALMER

Then read from the treasured volume
The poem of thy choice,
And add to the rhyme of the poet
The beauty of thy voice.

HENRY WADSWORTH LONGFELLOW

INTRODUCTION

THIS collection of verses is the result of many years of close search for poems suitable for reading to assembled schools. It is offered in the hope that it will lighten the task of those who prefer to plan their own services but have difficulty in sparing the time to find suitable verses.

Verses chosen for this purpose should fulfil certain requirements. They should fall tunefully on the ear, holding the attention of the hearers by their music, and also giving pleasure to the reader. Their message must be clear. This does not mean that they must be entirely understood by all, for with a wide range of age, intelligence and temperament, one would be restricted to great simplicity if this were made a requirement. Finally they must be relevant to the experience of the listeners . . . concerned with a simple philosophy that can be accepted, relate to the pageant of life around or to the intimacies of school or home, or be a comment on national or international affairs. Above all there must be found in many of them an expression of that praise and thanksgiving which is an essential part of worship.

Apart from the use of verse in the actual school service there is a place for the reading of verse to the assembled school, just as there is for the playing of fine music. Children enjoy sharing together poems read for their beauty or as an expression of sheer fun. Such readings, usually of greater length, are better separated entirely from the service, that is—read immediately before the dismissal of the gathering. The public reading of them by children, staff or head-teacher in the dignified surroundings of the school assembly leads to poetry gaining a status in the eyes of sceptical youth, which can have a considerable influence on the appreciation of poetry in the form-room.

The collection includes many poems which have been chosen to illumine those opportune moments that occur so frequently in school . . . to emphasize the calm after a storm, to express in words the feelings engendered by a glorious spring morning, to sympathize with one another over the dreariness of prolonged rain, to comment on the first snow of winter, to chide gently those of bad habits, to provide a parting smile for Friday evening. Such poems are difficult to find at the moment which requires them, and discoveries must be treasured.

Most of the poems are given in their entirety. Some, such as Blake's 'Auguries of Innocence', lend themselves to a choice of extract. Others have verses which some might prefer to omit in their readings. Such verses have been included if they are essential to the full comprehension of the poem. They will enable the reader to absorb its spirit, and, when reading aloud, to pass it on by his own more complete understanding, even if he omits those verses which may be thought undesirable. Some of the shorter poems of more difficult meaning might be given an immediate second reading. Some are more effectively read without any introduction, whilst others have a greater impact if the title is given at the end. Children will enjoy hearing their favourites on many occasions, rejoicing in the satisfaction of recognition . . . extending to the poem the same pleasure that is derived from hearing a familiar piece of music. Thorough understanding by the reader is essential. Children, staff and head-teacher, all should act as readers, for the interest given by variety holds the attention. Usually the effect is greater if the introduction is made by the leader, and then a reader being responsible for the verses only.

In the course of their school life many children are encouraged to build up and decorate their own anthologies; some produce very beautiful books in the course of four or five years. If this is the custom of the school it will soon be found that requests will be made to borrow the source of the reading so that the poem most recently read might be copied. Others will be glad to re-read it or to discuss it with a friend. For these reasons there should be a corner of the school where each day a copy of the book can be left open at the appropriate page.

Brief captions have been added to many of the poems to indicate their subject matter when it is not clear from the title. Biographical notes of authors have been provided where a knowledge of the poet's background helps the appreciation of the poem. In these notes any known facts regarding individual poems have been included. The extensive index provided will, it is hoped, ease the task of selection.

ACKNOWLEDGEMENTS

The author and publisher wish to thank those listed below for their kind permission to reproduce copyright material. Every endeavour has been made to trace the owners of copyright. Should a copyright poem be included without acknowledgement, the author and publisher would welcome any help to trace the owners of such copyright.

ROBERT ARMSTRONG and *The Poetry Review* for 'Prayer of the Breton Fisherman' and 'The Gauntlet'.

THE SOCIETY OF AUTHORS and Jonathan Cape Ltd. for 'Loveliest of Trees' from *Collected Poems of A. E. Housman*.

THE SOCIETY OF AUTHORS and the Literary Trustees of Walter de la Mare for 'Hi', 'Done For!' and 'Then as Now' by Walter de la Mare.

MRS. GEORGE BAMBRIDGE and Macmillan & Co. for 'The Thousandth Man' from *Rewards and Fairies* by Rudyard Kipling.

MRS. E. S. BARING-GOULD and J. Curwen & Sons for 'The Olive Tree' by Sabine Baring-Gould.

ERNEST BENN LTD. for 'The Piper' by Seumas O'Sullivan.

JOHN BETJEMAN and John Murray Ltd. for 'Christmas' from *Collected Poems*.

CICELY BINYON and The Society of Authors for 'For the Fallen' and 'O Summer Sun' by Laurence Binyon.

SHEILA BLANCHARD for 'Manifold'.

EDMUND BLUNDEN and A. D. Peters for 'Forefathers' from *Poems, 1914–1950*.

MRS. FRANCIS BRETT YOUNG and David Higham Associates Ltd. for 'February' by Francis Brett Young.

ALFRED J. BROWN for 'Easter Birds'.

THE CLARENDON PRESS for 'Laus Deo', 'January' and 'Spring' from *The Shorter Poems of Robert Bridges*; and for 'St. Francis' Song' by Jessie Pope.

ELIZABETH COATSWORTH for 'On a Night of Snow'.

PADRAIC COLUM and The Oxford University Press for 'An Old Woman of the Roads' from *The Wild Earth and Other Poems*.

ELLA KATE CONE for 'The Common Street' by Helen Gray Cone.

DR. T. P. CONWELL-EVANS for 'Prayer for Donkeys', 'In the Temple', 'Time' and 'All Night the Waves' from *Poems of Eva Gore-Booth*, published by Longmans, Green & Co.

COUNTRY LIFE for 'A Sealess World' by Joan Campbell.

THE CRESSET PRESS LTD. for 'London Spring' by Frances Cornford.

SIR MAURICE BOWRA and Macmillan & Co. for 'The Coach of Time' by Alexander Pushkin from *A Second Book of Russian Verse*.

MACMILLAN & CO. for 'Rest' by Margaret L. Woods.

REV. J. MAGEE and *The Teachers' World* for 'High Flight' by J. G. Magee.

DR. JOHN MASEFIELD, O.M., and The Society of Authors for 'Laugh and be Merry', 'Little lower than the Angels', 'Roadways', 'The Will', and an extract from *On England*.

METHUEN & CO. for 'For Any Boy' by G. W. Young.

JOAQUIN MILLER and Routledge & Kegan Paul Ltd. for 'For those who fail'.

MISS STURGE MOORE and Macmillan & Co. for 'Beautiful Meals' by Thomas Sturge Moore.

THE MOTHERS' UNION JOURNAL for 'A Thanksgiving' by J.D.

THOMAS MOULT and *The Poetry Review* for 'Refugees'.

ALFRED NOYES and William Blackwood & Sons Ltd. for 'February Fill-dyke' and 'Snow'.

THE OXFORD UNIVERSITY PRESS for 'Father, we praise Thee' by Percy Dearmer, reprinted from the *B.B.C. Hymn Book*; for 'Winter Creeps' by Percy Dearmer from *Songs of Praise* (enlarged edition); for 'Fame is a Food' and 'July' from *The Poems of Austin Dobson*.

MRS. A. G. PAIN for 'For the Strength of His Body' by Godfrey S. Pain.

HERBERT PALMER for 'Let there be singing' from *Counsels to a Young Poet* and Rupert Hart-Davis for 'Prayer for Rain' and 'Lord of All'.

SIEGFRIED SASSOON and Faber & Faber Ltd. for 'To My Son' from *The Collected Poems of Siegfried Sassoon*.

MRS. STEPHENS and Macmillan & Co. for 'Blue Stars and Gold', 'Danny Murphy', 'Hesperus', 'Donnybrook', 'Little Things that run and quail' and 'This Way to Winter' from *Collected Poems* by James Stephens.

MRS. HELEN THOMAS for 'Digging' by Edward Thomas.

HARRY WAINE and The Northumberland Press Ltd. for 'Those Older Men' and 'The Balanced Mind'.

ELLA WHEELER WILCOX and A. C. Black & Co. Ltd. for 'Solitude' and 'Let me to-day do something' from *The Collected Poems of Ella Wheeler Wilcox*.

KENNEDY WILLIAMSON for 'They Work who Dream'.

MRS. W. B. YEATS and Macmillan & Co. for 'The Lake Isle of Innisfree' from *Collected Poems of W. B. Yeats*.

MRS. A. MONRO and Duckworth & Co. for 'In the Fields' and 'Old Shepherd's Prayer' by Charlotte Mew.

EDWIN MUIR and Faber & Faber Ltd. for 'The Way' from *The Labyrinth, 1949*.

CONTENTS

PAGE

GENERAL INTRODUCTION ix

PART I—GOD'S WORLD

PRAISE AND THANKSGIVING 2
PRAYER 11
THE SON OF GOD 18
GOD AND MAN 24
THE LORD THE CREATOR 32
BEAUTY 40
FLOWERS AND TREES 48
ANIMALS 55
BIRDS 65
CREATURES THAT ARE SMALL 70
THE WEATHER 73
THE WATERS 83
THE HEAVENS 90
THE MORNING 96
THE EVENING 104
SPRING 112
SUMMER 117
AUTUMN AND HARVEST 121
WINTER 128
THROUGH THE YEAR 134
THE CHRISTIAN YEAR 146

PART II—MAN'S WORLD

PAGE

MAN-MAKING 156
THE WHOLE MAN 161
THE VIRTUES 166
OUR FELLOW MEN 172
FRIENDS 184
LOVE OF HOME 190
THE TOWN 199
THE COUNTRYSIDE 205
OUR NATIVE LAND 212
BETWEEN NATIONS 216
THE AGES OF MAN 221
CHILDHOOD 226
YOUTH 231
WISDOM AND LEARNING . . . 238
OUR DAILY WORK 242
CRAFTSMANSHIP 252
SERVICE 258
ENDEAVOUR 264
PIONEERS 271
CHANCES AND CHANGES . . . 273
GAIETY AND PLEASURE . . . 278
OLD AGE 287
CONTENTMENT 297
CONCLUDING VERSES 306
NOTES ON AUTHORS 308
INDEX OF FIRST LINES . . . 319
INDEX OF SUBJECTS 328

PART I

GOD'S WORLD

I was glad when they said unto me,
Let us go into the house of the Lord.

Psalm CXXII. 1

We took sweet counsel together,
And walked unto the house of God in company.

Psalm LV. 14

And many people shall go and say,
Come ye, and let us go up to the mountain of the Lord
And he will teach us of his ways,
And we will walk in his paths.   *Isaiah* II. 3

Exalt ye the Lord our God,
And worship at his footstool;
For he is holy.   *Psalm* XCIX. 5

Give unto the Lord the glory due unto his name;
Worship the Lord in the beauty of holiness.

1 *Chronicles* XVI. 29

Sing unto the Lord;
For he hath done excellent things:
This is known in all the earth.   *Isaiah* XII. 5

O come, let us sing unto the Lord:
Let us make a joyful noise to the rock of our salvation.

Psalm XCV. 1

1

PRAISE AND THANKSGIVING

1. Verses: On Praise
2. Verses: On Grace and Thanksgiving
3. Miracles . . . . *Walt Whitman*
4. Lovely Things . . . . *H. M. Sarson*
5. Song of Health . . . . *F. W. Harvey*
6. 'For faith and works and gentle charity'
   John Oxenham
7. 'We thank thee, Lord, for this fair earth'
   Bishop G. E. L. Cotton
8. The Robin's Song . . . *Old English Rhyme*
9. 'We thank you, Lord of Heaven' . *Jan Struther*
10. Grace and Thanksgiving . *Elizabeth Gould*
11. A Thanksgiving . . . . . *J.D.*

I

ON PRAISE

Praise ye the Lord.
Praise ye the name of the Lord;
Praise him, O ye servants of the Lord,
Praise the Lord; for the Lord is good:
Sing praises unto his name; for it is pleasant.

Psalm CXXXV. 1, 3

Bless God, praise him, and magnify him,
And praise him for the things which he hath done unto
　　you in the sight of all that live.

Tobit XII. 6

I will praise thee, O Lord my God, with all my heart:
And I will glorify thy name for evermore.

Psalm LXXXVI. 12

2

I will bless the Lord at all times:
His praise shall continually be in my mouth.
O magnify the Lord with me,
    And let us exalt his name together.

Psalm XXXIV. 1, 3

It is good to praise God,
    And exalt his name,
    And honourably to show forth the works of God;
Therefore be not slack to praise him.

Tobit XII. 6

Oh that men would praise the Lord for his goodness,
And for his wonderful works to the children of men!

Psalm CVII. 21

The Lord is King! Lift up thy voice,
O earth, and all the heavens, rejoice;
From world to world the joy shall ring,
'The Lord omnipotent is King!'

J. Conder

Praise ye and bless ye the Lord,
And give thanks unto Him,
And serve Him with great humility.

*Canticle of the Sun
St. Francis*

O Most High Almighty Good Lord God,
To Thee belong praise, glory, honour and all blessing.

*Canticle of the Sun
St. Francis*

Blessing, and glory, and wisdom, and thanksgiving,
And honour, and power, and might,
Be unto our God for ever and ever.
Amen.

Revelation VII. 12

3

ON GRACE AND THANKSGIVING

Every good gift and every perfect gift is from above,
And cometh down from the Father of lights.

St. James I. 17

Enter into his gates with thanksgiving,
And into his courts with praise:
Be thankful unto him,
And bless his name. *Psalm* C. 4

I will thank thee, O Lord and King,
And praise thee, O God my Saviour:

Ecclesiasticus LI. 1

O give thanks unto the Lord;
For he is good:
For his mercy endureth for ever. *Psalm* CXVIII. 29

O all ye that worship the Lord,
Bless the God of gods,
Praise him, and give him thanks:
For his mercy endureth for ever. *Three Holy Children* 68

We thank Thee, loving Father,
For all Thy tender care,
For food and clothes and shelter
And all the world so fair. *Anonymous*

Thank you for the world so sweet;
Thank you for the food we eat;
Thank you for the birds that sing;
Thank you, God, for everything.

E. Rutter Leatham

The ordinary things which we enjoy so much but take for granted are, themselves, miracles.

MIRACLES
WALT WHITMAN

Why, who makes much of a miracle?
As to me I know of nothing else but miracles,
Whether I walk in the streets of Manhattan,
Or dart my sight over the roofs of houses towards
    the sky,
Or wade with naked feet along the beach just in the edge
    of the water,
Or stand under trees in the woods,
Or talk by day with anyone I love,
Or sit at table at dinner with the rest,
Or look at strangers riding opposite me in the car,
Or watch honey-bees busy around the hive of a summer
    fore-noon,
Or animals feeding in the fields,
Or birds, or the wonderfulness of insects in the air,
Or the wonderfulness of the sundown, or of stars shining
    so quiet and bright,
Or the exquisite delicate thin curve of the new moon in
    spring;
These with the rest, one and all, are to me miracles. . . .

Here is thankfulness for the basic gifts . . . food, air, being alive, the company of others.

LOVELY THINGS
H. M. SARSON

Bread is a lovely thing to eat—
God bless the barley and the wheat!

A lovely thing to breathe is air—
God bless the sunshine everywhere!

The earth's a lovely place to know—
God bless the folks that come and go!

Alive's a lovely thing to be—
Giver of life—we say—bless Thee!

A poem of thanks for those gifts which are offered to normal, well-balanced people, but which so many of us may be taking for granted.

SONG OF HEALTH
F. W. HARVEY

For friends to stand beside, for foes to fight,
For devil's work to break, for Wrong and Right,
And will (however hard) to choose between them:
For merry tales, no matter where you glean them:
Songs, stars, delight of birds, and summer roses,
Sunshine, wherein my friend the dog now dozes:

Danger—the zest of life, and Love, the Lord
Of Life and Death: for every open word
Spoken in blame or praise by friend o' mine
To spur me on: for old, good memories,
Keeping in my soul's cellar like good wine:
For Truth that's strong, and Beauty so divine:
For animals, and children, and for trees,
Both wintry-black and blossoming in white:
For homely gardens and for humming bees:
For drink, and dreams, and daisies on the sod,
Plain food, and fire (when it will light)—
                    Thank God.

6

*A thanksgiving for all that makes the world a pleasanter place
in which to live, and especially for companionship.*

'FOR FAITH AND WORKS AND GENTLE CHARITY'

JOHN OXENHAM

For faith and works and gentle charity;
For all that makes for quiet in the world;
For all that lifts man from his common rut;
For all that knits the silken bonds of peace;
For all that lifts the fringes of the night,
And lights the darkened corners of the earth;
For kinship, sonship, friendship, brotherhood
Of man—one Father, one great family,
We thank Thee, Lord.

From 'A Little Te Deum of the Commonplace'

Though precious and lovely may be the things which we can see, more precious is the nature of our actions and the spirit in which we perform them.

'WE THANK THEE, LORD, FOR THIS FAIR EARTH'
BISHOP G. E. L. COTTON

We thank Thee, Lord, for this fair earth,
    The glittering sky, the silver sea;
For all their beauty, all their worth,
    Their light and glory come from thee.

Thanks for the flowers that clothe the ground,
    The trees that wave their arms above,
The hills that gird our dwellings round,
    As thou dost gird thine own with love.

Yet teach us still how far more fair,
    More glorious, Father, in thy sight,
Is one pure deed, one holy prayer,
    One heart that owns thy Spirit's might.

8

A wish for the good of everything and everybody.

THE ROBIN'S SONG
OLD ENGLISH RHYME

God bless the field and bless the furrow,
Stream and branch and rabbit burrow,
Hill and stone and flower and tree,
From Bristol town to Wetherby—
Bless the sun and bless the sleet,
Bless the lane and bless the street,
Bless the night and bless the day,
From Somerset and all the way
To the meadows of Cathay;
Bless the minnow, bless the whale,
Bless the rainbow and the hail,

Bless the nest and bless the leaf,
Bless the righteous and the thief,
Bless the wing and bless the fin,
Bless the air I travel in,
Bless the mill and bless the mouse,
Bless the miller's bricken house,
Bless the earth and bless the sea,
God bless you and God bless me!

9

A 'thank you' for ordinary things.

'WE THANK YOU, LORD OF HEAVEN'
JAN STRUTHER

We thank you, Lord of Heaven,
　For all the joys that greet us,
For all that you have given
　　To help us and delight us
　　　In earth and sky and seas;
The sunlight on the meadows,
　The rainbow's fleeting wonder,
The clouds with cooling shadows,
　　The stars that shine in splendour—
　　　We thank you, Lord, for these.

For swift and gallant horses,
　For lambs in pastures springing,
For dogs with friendly faces,
　　For birds with music thronging
　　　Their chantries in the trees;
For herbs to cool our fever,
　For flowers of field and garden,
For bees among the clover
　　With stolen sweetness laden—
　　　We thank you, Lord, for these.

For homely dwelling-places
　Where childhood's visions linger,
For friends and kindly voices,
　For bread to stay our hunger

And sleep to bring us ease;
For zeal and zest of living,
    For faith and understanding,
For words to tell our loving,
    For hope of peace unending—
        We thank you, Lord, for these.

10

GRACE AND THANKSGIVING
ELIZABETH GOULD

We thank Thee, Lord, for quiet upland lawns,
For misty loveliness of autumn dawns,
For gold and russet of the ripened fruit,
For yet another year's fulfilment, Lord,
    We thank Thee now.

For joy of glowing colour, flash of wings,
We thank Thee, Lord, for all the little things
That make the love and laughter of our days,
For home and happiness and friends, we praise
    And thank Thee now.

11

A particular 'thank you' for the hands that enable labour, skill, travel and homely care to enrich our lives.

A THANKSGIVING
J.D.

For all skilled hands, both delicate and strong—
Doctors' and nurses', soothing in their touch;
Sensitive artist-hands: musicians' hands
Vibrant with beauty: for the hands that guide
Great ships amid great seas: for all brave hands,
Where'er they be, that ply their busy trades
With daily courage: homely mother-hands
Busy with countless differing tasks each day;
For miners' hands that labour for our sakes;
For all hands rough and hard with honest work,
For old hands, frail and lovely, interlaced
With tell-tale wrinkles left by work and age:
For these we thank Thee, Lord.

PRAYER

12. Verses
13. 'But thou, when thou prayest' *St. Matthew* VI. 6–15
14. 'Ask, and it shall be given you' *St. Matthew* VII. 7–12
15. 'What things soever ye desire' *St. Mark* XI. 24–26
16. 'Oft have I seen' . *Henry Wadsworth Longfellow*
17. Prayer . . . . *James Montgomery*
18. Proof . . . . . *Ethel Romig Fuller*
19. 'White captain of my soul, lead on' *Robert Freeman*
20. 'By the faith that the flowers show' *Henry Van Dyke*
21. 'If thou shouldst never see my face again'
  Alfred Lord Tennyson
22. The Olive Tree . . . *Sabine Baring-Gould*

12

VERSES

In every thing by prayer and supplication with thanksgiving let your requests be made known unto God.
Philippians IV. 6

Hearken unto the voice of my cry, my King, and my
  God:
For unto thee will I pray.
My voice shalt thou hear in the morning, O Lord;
In the morning will I direct my prayer unto thee, and
  will look up.
Psalm V. 2, 3

All things, whatsoever ye shall ask in prayer, believing,
  ye shall receive.
St. Matthew XXI. 22

Confess your faults one to another,
And pray one for another, that ye may be healed.
The effectual fervent prayer of a righteous man availeth
    much.

St. James v. 16

Look at the generations of old, and see;
Did ever any trust in the Lord, and was confounded?
Or did any abide in his fear, and was forsaken?
Or whom did he ever despise, that called upon him?

Ecclesiasticus II. 10, 11

Be not afraid to pray—to pray is right,
    Pray, if thou canst, with hope; but ever pray,
    Though hope be weak, or sick with long delay;
Pray in the darkness, if there be no light.

Hartley Coleridge

He prayeth well who loveth well
Both man and bird and beast;
He prayeth best who loveth best
All things both great and small,
For the dear God who loveth us
He made and loveth all.

Samuel Taylor Coleridge

My soul, thou shouldst to thy knees
When daylight draweth to a close,
And let thy Master lift the load
    And grant repose.

Source unknown

READINGS

13

'BUT THOU, WHEN THOU PRAYEST'
$$\text{St. Matthew VI. 6–15}$$
Christ tells His disciples how to pray.

14

'ASK, AND IT SHALL BE GIVEN YOU'
$$\text{St. Matthew VII. 7–12}$$
Christ promises that prayer shall be answered.

15

'WHAT THINGS SOEVER YE DESIRE' St. Mark XI. 24–26

Prayer should be accompanied by the forgiving of those who have given offence.

16

In prayer, anxieties disappear.

'OFT HAVE I SEEN'
HENRY WADSWORTH LONGFELLOW

Oft have I seen at some cathedral door
  A labourer, pausing in the dust and heat,
  Lay down his burden, and with reverent feet
Enter, and cross himself, and on the floor
Kneel to repeat his paternoster o'er;
  Far off the noises of the world retreat;
  The loud vociferations of the street
Become an indistinguishable roar.

So, as I enter here from day to day,
  And leave my burden at this minster gate,
Kneeling in prayer, and not ashamed to pray,
  The tumult of the time disconsolate
To inarticulate murmurs dies away,
  While the eternal ages watch and wait.

From 'Divina Commedia'

Words are not needed for prayer. It is a feeling after God rather than a form of expression to Him.

PRAYER

JAMES MONTGOMERY

Prayer is the soul's sincere desire,
    Uttered or unexpressed;
The motion of a hidden fire,
    That trembles in the breast.

Prayer is the burthen of a sigh;
    The falling of a tear;
The upward glancing of an eye,
    When none but God is near.

Prayer is the simplest form of speech
    That infant lips can try;
Prayer, the sublimest strains that reach
    The Majesty on high.

18

Could not there be a similarity between the way in which our prayers reach God, and the radio? If we can believe in one, why not in the other?

PROOF

ETHEL ROMIG FULLER

If radio's slim fingers can pluck a melody
From night—and toss it over a continent or sea;
If the petalled white notes of a violin
Are blown across the mountains or the city's din;
If songs like crimson roses are culled from thin blue air—
Why should mortals wonder if God hears prayer?

A prayer which particularly asks for help in times of temptation.

'WHITE CAPTAIN OF MY SOUL, LEAD ON'
ROBERT FREEMAN

White Captain of my soul, lead on;
I follow thee, come dark or dawn.
Only vouchsafe three things I crave:
Where terror stalks, help me be brave!
Where righteous ones can scarce endure
The siren call, help me be pure!
Where vows grow dim, and men dare do
What once they scorned, help me be true!

We are advised to leave God to direct our lives and to show the same confidence in Him that plants, animals and birds appear to show.

'BY THE FAITH THAT THE FLOWERS SHOW'
HENRY VAN DYKE

By the faith that the flowers show when they bloom
    unbidden,
By the calm of the river's flow to a goal that is hidden,
By the trust of the tree that clings to its deep foundation,
By the courage of wild birds' wings on the long migration,
(Wonderful secret of peace that abideth in Nature's
    breast!)
Teach me how to confide, and live my life, and rest.

Prayer for oneself and for one's friends can be a way of uniting mankind through God. Here these thoughts are put in the words of the dying King Arthur speaking from his funeral barge to the last of the Knights of the Round Table.

'IF THOU SHOULDST NEVER SEE MY FACE AGAIN'

ALFRED LORD TENNYSON

If thou shouldst never see my face again,
Pray for my soul. More things are wrought by prayer
Than this world dreams of. Wherefore let thy voice
Rise like a fountain for me night and day.
For what are men better than sheep or goats
That nourish a blind life within the brain,
If, knowing God, they lift not hands of prayer
Both for themselves and those who call them friend?
For so the whole round world is every way
Bound by gold chains about the feet of God,

From 'Morte d'Arthur'

22

Here is a simple story illustrating the belief that God knows better than man what is good for the world, and it is better to trust in Him.

THE OLIVE TREE

SABINE BARING-GOULD

Said an ancient hermit, bending
    Half in prayer upon his knee,
'Oil I need for midnight watching,
    I desire an olive tree.'

Then he took a tender sapling,
    Planted it before his cave,
Spread his trembling hands above it,
    As his benison he gave.

But he thought, the rain it needeth,
  That the root may drink and swell:
'God! I pray Thee send Thy showers!'
  So a gentle shower fell.

'Lord! I ask for beams of summer,
  Cherishing this little child.'
Then the dripping clouds divided,
  And the sun looked down and smiled.

'Send it frost to brace its tissues,
  O my God!' the hermit cried.
Then the plant was bright and hoary,
  But at evensong it died.

Went the hermit to a brother
  Sitting in his rocky cell:
'Thou an olive tree possessest;
  How is this, my brother, tell!

'I have planted one, and prayed,
  Now for sunshine, now for rain;
God hath granted each petition,
  Yet my olive tree hath slain!'

Said the other, 'I intrusted
  To its God my little tree;
He who made knew what it needed
  Better than a man like me.

'Laid I on Him no condition,
  Fixed not ways and means; so I
Wonder not my olive thriveth,
  Whilst thy olive tree did die.'

23. Verses
24. 'I am the good shepherd' . . *St. John* x. 11–16
25. 'I am the true vine' . . *St. John* xv. 1–8
26. All our Days . . . . *Anonymous*
27. 'I have a guide' . . . . *T. T. Lynch*
28. 'Christ be with me' . . *Frances Alexander*
29. A Wish . . . . . *M. Savidge*
30. 'For the strength of his body' . *Godfrey S. Pain*
31. In the Temple . . . *Eva Gore-Booth*

23

VERSES

Whatsoever ye do in word or deed,
Do all in the name of the Lord Jesus,
Giving thanks to God and the Father by him.

Colossians III. 17

He shall feed his flock like a shepherd:
He shall gather the lambs with his arm,
    and carry them in his bosom,
And shall gently lead those that are with young.

Isaiah XL. 11

Day by day,
    Dear Lord, of Thee three things I pray:
        To see Thee more clearly,
        Love Thee more dearly,
        Follow Thee more nearly,
            Day by day. *St. Richard of Chichester*

READINGS

24

'I AM THE GOOD SHEPHERD' . St. John x. 11–16

Christ compares Himself to a shepherd caring for His sheep.

25

'I AM THE TRUE VINE' . . St. John xv. 1–8

Christ compares Himself to the vine and His followers to the branches which will bear fruit.

26

ALL OUR DAYS
ANONYMOUS

Lord of the loving heart,
May mine be loving too;
Lord of the gentle hands,
May mine be gentle too;
Lord of the willing feet,
May mine be willing too;
So may I grow more like to Thee
In all I say and do.

27

The example of Christ enables us to follow the path to God regardless of circumstances, good or bad.

'I HAVE A GUIDE'
T. T. LYNCH

I have a Guide, and in His steps
    When travellers have trod,
Whether beneath was flinty rock
    Or yielding grassy sod,
They cared not, but with force unspent,
Unmoved by pain, they onward went,
Unstayed by pleasures, still they bent,
    Their zealous course to God.

A hope that thoughts of Christ may be ever-present to help.

'CHRIST BE WITH ME'
FRANCES ALEXANDER

Christ be with me, Christ within me,
   Christ behind me, Christ before me,
Christ beside me, Christ to win me,
Christ to comfort and restore me,
   Christ in quiet, Christ in danger,
Christ in hearts of all that love me,
Christ in mouth of friend and stranger.

From 'The Breastplate of St. Patrick'

*The writers of the New Testament describe many of the
actions and words of Christ, but omit to tell us of His happiness
and merriment when He was young, gay and carefree.*

A WISH
M. SAVIDGE

They told us how they walked with Him
And blessed and healed and talked with Him
How men and children followed Him
By Tiber's Sea.

Of themselves who broke bread with Him,
How they betrayed and fled from Him,
While thief and soldier turned to Him
Upon a tree.

How women stood and wept for Him
And angels rolled the stone for Him,
Of skies that made a throne, for Him
From Galilee.

I wish that as they wrote of Him
They'd told us how they laughed with Him;
He must have laughed, with heart of Him
So young and free.

30

*God is thanked for the example of Christ . . . for His health,
His sense of fun, His courage, His love and His friendship for
man.*

'FOR THE STRENGTH OF HIS BODY'

GODFREY S. PAIN

For the strength of His body, and the firmness of His
    tread:
For the beauty of His spirit, and the laughter in His eyes:
For the courage of His heart, and the greatness of His
    deeds:
For the depth of His love, and the men it makes anew:
For the strength of His friendship when we dare to trust
    His love:
For the knowledge of His presence at each turn of the
    road,
  We thank Thee, Lord.

'I came to put an end to sacrifices.'—Traditional saying of Christ.

IN THE TEMPLE

EVA GORE-BOOTH

Mary, young but very wise,
Pondered many mysteries.

Likely to her Son she told
How she went in days of old

To the Temple with a song,
Praising God the whole day long,

(Soul that prays and heart that loves),
In her hand a cage of Doves!

Two live pigeons prisoned there,
(Heart of Love and soul of prayer!)

How the old indifferent priest
Sacrificed them at the Feast. . . .

Did she pray in broken words
For the fluttering dying birds?

Soilèd silver, lifeless wings—
God's pity on all helpless things!

Did she stand and weep alone
By the bloodstained altar stone?

Haply even then the Child
Out of His deep wisdom smiled,

Knowing that from God He came,
To lighten every dying flame;

Knowing He Himself would pay
Her debt to the wild birds one day.

II

When Christ, in the Father's name,
Into the bloodstained Temple came,

All the Doves began to sing,
Stretching every prisoned wing.

And He said, 'The Spirit of Love
Is as a living, flying dove.'

As once in His babyhood,
Sheep and oxen round Him stood.

'God made them living souls,' He said. . . .
(Jesus, raise us from the dead.)

Did life stir in caverns dim,
Whilst patient eyes were fixed on Him?

None so merciful as He, . . .
He sets them free, He sets them free.

He opens every cage of pain,
He will not have the oxen slain.

The sheep as His own people seem,
He leads them to the living stream.

The birds have heard the story now,
It shrills and thrills from bough to bough.

Lord, of Thee the skylark sings,
Give Life, more Life, unto all things.

GOD AND MAN

32. Verses

33. 'Teach me, O Lord, the way of thy statutes'
Psalm CXIX. 33–40

34. 'Seek ye the Lord while he may be found'
Isaiah LV. 6–11

35. 'Finally, my brethren, be strong in the Lord'
Ephesians VI. 10–17

36. 'The Lord rewarded me' . *Psalm* XVIII. 20–24

37. 'I will lift up mine eyes unto the hills' *Psalm* CXXI

38. Time . . . . . *Eva Gore-Booth*

39. Each in his own Tongue . . *W. H. Carruth*

40. The Lord of All . . . *Herbert Palmer*

41. Manifold . . . . *Sheila Blanchard*

42. 'O Little Self' . . . *John Masefield*

32

VERSES

The Lord our God is one Lord:
And thou shalt love the Lord thy God with all thine
heart,
And with all thy soul,
And with all thy might. *Deuteronomy* VI. 4, 5

I am persuaded,
That neither death, nor life,
Nor angels, nor principalities, nor powers,
Nor things present, nor things to come,
Nor height, nor depth, nor any other creature,
Shall be able to separate us from the love of God.
Romans VIII. 38, 39

Shew me thy ways, O Lord;
Teach me thy paths.
Lead me in thy truth, and teach me:
For thou art the God of my salvation;
On thee do I wait all the day.

Psalm xxv. 4, 5

Ye shall diligently keep the commandments of the Lord
    your God,
And his testimonies, and his statutes,
Which he hath commanded thee.
And thou shalt do that which is right and good in the
    sight of the Lord.

Deuteronomy vi. 17, 18

My son, be mindful of the Lord our God all thy days,
And let not thy will be set to sin,
Or to transgress his commandments:
Do uprightly all thy life long,
And follow not the ways of unrighteousness.

Tobit iv. 5

Let your heart therefore be perfect with the Lord our
    God,
To walk in his statutes,
And to keep his commandments.

1 *Kings* viii. 61

Bless the Lord, O my soul:
And all that is within me, bless his holy name.
Bless the Lord, O my soul,
And forget not all his benefits.

Psalm ciii. 1, 2

The Lord our God be with us, as he was with our fathers:
Let him not leave us, nor forsake us:

1 *Kings* viii. 57

25

Let us hear the conclusion of the whole matter:
Fear God, and keep his commandments:
For this is the whole duty of man.

Ecclesiastes XII. 13, 14

The earth, O Lord, is full of thy mercy:
Teach me thy statutes.

Psalm CXIX. 64

Dear Lord and Father of mankind,
  Forgive our foolish ways;
Reclothe us in our rightful mind;
In purer lives thy service find,
  In deeper reverence, praise.

John Greenleaf Whittier

Enrich, Lord, heart, mouth, hands in me,
With faith, with hope, with charity:
That I may run, rise, rest with thee.

George Herbert

God's might to direct me,
God's power to protect me,
God's wisdom for learning,
God's eye for discerning,
God's ear for my hearing,
God's word for my clearing.

St. Patrick

READINGS

33

'TEACH ME, O LORD, THE WAY OF THY STATUTES'

Psalm CXIX. 33–40

A promise to follow the path of righteousness once the way is clear.

26

'SEEK YE THE LORD WHILE HE MAY BE FOUND'

Isaiah LV. 6–11

A reminder that forgiveness is offered to all who regret their misdeeds.

'FINALLY, MY BRETHREN, BE STRONG IN THE LORD'

Ephesians VI. 10–17

A description of the whole armour of God.

'THE LORD REWARDED ME' . Psalm XVIII. 20–24

David claims to have been rewarded because he had done that which was right.

'I WILL LIFT UP MINE EYES UNTO THE HILLS' Psalm CXXI

An assurance of God's care for His people.

Here is faith that has hopes of better things.

TIME

EVA GORE-BOOTH

In time the whole of things shall alter,
  And the earth shine as shines the sun,
In time the hangman's hands shall falter,
  In time the gunner shall leave the gun.

In time the hater shall cease from hating,
  In time the judge shall judge no more,
In time the wave of Life is waiting
  To thunder on the Eternal Shore.

In time no man shall kill his brother;
  Of every living thing the friends,
We shall all see God in one another
  Before the day when Time ends.

The scientist is acquainted with the work of God through his deep knowledge of scientific facts and the theories that he can deduce from them. Other men feel His existence through the beauty of ordinary things.

EACH IN HIS OWN TONGUE

W. H. CARRUTH

A fire-mist and a planet,
    A crystal and a cell,
A jelly-fish and a saurian,
    And caves where the cave-men dwell;
Then a sense of law and beauty,
    And a face turned from the clod—
Some call it Evolution,
    And others call it God.

A haze on the far horizon,
    The infinite, tender sky,
The ripe, rich tint of the cornfields,
    And the wild geese sailing high;
And all over upland and lowland
    The charm of the golden rod—
Some of us call it Autumn,
    And others call it God.

Like tides on a crescent sea-beach,
    When the moon is new and thin,
Into our hearts high yearnings
    Come welling and surging in—
Come from the mystic ocean
    Whose rim no foot has trod—
Some of us call it Longing,
    And others call it God.

A picket frozen on duty—
    A mother starved for her brood—
Socrates drinking the hemlock,
    And Jesus on the rood;
And millions who, humble and nameless,
    The straight, hard pathway plod—
Some call it Consecration,
    And others call it God.

40

God is all that is good in us.

THE LORD OF ALL
HERBERT PALMER

Thou comest plainly, Lord of All,
Or strangely, as the chance may be,
In firm uplift or breaking fall,
In scent of flowers or surge of sea,
In wet of rain or scorch of fire,
In cloak of bright or sombre sheen,
In ring of bell or singing wire,
In fruit of sweet or bitter bean.

But what Thou art is always plain,
For Thou art Rapture, Life, and Song,
And Valour in the pit of pain,
And Punishment for grievous wrong;
And Thou art Honour, Truth, and Love,
And Triumph over death and vice,
And Gentleness of lamb or dove,
Bright Mercy, Justice, Sacrifice.

Great power wrongly used can be devastating: so it is necessary for us to take care that a few twisted minds cannot nullify the benefits that it can bring.

MANIFOLD

SHEILA BLANCHARD

Power from the sun
To earth descending,
All that has life
With life befriending;
But sun's rays trapped
In a burning glass
Can make a desert
That none dare pass.

Power by the earth
To mankind given,
Giant machines
By nature driven;
But a faulty part
Or a weakened wire
Can waste the work
In a blaze of fire.

Power from God
The Spirit burning,
Through all his saints
To God returning,
Love, compassion,
Humility,
Teaching the world
True sanity.

From heart to heart
God's power flowing
All that is good
On men bestowing;
But twisted minds
In the human chain
May make at last
A world insane.

42

*Although man has in his small body the ability to understand
all knowledge, he does not use it to give God His proper due.
This poem asks God to give man a sense of appreciation.*

'O LITTLE SELF'

JOHN MASEFIELD

O little self, within whose smallness lies
All that man was, and is, and will become,
Atom unseen that comprehends the skies
And tells the tracks by which the planets roam;
That, without moving, knows the joys of wings,
The tiger's strength, the eagle's secrecy,
And in the hovel can consort with kings,
Or clothe a God with his own mystery.
O with what darkness do we cloak thy light,
What dusty folly gather thee for food,
Thou who alone art knowledge and delight,
The heavenly bread, the beautiful, the good.
O living self, O God, O morning star,
Give us thy light, forgive us what we are.

43. Verses

44. 'The works of the Lord are great'   *Psalm* CXI. 2–4

45. 'Praise the Lord, from the earth'

Psalm CXLVIII. 7–13

46. 'The law the lawyers know about'   *H. D. C. Pepler*

47. 'His praise, ye winds'   .   .   .   *John Milton*

48. St. Francis' Song of the Creatures .   *Jessie Pope*

49. Rest   .   .   .   .   .   *Margaret L. Woods*

50. 'There lives and works a soul in all things'

William Cowper

51. Universal Goodness   .   .   .   *John Clare*

43

VERSES

Seek him that maketh the seven stars and Orion,
And turneth the shadow of death into the morning,
And maketh the day dark with night:
That calleth for the waters of the sea,
And poureth them out upon the face of the earth.
The Lord is his name.

Amos V. 8

For, lo, he that formeth the mountains, and createth
    the wind,
And declareth unto man what is his thought,
That maketh the morning darkness,
And treadeth upon the high places of the earth,
The Lord, the God of hosts, is his name.

Amos IV. 13

By him were all things created, that are in heaven,
    and that are in earth,
Visible and invisible,
Whether they be thrones, or dominions,
Or principalities or powers;
All things were created by him, and for him.

Colossians I. 16

O Lord, how manifold are thy works!
In wisdom hast thou made them all:
The earth is full of thy riches.

Psalm CIV. 24

Who hath measured the waters in the hollow of his hand,
And meted out heaven with the span,
And comprehended the dust of the earth in a measure,
And weighed the mountains in scales, and the hills in a
    balance?
Who hath directed the Spirit of the Lord,
Or being his counsellor hath taught him?

Isaiah XL. 12, 13

All the works of the Lord are good:
And he will give every needful thing in due season.
And therefore praise ye the Lord with the whole heart
    and mouth,
And bless the name of the Lord.

Ecclesiasticus XXXIX. 33, 35

O Lord, thou art my God;
I will exalt thee,
I will praise thy name;
For thou hast done wonderful things.

Isaiah XXV. 1

The Lord is good to all: and his tender mercies are over
all his works.
All thy works shall praise thee, O Lord;
And thy saints shall bless thee.

Psalm CXLV. 9, 10

I will praise thee, O Lord, with my whole heart;
I will shew forth all thy marvellous works.

Psalm IX. 1

One generation passeth away, and another generation
cometh;
But the earth abideth for ever.

Ecclesiastes I. 4

And God saw every thing that he had made, and, behold,
it was very good.

Genesis I. 31

Beneath thy all-directing rod
Both worlds and worms are equal, God.
Thy hand the comet's orbit drew,
And lighted yonder glow-worm too.
Thou didst the dome of heaven build up,
And form yon snowdrop's silver cup.

Sir John Bowring

Talk not of temples, there is one
    Built without hands, to mankind given:
Its lamps are the meridian sun
    And all the stars of heaven,
Its walls are the cerulean sky,
    Its floor the earth so green and fair,
The dome its vast immensity
    All Nature worships there!

David Vedder

God of the granite and the rose,
Soul of the sparrow and the bee,
The mighty tide of being flows
Thro' countless channels, Lord, from Thee.

Elizabeth Doten

READINGS

44

'THE WORKS OF THE LORD ARE GREAT' . Psalm CXI. 2–4

45

'PRAISE THE LORD FROM THE EARTH, YE DRAGONS, AND
ALL DEEPS' . . . . . Psalm CXLVIII. 7–13

The call to all Creation to offer praise.

46

*Often even the most highly trained and learned men do not
understand simple facts about Nature and the human heart.*

'THE LAW THE LAWYERS KNOW ABOUT'

H. D. C. PEPLER

The law the lawyers know about
Is property and land;
But why the leaves are on the trees,
And why the winds disturb the seas,
Why honey is the food of bees,
Why horses have such tender knees,
Why winters come and rivers freeze,
Why Faith is more than what one sees,
And Hope survives the worst disease,
And Charity is more than these,
    They do not understand.

A call to all moving things to praise God according to their individual powers.

'HIS PRAISE, YE WINDS'

JOHN MILTON

His praise, ye Winds, that from four Quarters blow,
Breathe soft or loud; and wave your tops, ye Pines,
With every Plant, in sign of Worship wave.
Fountains and ye that warble, as ye flow,
Melodious murmurs, warbling tune his praise.
Join voices all ye living Souls, ye Birds,
That singing up to Heaven Gate ascend,
Bear on your wings and in your notes his praise;
Ye that in waters glide, and ye that walk
The Earth, and stately tread, or lowly creep;
Witness if I be silent, Morn or Even,
To Hill, or Valley, Fountain, or fresh shade
Made vocal by my Song, and taught his praise.
Hail, universal Lord, be bounteous still
To give us only good; and if the night
Have gathered aught of evil or concealed,
Disperse it, as now light dispels the dark.

Paradise Lost, Book v. 196

48

A thanksgiving for the whole of creation.

ST. FRANCIS' SONG OF THE CREATURES

JESSIE POPE

Great Lord and King of Earth and Sky and Sea,
Who yet can hear a little child like me,
Who gives us everything we ask and more,
These are the things I want to thank You for—

For Brother Sun, whose bright and welcome face
Brings light and colour to each dingy place;
Who, in the golden rays he flashes down,
Reveals the shining glory of Thy crown.

For Sister Moon, whose splendour soft and white
Makes out-of-doors so beautiful at night.
For all the tiny silver stars on high,
A shower of sparkling snowflakes in the sky.

For Brother Wind, who sweeps the clouds away,
And cools my cheeks when I am hot with play.
For all the crisp, inviting open air
That carries life and freshness everywhere.

For Sister Water, precious, sweet and clean,
Who humbly serves a beggar and a queen;
And who, where sea and sliding pebbles meet,
Comes rippling gently round my naked feet.

For Brother Fire, whose light and shadow falls
In merry dances on my nursery walls;
And who, though very powerful and bold,
Will warm my fingers when they ache with cold.

For Mother Earth, so solid, firm and wide,
I could not move or shake her if I tried;
Who bears the forests and the waving grass,
And little flowers that beckon as we pass.

For all kind people, wheresoe'er they live,
Who help each other, suffer and forgive;
And who, with loving reverence, unite
In serving Thee, by trying to do right.

*Just hearing and seeing the small happenings of out-of-doors
in peace and quiet relaxation can give great pleasure.*

REST
MARGARET L. WOODS

To spend the long warm days
Silent beside the silent-stealing streams,
 To see, not gaze,
To hear, not listen, thoughts exchanged for dreams:

 See clouds that slowly pass
Trailing their shadows o'er the far faint down,
 And ripening grass,
While yet the meadows wear their starry crown.

 To hear the breezes sigh
Cool in the silver leaves like falling rain,
 Pause and go by,
Tired wanderers o'er the solitary plain:

 See far from all affright
Shy river creatures play hour after hour,
 And night by night
Low in the West the white moon's folding flower.

 Thus lost to human things,
To blend at last with Nature and to hear
 What song she sings
Low to herself when there is no one near.

50

The beauties of Nature are evidence of the existence of God.

'THERE LIVES AND WORKS A SOUL IN ALL THINGS'
WILLIAM COWPER

There lives and works
A soul in all things, and that soul is God.

The beauties of the wilderness are his,
That make so gay the solitary place
Where no eye sees them. And the fairer forms
That cultivation glories in, are his.
He sets the bright procession on its way,
And marshals all the order of the year;
He marks the bounds which winter may not pass,
And blunts its pointed fury; in its case,
Russet and rude, folds up the tender germ,
Uninjured, with inimitable art;
And, ere one flowery season fades and dies,
Designs the blooming wonders of the next.

The Lord of all, himself through all diffused,
Sustains, and is the life of all that lives.
Nature is but a name for an effect
Whose cause is God.
From 'The Winter Walk at Noon'

51

*A great lover of the countryside finds in the presence and
quietness of ordinary things a feeling of the companionship of
God which is a source of comfort.*

UNIVERSAL GOODNESS
JOHN CLARE

I look on nature less with critic's eyes
Than with that feeling every scene supplies,
Feeling of reverence that warms and clings
Around the heart while viewing pleasing things;
And heath and pastures, hedgerow-stunted trees,
Are more than Alps with all its hills to me;
The bramble for a bower, the old mole-hill
For seat, delights me, wander where I will;
I feel a presence of delight and fear,
Of love and majesty far off and near;
Go where I will, its absence cannot be,
And solitude and God are one to me;
A presence that one's gloomiest cares caress
And fills up every place to guard and bless.

BEAUTY

52. Verses
53. Lines . . . . . *Ralph Hodgson*
54. In the Fields . . . . *Charlotte Mew*
55. 'A Thing of Beauty' . . . *John Keats*
56. Memory . . . *Thomas Bailey Aldrich*
57. 'These I have loved' . . . *Rupert Brooke*
58. Pied Beauty . . *Gerard Manley Hopkins*
59. Gossamer . . . . *Eleanor Farjeon*
60. Apple Blossoms . . . *Helen Adams Parker*
61. Beautiful Meals . . . *T. Sturge Moore*
62. The Blind Man . . . *Douglas Gibson*

52

VERSES

He hath made every thing beautiful in his time.
Ecclesiastes III. 11

Whatsoever things are true,
Whatsoever things are honest,
Whatsoever things are just,
Whatsoever things are pure,
Whatsoever things are lovely,
Whatsoever things are of good report;
If there be any virtue,
And if there be any praise,
Think on these things.
Philippians IV. 8

To see a World in a grain of sand,
And a Heaven in a wild flower,
Hold Infinity in the palm of your hand,
And Eternity in an hour.

William Blake

Beauty remains, but we are transitory,
Ten thousand years from now will fall the dew,
And high in heaven still hang that arch of blue;
The rose will still repeat its perfect story.

Charles Hanson Towne

Beauty—what is it? A perfume without name:
A sudden hush where clamour was before:
Across the darkness a faint ghost of flame:
A far sail seen from a deserted shore.

Arthur D. Ficke

53

There is beauty somewhere in all things, though, perhaps, not immediately obvious; and this links the very humblest with heaven.

LINES

RALPH HODGSON

No pitted toad behind a stone
    But hoards some secret grace;
The meanest slug with midnight gone
    Has left a silver trace.

No dullest eye to beauty blind,
    Uplifted to the beast,
But prove some kin with angel kind,
    Though lowliest and least.

The earth seems so beautiful at times that it is difficult to believe that greater beauty is possible.

IN THE FIELDS
CHARLOTTE MEW

Lord, when I look at lovely things which pass,
  Under old trees the shadows of young leaves
Dancing to please the wind along the grass,
  Or the gold stillness of the August sun on the August
    sheaves;
Can I believe there is a heavenlier world than this?
  And if there is
Will the strange heart of any everlasting thing
  Bring me these dreams that take my breath away?
They come at evening with the home-flying rooks and
    the scent of hay,
Over the fields. They come in Spring.

The everlasting pleasure given by beautiful things helps us to endure the unpleasant parts of life.

'A THING OF BEAUTY'
JOHN KEATS

A thing of beauty is a joy for ever:
Its loveliness increases; it will never
Pass into nothingness; but still will keep
A bower quiet for us, and a sleep
Full of sweet dreams, and health, and quiet breathing.
Therefore, on every morrow, are we wreathing
A flowery band to bind us to the earth,
Spite of despondence, of the inhuman dearth
Of noble natures, of the gloomy days,
Of all the unhealthy and o'er-darkened ways
Made for our searching: yes, in spite of all,

Some shape of beauty moves away the pall
From our dark spirits. Such the sun, the moon,
Trees old and young, sprouting a shady boon
For simple sheep; and such are daffodils
With the green world they live in; and clear rills
That for themselves a cooling covert make
'Gainst the hot season; the mid-forest brake,
Rich with a sprinkling of fair musk-rose blooms.

56

*It is easier for us to forget great national events than to forget
those things whose beauty has caused us pleasure.*

MEMORY

THOMAS BAILEY ALDRICH

My mind lets go a thousand things,
Like dates of wars and deaths of kings,
And yet recalls the very hour—
'Twas noon by yonder village tower,
And on the last blue noon in May—
The wind came briskly up this way,
Crisping the brook beside the road;
Then, pausing here, set down its load
Of pine-scents, and shook listlessly
Two petals from that wild-rose tree.

Here is a list of ordinary things which please our senses through their beauty.

'THESE I HAVE LOVED'
RUPERT BROOKE

These I have loved:
  White plates and cups, clean-gleaming,
Ringed with blue lines; and feathery, faery dust;
Wet roofs, beneath the lamp-light; the strong crusts
Of friendly bread; and many-tasting food;
Rainbows; and the blue bitter smoke of wood;
And radiant raindrops couching in cool flowers;
And flowers themselves, that sway through sunny hours,
Dreaming of moths that drink them under the moon;
Then, the cool kindliness of sheets, that soon
Smooth away trouble; and the rough male kiss
Of blankets; grainy wood; live hair that is
Shining and free; blue-massing clouds; the keen
Unpassioned beauty of a great machine;
The benison of hot water; furs to touch;
The good smell of old clothes; and others such—
The comfortable smell of friendly fingers,
Hair's fragrance, and the musty reek that lingers
About dead leaves and last year's ferns. . . .

58

An offering of praise for contrasting colours and ideas.

PIED BEAUTY
GERARD MANLEY HOPKINS

Glory be to God for dappled things—
  For skies of couple-colour as a brinded cow;
  For rose-moles all in stipple upon trout that swim;

Fresh-firecoal chestnut-falls; finches' wings;
   Landscape plotted and pieced—fold, fallow, and
      plough;
     And all trades, their gear and tackle and trim.
All things counter, original, spare, strange;
   Whatever is fickle, freckled (who knows how?)
    With swift, slow; sweet, sour; adazzle, dim;
He fathers-forth whose beauty is past change:
   Praise him.

59

A spider's web is a finer piece of craftsmanship than any of those of the world's most skilful workers.

GOSSAMER

ELEANOR FARJEON

To-day I broke a lovelier thing
Than the most precious piece of Ming,
Tore a design of airier grace
Than any scrap of Mechlin lace,
Pulled down a pile more marvellous
Than Gothic monks have left for us,
Destroyed a craft more exquisite
Than any silver-worker's bit
Of ancient art; no fine-blown glass
That which I shattered could surpass,
Cellini would have given his ears
Could he, by labouring for years,
Have been by curious toil delivered
Of what to-day at dawn I shivered.

Artist! had you not hung before
The opening of my garden-door
Your masterpiece stretched taut on air,
That silver web would still be there.

APPLE BLOSSOMS

HELEN ADAMS PARKER

Is there anything in Spring so fair
As apple blossoms falling through the air?

When from a hill there comes a sudden breeze
That blows freshly through all the orchard trees.

The petals drop in clouds of pink and white,
Noiseless like snow and shining in the light,

Making beautiful an old stone wall,
Scattering a rich fragrance as they fall.

There is nothing I know of to compare
With apple blossoms falling through the air.

Approval of a beautifully laid table.

BEAUTIFUL MEALS

THOMAS STURGE MOORE

How nice it is to eat!
All creatures love it so,
That they who first did spread,
Ere breaking bread,
A cloth like level snow,
Were right, I know.

And they were wise and sweet
Who, glad that meats taste good,
Used speech in an arch style,
And oft would smile
To raise the cheerful mood,
While at their food.

And those who first, so neat,
Placed fork and knife quite straight,

The glass on the right hand;
And all, as planned,
Each day set round the plate—
Be their praise great!

For then, their hearts being light,
They plucked hedge-posies bright—
Flowers who, their scent being sweet,
Give nose and eye a treat:
'Twas they, my heart can tell,
Not eating fast but well,
Who wove the spell
Which finds me every day,
And makes each meal-time gay;
I know 'twas they.

62

*Has a blind man some gift which is a recompense for the loss
of all the experiences of beauty that sight can give?*

THE BLIND MAN

DOUGLAS GIBSON

Out of the house I saunter into sun
And through my body feel the sensuous light
Steal like a lover. Down the street goes one
Condemned to live his days in endless night;
His white stick tapping, tapping out the hours
Of unseen beauty—how can he forgive
The limpid sunlight and the burning flowers
That need the loving of the eyes to live?

They say that men whose eyes are closed to light
Have other senses, wonderful and rare—
But oh! the beauty of a swallow's flight,
Of poplars swaying in the evening air!
But what dark thought is tapping in my mind
(The blossom falls around like summer snow)
Tormenting me with hints that I am blind
To some great secret that all blind men know?

47

63. Verses
64. 'Blessed is the man' . . . *Psalm* I. 1–3
65. 'Behold, the Assyrian was a cedar in Lebanon'
Ezekiel XXXI. 3–9
66. 'The carpenter stretcheth out his rule'
Isaiah XLIV. 13–16
67. 'Flower in the crannied wall' . *Alfred Lord Tennyson*
68. First Snowdrop . . . . *B. R. Gibbs*
69. A Field Flower . . . *James Montgomery*
70. 'Much can they praise the trees' . *Edmund Spenser*
71. Tree . . . . . . *Teresa Hooley*
72. Of Trees . . . . . *Pamela Tennant*
73. A London Plane Tree . . . *Amy Levy*

63

VERSES

God said,
Let the earth bring forth grass,
The herb yielding seed,
And the fruit tree yielding fruit after his kind, whose seed
is in itself, upon the earth:
And it was so.

Genesis I. 11

As the earth bringeth forth her bud,
And as the garden causeth the things that are sown in it
to spring forth;
So the Lord God will cause righteousness and praise to
spring forth before all the nations.

Isaiah LXI. 11

Consider the lilies of the field, how they grow;
They toil not, neither do they spin:
And yet I say unto you, that even Solomon in all his
glory was not arrayed like one of these.

St. Matthew VI. 28, 29

Praised be my Lord for our sister the Earth, the which
   doth sustain us and keep us and bringeth forth
   divers fruits—and flowers of many colours and grass.

> *Canticle of the Sun*
> *St. Francis*

Were I, O God, in churchless lands remaining,
   Far from all voice of teachers or divines,
My soul would find, in flowers of thy ordaining,
   Priests, sermons, shrines!   *Horace Smith*

Blessed is the man that trusteth in the Lord, and whose
   hope the Lord is.
For he shall be as a tree planted by the waters,
And that spreadeth out her roots by the river,
And shall not see when heat cometh,
But her leaf shall be green;
And shall not be careful in the year of drought,
Neither shall cease from yielding fruit.

> *Jeremiah* XVII. 7, 8

READINGS

64

'BLESSED IS THE MAN THAT WALKETH NOT' Psalm I. 1–3
The righteous man is compared to a flourishing tree.

65

'BEHOLD, THE ASSYRIAN WAS A CEDAR IN LEBANON'
Ezekiel XXXI. 3–9
A great nation is compared to a mighty tree.

66

'THE CARPENTER STRETCHETH OUT HIS RULE'
Isaiah XLIV. 13–16
A description of the usefulness of timber to man.

If we could only understand the working of a small flower we should understand the meaning of God and why we exist.

'FLOWER IN THE CRANNIED WALL'
ALFRED LORD TENNYSON

Flower in the crannied wall,
I pluck you out of the crannies,
I hold you here, root and all, in my hand,
Little flower—but if I could understand
What you are, root and all, and all in all,
I should know what God and man is.

The snowdrop is praised for its early courage and the promise that it brings.

FIRST SNOWDROP
B. R. GIBBS

Snow-waxen point of life, untimely come
  While still unready earth is iron-dead,
When finger-tips on tree and hedge are numb,
  And crystalled is the holly overhead,
Your cloak of powdered green is thin and small
  To shield you from these tentacles of snow,
There is no comfort in the driven squall,
  No tenderness about you as you grow;
Warm in the blankets of the earth you lay,
  But you have dared to thrust aside the night
And tilt your chalk-soft spear against the day,
  While still his armour glitters, winter-white;
Yet, foolish snowdrop, for the hope you bring
These eyes have never seen a lovelier thing.

*An appreciation of the cheering sight of a daisy flower, to be
found at all seasons, in all weathers, in the most unlikely places.*

A FIELD FLOWER
On finding a daisy in bloom on Christmas Day.

JAMES MONTGOMERY

There is a flower, a little flower,
With silver crest and golden eye,
That welcomes every changing hour,
And weathers every sky.

.   .   .   .

It smiles upon the lap of May,
To sultry August spreads its charms,
Lights pale October on his way,
And twines December's arms.

The purple heath and golden broom
On moory mountains catch the gale,
O'er lawns the lily sheds perfume,
The violet in the vale.

But this bold flowerlet climbs the hill,
Hides in the forest, haunts the glen,
Plays on the margin of the rill,
Peeps round the fox's den.

.   .   .   .

On waste and woodland, rock and plain,
Its humble buds unheeded rise;
The Rose has but a summer reign,
The Daisy never dies.

Lines spoken in praise of trees by one who appreciated their uses.

'MUCH CAN THEY PRAISE THE TREES'
EDMUND SPENSER

Much can they praise the trees so straight and high,
The sailing pine, the cedar proud and tall,
The vine-prop elm, the poplar never dry,
The builder oak, sole king of forests all,
The aspen good for staves, the cypress funeral,
The laurel, meed of mighty conquerors
And poets sage, the fir that weepest still,
The willow worn of forlorn paramours,
The yew obedient to the bender's will,
The birch for shafts, the sallow for the mill,
The myrrh sweet-bleeding in the bitter wound,
The warlike beech, the ash for nothing ill,
The fruitful olive, and the plane tree round,
The carver holme, the maple seldom inward sound.

From 'Faerie Queen', I. I. 8

71

A tribute to the tree for its usefulness.

TREE
TERESA HOOLEY

Days present, days to come, days gone,
Tree is my good companion.

In sleep of helpless infancy
Tree was the cot that cradled me;
On Tree my daily food is spread,
Tree is my chair and Tree my bed.
Fibre of Tree the books I con,
And Tree the shelf they stand upon.
Primeval Tree burns clear and bright
To warm me on a winter night.

I hear, to wind in woods akin,
Tree-music of the violin;
And at the last, when I shall die,
My tired dust in Tree will lie.

72

In praise of the chestnut tree.

OF TREES

PAMELA TENNANT

Winter Willow is ruddy red,
Pollarded in the withy-bed,
Summer Willow is green and grey,
Bending white on a windy day.

Autumn Beech is a stately creature,
Well she made her pact with Nature;
While she casts her russet gown,
She wears her new buds, sharp and brown.

If Birch beside the Broom be found,
Her satin is the more renown'd;
And yet of seasonable trees,
There is a better one than these.

For Chestnut goes to meet the Spring
While Oak and Ash are lingering.
He holds his boughs, when Winter's by,
Like altar candles to the sky.

He makes it his to be the first,
The East may blow, his bonds must burst,
And leader of the budding rout,
In one green stride the Chestnut's out.

A tribute to a tree that has accepted the town.

A LONDON PLANE TREE

AMY LEVY

Green is the plane tree in the square,
  The other trees are brown;
They droop and pine for country air;
  The plane tree loves the town.

Here from my garret-pane I mark
  The plane tree bud and blow,
Shed her recuperative bark,
  And spread her shade below.

Among her branches, in and out,
  The city breezes play;
The dull fog wraps her round about;
  Above, the smoke curls grey.

Others the country take for choice,
  And hold the town in scorn;
But she has listen'd to the voice
  On city breezes borne.

ANIMALS

74. Verses
75. Little Things . . . . *James Stephens*
76. The Tyger . . . . . *William Blake*
77. The Human Attitude . . *Geoffrey Dearmer*
78. A Prayer for Donkeys . . *Eva Gore-Booth*
79. Prayer for Gentleness to all Creatures
John Galsworthy
80. On a Night of Snow . . *Elizabeth Coatsworth*
81. Hi! . . . . . *Walter de la Mare*
82. Done For . . . . *Walter de la Mare*
83. 'A robin redbreast in a cage' . . *William Blake*
84. 'I think I could turn and live with animals'
Walt Whitman
85. The Bells of Heaven . . . *Ralph Hodgson*
86. Master and Man . . . . *Robert Bell*
87. The Church Mouse . . . *Gerald Bullett*

74

VERSES

God said,
Let the earth bring forth the living creature after his
kind,
Cattle, and creeping thing, and beast of the earth after
his kind:
And it was so.
And God made the beast of the earth after his kind,
And cattle after their kind,
And every thing that creepeth upon the earth after his
kind:
And God saw that it was good.

Genesis I. 24, 25

I am God, even thy God.

I will take no bullock out of thy house, or he goats out
    of thy folds.

For every beast of the forest is mine, and the cattle upon
    a thousand hills.

I know all the fowls of the mountains: and the wild
    beasts of the field are mine.

Psalm L. 7, 9–11

A righteous man regardeth the life of his beast: but the
tender mercies of the wicked are cruel.

Proverbs XII. 10

Who believes that equal grace
God extends in every place
Little difference he scans
'Twixt a rabbit's God and Man's.

Bret Harte

75

*A simple poem asking that man shall be forgiven for his many
acts of unkindness towards animals.*

LITTLE THINGS
JAMES STEPHENS

Little things, that run, and quail,
And die, in silence and despair!

Little things, that fight, and fail,
And fall, on sea, and earth, and air!

All trapped and frightened little things,
The mouse, the coney, hear our prayer!

As we forgive those done to us,
The lamb, the linnet, and the hare—

Forgive us all our trespasses,
Little creatures, everywhere.

Who dare make such an awe-inspiring creature as a tiger?

THE TYGER

WILLIAM BLAKE

Tyger! tyger! burning bright
In the forests of the night,
What immortal hand or eye
Could frame thy fearful symmetry?

In what distant deeps or skies
Burnt the fire of thine eyes?
On what wings dare he aspire?
What the hand dare seize the fire?

And what shoulder, and what art,
Could twist the sinews of thy heart?
And when thy heart began to beat,
What dread hand? and what dread feet?

What the hammer? what the chain?
In what furnace was thy brain?
What the anvil? what dread grasp
Dare its deadly terrors clasp?

When the stars threw down their spears,
And watered heaven with their tears,
Did he smile his work to see?
Did he who made the Lamb make thee?

Tyger! tyger! burning bright
In the forests of the night,
What immortal hand or eye
Dare frame thy fearful symmetry?

We laugh at or abuse the peculiarities of animals, but they ignore the silly dress and habits of men and are without our faults. Perhaps a reward is prepared for them.

THE HUMAN ATTITUDE
GEOFFREY DEARMER

When I catch myself agape
Grinning at a Barbary ape,
Or assuming hatred lies
In the hungry tiger's eyes—
When I call the vulture 'vile',
Or 'devilish' the crocodile,
Tigers 'cruel', camels' humps
'Ugly', or the roseate rumps
Which baboons so proudly show
As they swing from bough to bough.
When I call the boar 'malicious',
Kite 'revolting', grizzly 'vicious',
'Quaint' the lithe prehensile nose
The elephant so blithely blows.
When I say of birds, 'The He-male
Warbles to attract the She-male,'
Or 'Brute beasts are soulless',—I
Do not merely simply lie—
I commit a sheer enormity,
Like one jeering at deformity—
I curse the day and bless the night;
In short, I sin against the light.
When I reluctantly arise,
Breakfast, and after exercise,
With dispassionate disdain
And breathlessly approach my train
With my bowler on and spats:
Do the sparrows, dogs and cats
Mock me in amused delight?
No, they don't, but well they might.
Animals have no pretence
Veiling their indifference.

They don't overeat nor whine,
Label all things 'yours' and 'mine'.
Never vulgar, avaricious,
Sentimental, superstitious;
Never snobbish, vengeful, vain.
Pleasure they accept and pain.
Vice is unknown, filth abhorred.
They do good without reward.
When their lives on earth are done,
Happily, I think, they run
Over death's dividing dark;
Where those saints, who ran the Ark—
Noah and Japhet, Ham and Shem—
Probably look after them.

A PRAYER FOR DONKEYS
EVA GORE-BOOTH

The Wise Ass turned from the hay
Where the Child in the manger lay.
Lord, pity the poor Ass, we pray.

Lo, with Joseph old and bent,
And Mary, on the Child intent,
The Wise Ass into Egypt went.

Yet once again, with God his Guide,
And blessed Mary at his side,
The Lord did to his Passion ride.

Thrice did the patient beast and wise
Gaze into those strange secret eyes
That hid Life's uttermost surprise.

Lord, whom the stars and suns obey,
Remember the poor Ass, we pray,
In thy Resurrection Day.

A plea to God to protect all animals, and to influence mankind to do the same.

PRAYER FOR GENTLENESS TO ALL CREATURES
JOHN GALSWORTHY

To all the humble beasts there be,
To all the birds on land and sea,
Great Spirit! sweet protection give,
That free and happy they may live!

And to our hearts the rapture bring
Of love for every living thing;
Make of us all one kin, and bless
Our ways with Christ's own gentleness!

Why cats go out at night in spite of the weather.

ON A NIGHT OF SNOW
ELIZABETH COATSWORTH

Cat, if you go outdoors you must walk in the snow,
You will come back with little white shoes on your feet,
Little white slippers of snow that have heels of sleet.
Stay by the fire, my Cat. Lie still, do not go.
See how the flames are leaping and hissing low,
I will bring you a saucer of milk like a marguerite,
So white and so smooth, so spherical and so sweet—
Stay with me, Cat. Out-doors the wild winds blow.

Outdoors the wild winds blow, Mistress, and dark is the
    night.
Strange voices cry in the trees, intoning strange lore,
And more than cats move, lit by our eyes' green light,
On silent feet where the meadow grasses hang hoar—
Mistress, there are portents abroad of magic and might,
And things that are yet to be done. Open the door!

Two short poems which cast doubt on the 'fun' of shooting.

HI!

WALTER DE LA MARE

Hi! handsome hunting man,
Fire your little gun.
Bang! Now the animal
Is dead and dumb and done.
Nevermore to peep again, creep again, leap again,
Eat or sleep or drink again. Oh, what fun!

82

DONE FOR

WALTER DE LA MARE

Old Ben Bailey
He's been and done
For a small brown bunny
With his long gun.

Glazed are the eyes
That stared so clear,
And no sound stirs
In that hairy ear.

What once was beautiful
Now breathes not,
Bound for Ben Bailey's
Smoking pot.

A tragic list of the various ways in which animals and birds are ill-treated.

'A ROBIN REDBREAST IN A CAGE'

WILLIAM BLAKE

A robin redbreast in a cage
Puts all Heaven in a rage.
A dove-house fill'd with doves and pigeons
Shudders Hell thro' all its regions.
A dog starv'd at his master's gate
Predicts the ruin of the State;
A game-cock clipped and arm'd for fight
Does the rising sun affright;
A horse misus'd upon the road
Calls to Heaven for human blood.
Every wolf's and lion's howl
Raises from Hell a Human soul.
Each outcry of the hunted hare
A fibre from the brain doth tear.
A skylark wounded on the wing,
A cherubim does cease to sing.
He who shall hurt the little wren
Shall never be belov'd by men.
He who the ox to wrath has mov'd
Shall never be by woman lov'd.
The bleat, the bark, bellow, and roar
Are waves that beat on Heaven's shore.

From 'Auguries of Innocence'

Perhaps in many ways animals are superior to men.

'I THINK I COULD TURN AND LIVE WITH ANIMALS'

WALT WHITMAN

I think I could turn and live with animals, they're so
    placid and self-contain'd,
I stand and look at them long and long.

They do not sweat and whine about their condition,
They do not lie awake in the dark and weep for their
    sins,
They do not make me sick discussing their duty to God,
Not one is dissatisfied—not one is demented with the
    mania of owning things,
Not one kneels to another, nor to his kind that lived
    thousands of years ago;
Not one is respectable or unhappy over the whole earth.

85

*What a wonderful thing it would be if everyone combined to
prevent animals from being ill-treated for the amusement of men.*

THE BELLS OF HEAVEN

RALPH HODGSON

'Twould ring the bells of Heaven
The wildest peal for years,
If Parson lost his senses
And people came to theirs,
And he and they together
Knelt down with angry prayers
For tamed and shabby tigers
And dancing dogs and bears,
And wretched, blind pit ponies,
And little hunted hares.

F

Perhaps this poem could have been called 'Who owns which?'

MASTER AND MAN
ROBERT BELL

No, Bob; I will not go a walk—
I am not feeling very fit;
I'd much prefer to sit and talk—
Or sit and read—or simply sit;
It's very hot—there's lots of dust—
I really do not think I can . . .
Well, if you look like that, I must—
Are you my Dog? No; I'm your Man.

A mouse-eye picture of church and congregation.

THE CHURCH MOUSE
GERALD BULLETT

Here in a crumbled corner of the wall,
Well stockt with food from harvest festival,
My twitching ears and delicate small snout
And velvet feet that know their way about
From age to age in snug contentment dwell,
Unseen, and serve my hungry nestlings well.

The slanting light makes patterns on the floor
Of nave and chancel. At my kitchen door
God's acre stretches greenly, should I wish
To take the air and seek a daintier dish.
And week by week the shuddering organ mews,
And all my world is filled with books and shoes.

Sometimes, on Sundays, from my living tomb
I venture out into the vast room,
Smelling my way, as pious as you please,
Among the hassocks and the bended knees,
To join with giants, being filled with food,
In worship of the Beautiful, the Good:
The all-creative Incorporeal Mouse,
Whose radiant odours warm this holy house.

BIRDS

88. Verses

89. 'When God had finished the stars' . *F. W. Harvey*

90. 'For songbirds answering song' . *John Oxenham*

91. Blackbird . . . . *John Drinkwater*

92. Easter Birds . . . *Alfred J. Brown*

93. Birds' Nests . . . . *Anonymous*

94. The Thrush's Nest . . . *John Clare*

88

VERSES

God said,
Let the waters bring forth abundantly the moving creature that hath life,
And fowl that may fly above the earth in the open firmament of heaven.

Genesis I. 20

He sendeth the springs into the valleys, which run among
the hills.
By them shall the fowls of the heaven have their habitation, which sing among the branches.

Psalm CIV. 10, 12

Are not two sparrows sold for a farthing?
And one of them shall not fall on the ground without
your Father.
Fear ye not therefore, ye are of more value than many
sparrows.

St. Matthew X. 29, 31

As a bird that wandereth from her nest,
So is a man that wandereth from his place.

Proverbs XXVII. 8

89

Were ducks created to be an everlasting joke?

'WHEN GOD HAD FINISHED THE STARS'
F. W. HARVEY

When God had finished the stars and whirl of coloured
    suns
He turned His mind from big things to fashion little ones,
Beautiful tiny things (like daisies) He made, and then
He made the comical ones in case the minds of men

        Should stiffen and become
        Dull, humourless, and glum,

And so forgetful of their Maker be
As to take even themselves—quite seriously.
Caterpillars and cats are lively and excellent puns:
All God's jokes are good—even the practical ones!
And as for the duck, I think God must have smiled a bit
Seeing those bright eyes blink on the day He fashioned it.
And He's probably laughing still at the sound that came
    out of its bill!

90

A Thanksgiving for the songs of birds.

'FOR SONGBIRDS ANSWERING SONG'
JOHN OXENHAM

For songbirds answering song on topmost bough;
For myriad twittering of the simpler folk;
For that sweet lark that carols up the sky;
For that low fluting on the summer's night;
For hearts alive to earth's sweet minstrelsies;
We thank Thee, Lord.

        From 'A Little Te Deum of the Commonplace'

91

The song of a bird can cause one to forget the dullness of town surroundings.

BLACKBIRD
JOHN DRINKWATER

He comes on chosen evenings,
My blackbird bountiful, and sings
Over the gardens of the town
Just at the hour the sun goes down.
His flight across the chimneys thick,
By some divine arithmetic,
Comes to his customary stack,
And crouches there his plumage black,
And there he lifts his yellow bill,
Kindled against the sunset, till
These suburbs are like Dymock woods
Where music has her solitudes,
And while he mocks the winter's wrong
Rapt on his pinnacle of song,
Figured above our garden plots
Those are celestial chimney-pots.

92

The song of praise, heard morning and evening from the missel-thrush, can make us rejoice too.

EASTER BIRDS
ALFRED J. BROWN

A missel-thrush, I heard proclaim
At sun-rise, on this Easter morn,
His Matins from a greening thorn.
My own cold heart he set aflame:
So well he praised the Holy Name.

At sunset, from his sanctuary-stall,
His Vespers, with yet louder voice,
He toned: and bade the world rejoice.
And, high above, the sweet and small
Lark choristers renewed the call.

A poem for the student of Nature.

BIRDS' NESTS

ANONYMOUS

The skylark's nest among the grass
   And waving corn is found;
The robin's on a shady bank,
   With oak leaves strewn around.

The wren builds in an ivied thorn,
   Or old and ruined wall;
The mossy nest, so covered in,
   You scarce can see at all.

The martins build their nests of clay,
   In rows beneath the eaves;
While silvery lichens, moss and hair,
   The chaffinch interweaves.

The cuckoo makes no nest at all,
   But through the wood she strays
Until she finds one snug and warm,
   And there her egg she lays.

The sparrow has a nest of hay,
   With feathers warmly lined;
The ring-dove's careless nest of sticks
   On lofty trees we find.

Rooks build together in a wood,
   And often disagree;
The owl will build inside a barn
   Or in a hollow tree.

The blackbird's nest of grass and mud
    In brush and bank is found;
The lapwing's darkly spotted eggs
    Are laid upon the ground.

The magpie's nest is girt with thorns
    In leafless trees or hedge;
The wild duck and the water-hen
    Build by the water's edge.

Birds build their nests from year to year,
    According to their kind,
Some very neat and beautiful,
    Some easily designed.

94

THE THRUSH'S NEST
JOHN CLARE

Within a thick and spreading hawthorn bush
    That overhung a mole-hill large and round,
I heard from morn to morn a merry thrush
    Sing hymns to sunrise, while I drank the sound
With joy; and, often an intruding guest,
    I watched her secret toils from day to day—
How true she warped the moss to form a nest,
    And modelled it within with wood and clay;
And by and by, like heath-bells gilt with dew,
    There lay her shining eggs, as bright as flowers,
Ink-spotted over shells of greeny blue;
    And there I witnessed, in the sunny hours,
A brood of nature's minstrels chirp and fly,
Glad as that sunshine and the laughing sky.

CREATURES THAT ARE SMALL

95. 'There be four things which are little upon the earth'
Proverbs xxx. 24–28

96. 'Go to the ant, thou sluggard'   *Proverbs* vi. 6–11

97. Upon the Snail . . . . *John Bunyan*

98. The Wasp. . . . . *William Sharp*

99. The Night Moths . . *Edwin Markham*

100. The Grasshopper and the Cricket . *John Keats*

101. Sunday in October . . *Richard Eberhart*

READINGS

95

'THERE BE FOUR THINGS WHICH ARE LITTLE UPON THE
EARTH'   .   .   .   *Proverbs* xxx. 24–28
*The providence of the ant and the unity of the locusts are
commended.*

96

'GO TO THE ANT, THOU SLUGGARD'
Proverbs vi. 6–11
The ant is contrasted with a lazy person.

97

There is much to be learnt from the humble snail.

UPON THE SNAIL
JOHN BUNYAN

She goes but softly, but she goeth sure;
    She stumbles not as other creatures do:
Her journey's shorter, so she may endure
    Better than they that do much further go.

She makes no noise, but stilly seizeth on
    The flower or herb appointed for her food,
The which she quietly doth feed upon,
    While others range, and gare, but find no good.

70

And though she doth but very softly go,
    However 'tis not fast, nor slow, but sure;
And certainly they that do travel so,
    The prize they do aim at, they do procure.

98

An unusual comparison.

THE WASP
WILLIAM SHARP

Where the ripe pears droop heavily
    The yellow wasp hums loud and long
    His hot and drowsy autumn song:
A yellow flame he seems to be,
    When darting suddenly from on high
    He lights where fallen peaches lie:

Yellow and black, this tiny thing's
A tiger soul on elfin wings.

99

*Queries which arose through watching moths attracted by a
light.*

THE NIGHT MOTHS
EDWIN MARKHAM

Out of the night to my leafy porch they came,
A thousand moths. Did He who made the toad
Give them their wings upon the starry road?
Restless and wild, they circle round the flame,
Frail wonder-shapes that man can never tame—
Whirl like the blown flakes of December snows,
Tinted with amber, violet and rose,
Marked with hieroglyphs that have no name.
Out of the summer darkness pours the flight:
Unknown the wild processional they keep.
What lures them to this rush of mad delight?
Why are they called from nothingness and sleep?
Why this rich beauty wandering the night?
Do they go lost and aimless to the deep?

Two insects which take turn and turn about in maintaining the music of Nature.

THE GRASSHOPPER AND THE CRICKET
JOHN KEATS

The poetry of earth is never dead:
  When all the birds are faint with the hot sun,
  And hide in cooling trees, a voice will run
From hedge to hedge about the new-mown mead;
That is the grasshopper's—he takes the lead
  In summer luxury—he has never done
  With his delights; for when tired out with fun,
He rests at ease beneath some pleasant weed.
The poetry of earth is ceasing never;
  On a lone winter evening, when the frost
    Has wrought a silence, from the stove there shrills
The Cricket's song, in warmth increasing ever,
  And seems to one in drowsiness half lost,
    The Grasshopper's among some grassy hills.

The bee-keeper leaves his bees sufficient honey for the winter. Providence is not always so kind to us.

SUNDAY IN OCTOBER
RICHARD EBERHART

The farmer, in the pride of sea-won acres,
Showed me his honey mill, the honey-gate.
Late afternoon was hazy on the land,
The sun was a warm gauzy providence.

The honey mill, the honey-gate. And then,
Near by, the bees. They came in from the fields,
The sun behind them, from the fields and trees,
Like soft banners, waving from the sea.

He told me of their thousands, their ways,
Of pounds of honey in the homely apiaries.
The stores were almost full, in Autumn air,
Against the coming chill, and the long cold.

He was about ready to rob them now,
The combs. He'd leave them just enough to keep them.
I thought it a rather subtle point he made,
Wishing providence would be as sure of us.

THE WEATHER

102. Verses
103. 'He sendeth forth his commandment upon earth'
                                    Psalm CXLVII. 15–18
104. 'God thundereth marvellously with his voice'
                                    Job XXXVII. 5–11
105. 'Who hath divided a watercourse'
                                    Job XXXVIII. 25–27
106. 'For my thoughts are not your thoughts'
                                    Isaiah LV. 8–11
107. Weathers . . . . . *Thomas Hardy*
108. 'The hollow winds begin to blow' . *Edward Jenner*
109. A Windy Day . . . . *Andrew Young*
110. Storm . . . . . *R. N. Bartlett*
111. Prayer of the Breton Fisherman *Robert Armstrong*
112. Wild North-easter . . . *Charles Kingsley*
113. Prayer for Rain . . . . *Herbert Palmer*
114. 'Sometimes we see a cloud that's dragonish'
                                William Shakespeare
115. 'After a day of cloud and wind and rain'
                            Henry Wadsworth Longfellow

102

VERSES

He left not himself without witness,
In that he did good,
And gave us rain from heaven, and fruitful seasons,
Filling our hearts with food and gladness.
                                Acts XIV. 17

I will give you rain in due season,
And the land shall yield her increase,
And the trees of the field shall yield their fruit.
                                Leviticus XXVI. 4

The Lord shall open unto thee his good treasure,
The heaven to give the rain unto thy land in his season,
And to bless all the work of thine hand.

Deuteronomy XXVIII. 12

The earth which drinketh in the rain that cometh oft
    upon it,
And bringeth forth herbs meet for them by whom it is
    dressed,
Receiveth blessing from God.

Hebrews VI. 7

Ask ye of the Lord rain in the time of the latter rain;
So the Lord shall make bright clouds,
And give them showers of rain,
To every one grass in the field.

Zechariah X. 1

Blessed of the Lord be his land, for the precious things
    of heaven,
For the dew, and for the deep that coucheth beneath.

Deuteronomy XXXIII. 13

If ye shall hearken diligently unto my commandments
    which I command you this day,
To love the Lord your God,
And to serve him with all your heart,
And with all your soul,
That I will give you the rain of your land in his due
    season,
The first rain and the latter rain,
That thou mayest gather in thy corn.

Deuteronomy XI. 13, 14

Look upon the rainbow, and praise him that made it;
Very beautiful it is in the brightness thereof.
It compasseth the heaven about with a glorious circle,
And the hands of the most High have bended it.

Ecclesiasticus XLIII. 11, 12

74

He answered and said unto them, When it is evening, ye
    say,
    It will be fair weather: for the sky is red.
And in the morning,
    It will be foul weather to-day: for the sky is red and
    lowring.
                                        St. Matthew XVI. 2, 3

Praised be my Lord for our brother the Wind and for
    air and cloud, calms and all weather by the which
    Thou upholdest life in all creatures.
                                        Canticle of the Sun
                                        St. Francis

READINGS

103

'HE SENDETH FORTH HIS COMMANDMENT UPON EARTH'
                                        Psalm CXLVII. 15–18
Verses for a time of frost and snow.

104

'GOD THUNDERETH MARVELLOUSLY WITH HIS VOICE'
                                        Job XXXVII. 5–11
*Job illustrates the might of God by describing the changes
which He brings about in the weather.*

105

'WHO HATH DIVIDED A WATERCOURSE'
                                        Job XXXVIII. 25–27
Who is responsible for sending the changes in the weather?

106

'FOR MY THOUGHTS ARE NOT YOUR THOUGHTS'
                                        Isaiah LV. 8–11
*The word of God is likened to the rain in that both produce
a harvest.*

Showers can be enjoyed, but downpours . . . !

WEATHERS
THOMAS HARDY

This is the weather the cuckoo likes,
   And so do I;
When showers betumble the chestnut spikes,
   And nestlings fly:
And the little brown nightingale bills his best,
And they sit outside at 'The Travellers' Rest',
And maids come forth sprig-muslin drest,
And citizens dream of the south and west,
   And so do I.

This is the weather the shepherd shuns,
   and so do I;
When beeches drip in browns and duns,
   And thresh, and ply;
The hill-hid tides throb, throe on throe,
And meadow rivulets overflow,
And drops on gate-bars hang in a row,
And rooks in families homeward go,
   And so do I.

*Indications of bad weather to come . . . from before the days
of weather forecasts on the radio.*

'THE HOLLOW WINDS BEGIN TO BLOW'
EDWARD JENNER

The hollow winds begin to blow,
The clouds look black, the glass is low.
The soot falls down, the spaniels sleep,
The spiders from their cobwebs creep.
Last night the sun went pale to bed,
The moon in haloes hid her head.

The boding shepherd heaves a sigh,
For see! a rainbow spans the sky.
The walls are damp, the ditches smell,
Clos'd is the pink-eyed pimpernel.
Hark how the chairs and tables crack.
Old Betty's joints are on the rack;
Loud quack the ducks, the peacocks cry;
The distant hills are looking nigh;
How restless are the snorting swine,
The busy flies disturb the kine.
Low o'er the grass the swallow wings;
The cricket too, how loud it sings!
Puss on the hearth with velvet paws
Sits smoothing o'er her whiskered jaws.
Through the clear stream the fishes rise,
And nimbly catch the incautious flies.
The sheep are seen at early light,
Cropping the meads with eager bite.
Though June, the air is cold and chill;
The mellow blackbird's voice is still.
The glow-worms numerous and bright,
Illumed the dewy dell last night.
At dusk the squalid toad was seen
Hopping and crawling o'er the green.
The frog has lost his yellow vest,
And in a dingy suit is dressed.
The leech, disturbed, is newly risen,
Quite to the summit of his prison.
The whirling wind the dust obeys,
And in the rapid eddy plays.
My dog, so altered in his taste,
Quits marrow-bones on grass to feast.
And see, yon rooks, how odd their flight!
They imitate the gliding kite,
Or seem precipitate to fall,
As if they felt the piercing ball.
'Twill surely rain, I see with sorrow,
Our jaunt must be put off to-morrow.

For a windy morning.

A WINDY DAY
ANDREW YOUNG

This wind brings all dead things to life,
Branches that lash the air like whips
And dead leaves rolling in a hurry
Or peering in a rabbits' bury
Or trying to push down a tree;
Gates that fly open to the wind
And close again behind,
And fields that are a flowing sea
And make the cattle look like ships;
Straws glistening and stiff
Lying in air as on a shelf
And pond that leaps to leave itself;
And feathers too that rise and float,
Each feather changed into a bird,
And line-hung sheets that crack and strain;
Even the sun-greened coat,
That through so many winds has served,
The scarecrow struggles to put on again.

*For a morning when a boisterous wind is sweeping through
the streets. Here are mentioned many little scenes familiar to
the town-dweller.*

STORM
R. N. BARTLETT

Bursting on the suburbs with dynamic gusts of energy
  And concentrated fury comes the mad March-gale.
Blowing off the roofing-felt which lies atop the garden
  sheds,
Encountering the window with a splash of sleet and hail.
Distending all the trousers on the wildly waving washing-
  line,
  Drumming on the window like a hanged man's heels,
Swaying all the aitches of the television aerials,
Muddying the roadway 'neath the slowly turning wheels.

Gentlemen in overcoats pursuing trilbies hopelessly
  Cursing at the vigour of the brusque March gale,
And lightning lights the darkening sky with bright celes-
  tial clarity,
While women in their kitchens hear the thunder and turn
  pale.

Ear-lobes reddening at the slashing of the hail-stones,
  Nose-tips deadening at the coldness of the sleet,
Eyelids wincing at the brightness of the lightning,
Wet stones glistening beneath the hurried feet.

White marbles bouncing on the flat roofs of the garages,
  Black sky paling as the storm dies down.
Wet folk emerging from the haven of a doorway,
As the sun comes out again and shines upon the town.

III

*A prayer for safety from a fisherman almost overwhelmed by
his feeling of insignificance in the face of a mighty storm.*

PRAYER OF THE BRETON FISHERMAN
ROBERT ARMSTRONG

This boat of mine, oh Lord, is how so small;
This sail, oh master, scarce your winds can hold.
Weak are my arms to trim, to tack, to haul
Before grim waves that bludgeon, then to enfold.
These eyes of mine, oh Lord, cannot discern
Cliff, dune or harbour over high flung seas;
The angered skies deny my sure return
To cottage waiting by the sea-girt leas.
Your mercy, Lord, is kind and how so great,
To my inconsequence made manifest;
So for your servant may your winds abate;
Send home his boat to safe and certain rest.
So small my soul before the raging tide;
Your mercy, as your ocean, Lord, is wide.

79

G

A comforting thought for the time of that bitterest of winds,
the north-easter—at least it makes us bustle about to keep warm.

WILD NORTH-EASTER
CHARLES KINGSLEY

Welcome, wild North-easter!
   Shame it is to see
Odes to every zephyr;
   Ne'er a verse to thee.
Welcome, black North-easter!
   O'er the German foam,
O'er the Danish moorlands,
   From thy frozen home.
Tired we are of summer,
   Tired of gaudy glare,
Showers soft and steaming,
   Hot and breathless air.
Tired of listless dreaming,
   Through the lazy day:
Jovial wind of winter,
   Turns us out to play!
Sweep the golden reed-beds;
   Crisp the lazy dyke;
Hunger into madness
   Every plunging pike.
Fill the lake with wild-fowl;
   Fill the marsh with snipe;
While on dreary moorlands
   Lonely curlew pipe.
Through the black fir-forest
   Thunder harsh and dry,
Shattering down the snow-flakes
   Off the curdled sky.

        From 'Ode to the North-east Wind'

PRAYER FOR RAIN

HERBERT PALMER

O God, make it rain!
Loose the soft silver passion of the rain!
Send swiftly from above
This clear token of Thy love.
Make it rain!

Deck the bushes and the trees
With the tassels of the rain.
Make the brooks pound to the seas
And the earth shine young again.
God of passion, send the rain!

Oh, restore our ancient worth
With Thy rain!
Ease the heartache of the earth,
Sap the grain.
Fill the valleys and the dales
With Thy silver slanting gales;
And through England and wild Wales
Send the rain!

Lord, restore us to Thy will
With the rain!
Soak the valley, drench the hill,
Drown the stain;
Smite the mountain's withered hips,
Wash the rouge from sunset's lips,
Fill the sky with singing ships.
Send the rain!

The shape of clouds can remind us of many different pictures and often in the evening foretell bad weather.

'SOMETIMES WE SEE A CLOUD THAT'S DRAGONISH'

WILLIAM SHAKESPEARE

Sometimes we see a cloud that's dragonish;
A vapour sometime like a bear or lion,
A tower'd citadel, a pendant rock,
A forked mountain, or blue promontory
With trees upon't, that nod unto the world
And mock our eyes with air: thou hast seen these signs;
They are black vesper's pageants.

From 'Antony and Cleopatra', IV. 12

115

'AFTER A DAY OF CLOUD AND WIND AND RAIN'

HENRY WADSWORTH LONGFELLOW

After a day of cloud and wind and rain
Sometimes the setting sun breaks out again,
   And, touching all the darksome woods with light,
Smiles on the fields, until they laugh and sing,
Then like a ruby from the horizon's ring
   Drops down into the night.

From 'The Hanging of the Crane'

116. Verses
117. 'The waters saw thee, O God' *Psalm* LXXVII. 16–19
118. 'And when he was entered into a ship'
  St. Matthew VIII. 23–27
119. 'They that go down to the sea in ships'
  Psalm CVII. 23–31
120. A Sea-less World . . *Joan Campbell*
121. On the Quay . . . . *J. J. Bell*
122. 'Where lies the land' . . *Arthur Hugh Clough*
123. Roadways . . . . . *John Masefield*
124. The Fountain . . . *James Russell Lowell*

116

VERSES

Sing unto the Lord a new song,
And his praise from the end of the earth,
Ye that go down to the sea,
And all that is therein;
The isles, and the inhabitants thereof.

Isaiah XLII. 10

They that sail on the sea tell of the danger thereof;
And when we hear it with our ears, we marvel thereat.
For therein be strange and wondrous works,
Variety of all kinds of beasts and whales created.

Ecclesiasticus XLIII. 24, 25

O Lord God of hosts, who is a strong Lord like unto thee?
Thou rulest the raging of the sea:
When the waves thereof arise, thou stillest them.

The heavens are thine,
The earth also is thine:
As for the world and the fullness thereof, thou hast
  founded them.

Psalm LXXXIX. 8–11

The floods have lifted up, O Lord,
The floods have lifted up their voice;
The floods lift up their waves.
The Lord on high is mightier than the noise of many
    waters,
Yea, than the mighty waves of the sea.

Psalm XCIII. 3, 4

Praised be my Lord for our sister the Water who is very
    serviceable unto us and humble and precious and
    clean.   *Canticle of the Sun*

St. Francis

> The storm is laid, the winds retire
> Obedient to thy will;
> The sea that roars at thy command
> At thy command is still.
>
> In midst of dangers, fears and death,
> Thy goodness we'll adore;
> And praise thee for thy mercies past,
> And humbly hope for more.

Joseph Addison

The earth shall be filled with the knowledge of the glory
    of the Lord, as the waters cover the sea.

Habakkuk II. 14

117

'THE WATERS SAW THEE, O GOD' . Psalm LXXVII. 16–19
The Psalmist's description of a great storm.

118

'AND WHEN HE WAS ENTERED INTO A SHIP'
St. Matthew VIII. 23–27
Christ rebukes the sea.

119

'THEY THAT GO DOWN TO THE SEA IN SHIPS'
Psalm CVII. 23–31
*Men should praise God when He brings them safely through
the dangers of a great storm.*

120

To some lovers of the sea its closeness is essential to happiness.

A SEA-LESS WORLD
JOAN CAMPBELL

If when I come to Paradise
The Lord do not provide
The salt tang of seaweed
And the running of the tide,
And if as the book saith
There shall be no more sea,
Then all the peace of Paradise
Shall not comfort me.

If when I come to Paradise
The Lord do not provide
Pools fringed and sea pinks
And ribbed sands stretching wide,
If no gulls call shrilly
Across a ruffled sea,
Then all the songs of Paradise
Shall not solace me.

Even a landlubber can find the busyness of the ships attractive.

ON THE QUAY

J. J. BELL

I've never travelled for more'n a day,
   I never was one to roam,
     But I likes to sit on the busy quay,
     Watchin' the ships that says to me—
'Always somebody goin' away,
   Somebody gettin' home.'

I likes to think that the world's so wide—
   'Tis grand to be livin' there,
     Takin' a part in its goin's on. . . .
     Ah, now ye're laughin' at poor old John,
Talkin' o' works o' the world wi' pride
   As if he was doin' his share!

But laugh if ye will! When ye're old as me
   Ye'll find 'tis a rare good plan
     To look at the world—an' love it too!—
     Tho' never a job are ye fit to do. . . .
Oh! 'tisn't all sorrow, and pain to see
   The work o' another man.

'Tis good when the heart grows big at last,
   Too big for trouble to fill—
     Wi' room for the things that was only stuff
     When workin' an' winnin' seemed more'n enough—
Room for the world, the world so vast,
   Wi' its peoples an' all their skill.

That's what I'm thinkin' on all the days
   I'm loafin' an' smokin' here,
     An' the ships do make me think the most
     (Of readin' in books 'tis little I'd boast)—
But the ships, they carries me long, long ways,
   An' draws far places near.

I sees the things that a sailor brings,
   I hears the stories he tells. . . .
      'Tis surely a wonderful world, indeed!
      'Tis more'n the peoples can ever need!
An' I praises the Lord—to myself I sings—
   For the world in which I dwells.

An' I loves the ships more every day,
   Tho' I never was one to roam.
      Oh! the ships is comfortin' sights to see,
      An' they means a lot when they says to me—
'Always somebody goin' away,
   Somebody gettin' home.'

122

*In these lines the voyage is being compared with life, to which
a mixture of hardship and pleasure gives added zest.*

'WHERE LIES THE LAND'
ARTHUR HUGH CLOUGH

Where lies the land to which the ship would go?
Far, far ahead, is all her seamen know.
And where the land she travels from? Away,
Far, far behind, is all that they can say.

On sunny noons upon the deck's smooth face,
Linked arm in arm, how pleasant here to pace!
Or, o'er the stern reclining, watch below
The foaming wake far widening as we go.

On stormy nights when wild north-westers rave,
How proud a thing to fight with wind and wave!
The dripping sailor on the reeling mast
Exults to bear, and scorns to wish it past.

Where lies the land to which the ship would go?
Far, far ahead, is all her seamen know.
And where the land she travels from? Away,
Far, far behind, is all that they can say.

87

The beauty and grandeur of the sea can be an irresistible attraction.

ROADWAYS
JOHN MASEFIELD

One road leads to London,
   One road runs to Wales,
My road leads me seawards
   To the white dipping sails.

One road leads to the river,
   As it goes singing slow;
My road leads to shipping,
   Where the bronzed sailors go.

Leads me, lures me, calls me
   To salt green tossing sea;
A road without earth's road-dust
   Is the right road for me.

A wet road, heaving, shining,
   And wild with seagulls' cries,
And a salt sea-wind blowing
   The salt spray in my eyes.

My road calls me, lures me
   West, east, south and north;
Most roads lead men homewards,
   My road leads me forth.

To add more miles to the tally
   Of grey miles left behind,
In quest of that one beauty
   God put me here to find.

THE FOUNTAIN
JAMES RUSSELL LOWELL

Into the sunshine,
  Full of the light,
Leaping and flashing
  From morn till night;

Into the moonlight,
  Whiter than snow,
Waving so flower-like
  When the winds blow;

Into the starlight
  Rushing in spray,
Happy at midnight,
  Happy by day;

Ever in motion,
  Blithesome and cheery,
Still climbing heavenward,
  Never aweary;

Glad of all weathers,
  Still seeming best,
Upward or downward
  Motion thy rest;

Full of a nature
  Nothing can tame,
Changed every moment,
  Ever the same;

Ceaseless aspiring,
  Ceaseless content,
Darkness or sunshine
  Thy element;

Glorious fountain,
  Let my heart be
Fresh, changeful, constant,
  Upward, like thee!

THE HEAVENS

125. Verses
126. 'The heavens declare the glory of God'
                                    Psalm XIX. 1–6
127. 'O give thanks to the Lord of lords'
                                    Psalm CXXXVI. 3–9
128. 'By the word of the Lord were the heavens made'
                                    Psalm XXXIII. 6–8
129. 'Praise ye the Lord' . . *Psalm* CXLVIII. 1–5
130. 'All things are full of God' . *John Stuart Blackie*
131. Ode . . . . . . *Joseph Addison*
132. 'Glorious the sun in mid career' *Christopher Smart*
133. A Look at the Heavens . . *John Clare*
134. High Flight . . . . *J. G. Magee*
135. Donnybrook . . . *James Stephens*

125

VERSES

The heaven, even the heavens, are the Lord's:
But the earth hath he given to the children of men.
                                    Psalm CXV. 16

Lift up your eyes on high,
And behold who hath created these things,
That bringeth out their host by number:
He calleth them all by names by the greatness of his
    might,
For that he is strong in power;
Not one faileth.   *Isaiah* XL. 26

God made two great lights;
The greater light to rule the day,
And the lesser light to rule the night:
He made the stars also.
And God set them in the firmament of the heaven to
    give light upon the earth,
And to rule over the day and over the night,
And to divide the light from the darkness:
And God saw that it was good.   *Genesis* I. 16–18

The Lord, which giveth the sun for a light by day,
And the ordinances of the moon and of the stars for a
   light by night,
Which divideth the sea when the waves thereof roar,
The Lord of hosts is his name.   *Jeremiah* XXXI. 35

They that be wise shall shine as the brightness of the
   firmament;
And they that turn many to righteousness as the stars
   for ever and ever.   *Daniel* XII. 3

Praised be my Lord for our sister the Moon and for the
   stars which He has set clear and lovely in the
   heavens.   *Canticle of the Sun, St. Francis*

Praised be my Lord God with all his creatures and
   specially our brother the Sun who brings us the day
   and brings us the light: fair is he and shines with a
   very great splendour.
O Lord, he signifies to us Thee.
   Canticle of the Sun, St. Francis

READINGS

126

'THE HEAVENS DECLARE THE GLORY OF GOD'
   Psalm XIX. 1–6
A description of the glory of the sun.

127

'O GIVE THANKS TO THE LORD OF LORDS'
   Psalm CXXXVI. 3–9
A thanksgiving to God as the creator.

128

'BY THE WORD OF THE LORD WERE THE HEAVENS MADE'
   Psalm XXXIII. 6–8
God should be reverenced as the creator of the heavens.

129

'PRAISE YE THE LORD'   .   .   *Psalm* CXLVIII. 1–5
*The sun and the moon are constant reminders of the work of
the Creator.*

When man first began to think of the 'Why and Wherefore' of things, the Greeks realized that God was at the centre of all. No matter what further knowledge Science may reveal, it will only serve to emphasize this fact.

'ALL THINGS ARE FULL OF GOD'

JOHN STUART BLACKIE

All things are full of God. Thus spoke
  Wise Thales in the days
When subtle Greece to thought awoke
  And soared in lofty ways.
And now what wisdom have we more?
  No sage divining-rod
Hath taught than this a deeper lore,
  ALL THINGS ARE FULL OF GOD.

The Light that gloweth in the sky
  And shimmers in the sea,
That quivers in the painted fly
  And gems the pictured lea,
The million hues of Heaven above
  And Earth below are one,
And every lightful eye doth love
  The primal light, the Sun.

Even so, all vital virtue flows
  From life's first fountain, God;
And he who feels, and he who knows,
  Doth feel and know from God.
As fishes swim in briny sea,
  As fowl do float in air,
From Thy embrace we cannot flee;
  We breathe, and Thou art there.

Go, take thy glass, astronomer,
  And all the girth survey
Of sphere harmonious linked to sphere,
  In endless bright array.
All that far-reaching Science there
  Can measure with her rod,
All powers, all laws, are but the fair
  Embodied thoughts of God.

ODE
JOSEPH ADDISON

The spacious firmament on high,
With all the blue ethereal sky,
And spangled heavens, a shining frame.
Their great original proclaim.
Th' unwearied sun, from day to day,
Does his creator's power display;
And publishes to every land
The work of an almighty hand.

Soon as the evening shades prevail,
The moon takes up the wondrous tale,
And nightly to the listening earth
Repeats the story of her birth:
Whilst all the stars that round her burn,
And all the planets in their turn,
Confirm the tidings as they roll,
And spread the truth from pole to pole.

What though in solemn silence all
Move round the dark terrestrial ball?
What though nor real voice nor sound
Amid their radiant orbs be found?
In reason's ear they all rejoice,
And utter forth a glorious voice;
For ever singing as they shine,
'The hand that made us is divine'.

'GLORIOUS THE SUN IN MID CAREER'
CHRISTOPHER SMART

Glorious the sun in mid career;
Glorious the assembled fires appear;
Glorious the comet's train:
Glorious the trumpet and alarm.
Glorious the almighty stretch'd out arm,
Glorious the enraptured main:
Glorious the northern lights astream:
Glorious the song, when God's the theme.

Contemplation of the multitude of stars in the Heavens fills us with wonder at the omnipotence of God.

A LOOK AT THE HEAVENS
JOHN CLARE

Oh, who can witness with a careless eye
The countless lamps that light an evening sky,
And not be struck with wonder at the sight!
To think what mighty Power must there abound,
That burns each spangle with a steady light,
And guides each hanging world its rolling round.
What multitudes my misty eyes have found!
The countless numbers speak a Deity:
In numbers numberless the skies are crown'd,
And still they're nothing which my sight can see,
When science, searching through her aiding glass,
In seeming blanks to me can millions trace;
While millions more, that every heart impress,
Still brighten up throughout eternal space.
O Power Almighty! whence these beings shine,
All wisdom's lost in comprehending thine.

These are the feelings of a pilot flying high above the earth.

HIGH FLIGHT
J. G. MAGEE

Oh, I have slipped the surly bonds of Earth
And danced the skies on laughter-silvered wings;
Sunward I've climbed, and joined the tumbling mirth
Of sun-split clouds—and done a hundred things
You have not dreamed of—wheeled and soared and
    swung
High in the sunlight silence; hov'ring there,
I've chased the shouting wind along, and flung
My eager craft through footless halls of air.
Up, up the long, delirious, burning blue
I've topped the wind-swept heights with easy grace

Where never lark, or even eagle flew—
And, while with silent lifting mind I've trod
The high untrespassed sanctity of space,
Put out my hand and touched the face of God.

135

The high-sailing moon can engender a feeling of reverence.

DONNYBROOK
JAMES STEPHENS

I saw the moon, so broad and bright,
Sailing high on a frosty night!

And the air shone silverly between
The pearly queen, and the silver queen!

And here a white, and there a white
Cloud-mist swam in a mist of light!

And, all encrusted in the sky,
High, and higher, and yet more high,

Were golden star-points glimmering through
The hollow vault, the vault of blue!

And then I knew—that God was good,
And the world was fair! And, where I stood,

I bent the knee, and bent the head:
And said my prayers, and went to bed.

95

136. Verses
137. 'In the beginning God created the heaven and the earth' . . . . . *Genesis* I. 1–5
138. 'Why doth one day excel another?'
Ecclesiasticus XXXIII. 7–9
139. 'Lord, I my vows to thee renew' *Bishop Thomas Ken*
140. 'High o'er the lonely hills' . . *Jan Struther*
141. 'Faster and more fast' . . *Robert Browning*
142. 'Now that the daylight fills the sky' *J. M. Neale*
143. 'O Father, hear my morning prayer' *F. A. Percy*
144. 'And see—the sun himself!' . . *Thomas Moore*
145. Morning Thanksgiving . *John Drinkwater*
146. To-day . . . . *Thomas Carlyle*

136

VERSES

I laid me down and slept;
I awaked; for the Lord sustained me.

Psalm III. 5

Truly the light is sweet, and a pleasant thing it is for the
eyes to behold the sun.

Ecclesiastes XI. 7

Blessed be the name of the Lord from this time forth and
for evermore.
From the rising of the sun unto the going down of the
same the Lord's name is to be praised.

Psalm CXIII. 2, 3

This is the day which the Lord hath made:
We will rejoice and be glad in it.

Psalm CXVIII. 24

My voice shalt thou hear in the morning, O Lord;
In the morning will I direct my prayer unto thee, and
    will look up.

Psalm v. 3

The morning stars sang together,
And all the sons of God shouted for joy.

Job XXXVIII. 7

Father, we praise thee, now the night is over;
Active and watchful, stand we all before thee;
Singing we offer prayer and meditation:
    Thus we adore thee.

Ascribed to St. Gregory the Great
Tr. Percy Dearmer

Now that the sun is gleaming bright,
    Implore we, bending low,
That He, the Uncreated Light,
    May guide us as we go.

Adam de St. Victor

Holy, holy, holy, Lord God Almighty!
Early in the morning our song shall rise to Thee.

Bishop R. Heber

All night the waves of darkness broke about my head,
I prayed for sleep in vain, none seemed to hear my
    words.
Yet God who knows all deepest needs gave me instead
Dawn in the primrose garden, and the songs of birds.

Eva Gore-Booth

Hail, universal Lord, be bounteous still
To give us only good; and if the night
Have gathered aught of evil or concealed,
Disperse it, as now light dispels the dark.

John Milton

97

THE DAY—THE WAY

Not for a single day
Can I discern my way,
  But this I surely know—
Who gives the day,
Will show the way,
  So I securely go.   *John Oxenham*

Out of the scabbard of the night,
  By God's hand drawn,
Flashes his shining sword of light,
  And lo—the dawn!   *F. D. Sherman*

READINGS

137

'IN THE BEGINNING GOD CREATED THE HEAVEN AND THE
  EARTH' .   .   .   .   . Genesis I. 1–5
The creation of Day and Night.

138

'WHY DOTH ONE DAY EXCEL ANOTHER?'
                    Ecclesiasticus XXXIII. 7–9
Some of them are 'high days' and some are 'ordinary days'.

139

'LORD, I MY VOWS TO THEE RENEW'
BISHOP THOMAS KEN

Lord, I my vows to Thee renew,
Scatter my sins as morning dew;
Guard my first springs of thought and will,
And with Thyself my spirit fill.

Direct, control, suggest this day,
All I design, or do, or say,
That all my powers, with all their might,
In Thy sole glory may unite.
           From 'Awake my soul'

God's coming on earth is comparable to the way in which daylight follows darkness.

'HIGH O'ER THE LONELY HILLS'
JAN STRUTHER

High o'er the lonely hills
   Black turns to grey,
Birdsong the valley fills,
   Mists fold away;
Grey wakes to green again,
Beauty is seen again—
Gold and serene again
   Dawneth the day.

So, o'er the hills of life,
   Stormy, forlorn,
Out of the cloud and strife
   Sunrise is born;
Swift grows the light for us;
Ended is night for us;
Soundless and bright for us
   Breaketh God's morn.

Hear we no beat of drums,
   Fanfare nor cry,
When Christ the herald comes
   Quietly nigh;
Splendour he makes on earth;
Colour awakes on earth;
Suddenly breaks on earth
   Light from the sky.

'FASTER AND MORE FAST'

ROBERT BROWNING

Faster and more fast,
O'er night's brim, boils day at last;
Boils, pure gold, o'er the cloud-cup's brim
Where spurting and suppressed it lay,
For not a froth-flake touched the rim
Of yonder gap in the solid gray
Of the eastern cloud, an hour away;
But forth one wavelet, then another, curled,
Till the whole sunrise, not to be suppressed,
Rose, reddened, and its seething breast
Flickered in bounds, grew old, then overflowed the
    world.

From 'Pippa Passes'

'NOW THAT THE DAYLIGHT FILLS THE SKY'

J. M. NEALE

Now that the daylight fills the sky,
We lift our hearts to God on high,
That He, in all we do or say,
Would keep us free from harm to-day.

May He restrain our tongues from strife,
And shield from anger's din our life,
And guard with watchful care our eyes
From earth's absorbing vanities.

So we, when this day's work is o'er,
And shades of night return once more,
Our path of trial safely trod,
Shall give the glory to our God.

'O FATHER, HEAR MY MORNING PRAYER'

F. A. PERCY

O Father, hear my morning prayer,
　Thine aid impart to me,
That I may make my life to-day
　Acceptable to Thee.

May this desire my spirit rule,
　And, as the moments fly,
Something of good be born in me,
　Something of evil die.

Some grace, that seeks my heart to win,
　With shining victory meet;
Some sin, that strives for mastery,
　Find overthrow complete:

That so throughout the coming day
　The hours may carry me
A little farther from the world,
　A little nearer Thee.

'AND SEE—THE SUN HIMSELF!'

THOMAS MOORE

And see—the Sun himself!—on wings
Of glory up the East he springs.
Angel of God! who from the time
Those heavens began their march sublime,
Hath first of all the starry choir
Trod in his Maker's steps of fire!
From 'Lalla Rookh'

A thanksgiving for many ordinary things often taken for granted.

MORNING THANKSGIVING

JOHN DRINKWATER

Thank God for sleep in the long quiet night,
 For the clear day calling through the little leaded
  panes,
For the shining well-water and the warm golden light,
 And the paths washed white by singing rains.

We thank Thee, O God, for exultation born
 Of the kiss of Thy winds, for life among the leaves,
For the whirring wings that pass about the wonder of
  the morn,
 For the changing plumes of swallows gliding upwards
  to their eaves.

For the treasure of the garden, the gillyflowers of gold,
 The prouder petalled tulips, the primrose full of
  spring,
For the crowded orchard boughs, and the swelling buds
  that hold
 A yet unwoven wonder, to Thee our praise we bring.

Thank God for good bread, for the honey in the comb,
 For the brown-shelled eggs, for the clustered blossoms
  set
Beyond the open window in a pink and cloudy foam,
 For the laughing loves among the branches met.

For the kind-faced women we bring our thanks to Thee,
 With shapely mothering arms and grave eyes clear
  and blithe,
For the tall young men, strong-thewed as men may be,
 For the old man bent above his scythe.

For earth's little secret and innumerable ways,
　For the carol and the colour, Lord, we bring
What things may be of thanks, and that Thou hast lent
　　our days
　Eyes to see and ears to hear and lips to sing.

TO-DAY

THOMAS CARLYLE

So here hath been dawning
Another blue day:
Think wilt thou let it
Slip useless away.

Out of Eternity
This new Day is born;
Into Eternity,
At night, will return.

Behold it aforetime
No eye ever did:
So soon it forever
From all eyes is hid.

Here hath been dawning
Another blue Day:
Think wilt thou let it
Slip useless away.

EVENING

147. Verses
148. Twilight . . . . *Dorothy Una Ratcliffe*
149. Hesperus . . . . *James Stephens*
150. Day's End . . . . *Wilfred H. Bartlett*
151. 'Sweet is the breath of morn' . *John Milton*
152. To Sleep . . . . *William Wordsworth*
153. 'Time to go home' . . *James Reeves*
154. 'Night is the time for rest' . *James Montgomery*
155. 'Creator of the earth and sky' . *St. Ambrose*
156. For Sleep or Death . . . *Ruth Pitter*

147

VERSES

I will both lay me down in peace, and sleep: for thou,
Lord, only makest me dwell in safety.
Psalm IV. 8

It is a good thing to give thanks unto the Lord,
And to sing praises unto thy name, O most High:
To shew forth thy lovingkindness in the morning,
And thy faithfulness every night.
Psalm XCII. 1, 2

As the slow Evening gather'd in her grey,
And one clear star its ancient pathway trod—
With long, low cadences of dear delay,
The lark, descending, left his song with God!
Frederick G. Bowles
From 'Resurrection'

Live for to-day! to-morrow's light
To-morrow's cares shall bring to sight.
Go! sleep like closing flowers at night,
And Heaven thy morn will bless.
John Keble

NIGHT

The sun descending in the west,
The evening star does shine,
The birds are silent in their nest,
And I must seek for mine.
The moon, like a flower
In heaven's high bower,
With silent delight
Sits and smiles on the night.

William Blake

I must work the works of him that sent me, while it is
    day:
The night cometh, when no man can work.

St. John IX. 4

PRAYER: AFTER HEARING MUSIC

God keep my fingers clean and white
And give me peace to sleep at night;
May I be fair to outward view
And clean in spirit through and through.

Julian S. Huxley

DAY AND NIGHT

Said Day to Night,
'I bring God's light.
    What gift have you?'
    Night said, 'The dew.'

'I give bright hours,'
Quoth Day, 'and flowers.'
    Said Night, 'More blest,
    I bring sweet rest.'

Lady Lindsay

GOOD NIGHT

Good night! Good night!
Far flies the light;
But still God's love
Shall shine above
Making all bright.
Good night! Good Night!

Victor Hugo

148

TWILIGHT

DOROTHY UNA RATCLIFFE

The gentle Twilight Lady
  Is coming. Let her pass.
She scatters from her basket
  The dewdrops on the grass.
She closes up the lilies,
  She sends the bees to bed,
And throws a veil of silver
  Upon the rowans red.
And thro' the drowsy forest
  She bids the birds be still,
And listens, turns, and listens
  Unto the wakeful rill.
Then those who love the moortops,
  And to the hills belong,
May hear adown the valley
  The Twilight Lady's song,
Calling in lonely music,
  That breaks the heart o' the wild,
For Night, her star-eyed lover,
  To bring back Peace—their child.

HESPERUS

JAMES STEPHENS

Upon the sky
Thy sober robes are spread;

They drape the twilight,
Veil on quiet veil;

Until the lingering daylight all has fled
Before thee, modest goddess, shadow-pale!

The hushed and reverent sky
Her diadem of stars has lighted high!

II

The lamb, the bleating kid, the tender fawn;
All that the sunburnt day has scattered wide,

Thou dost regather; holding, till the dawn,
Each flower and tree and beast unto thy side:

The sheep come to the pen;
And dreams come to the men;

And to the mother's breast,
The tired children come, and take their rest.

III

Evening gathers everything
Scattered by the morning!

Fold for sheep, and nest for wing;
Evening gathers everything!

Child to mother, queen to king,
Running at thy warning!

Evening gathers everything
Scattered by the morning.

A description of the stealthy way in which darkness creeps over the land.

DAY'S END

WILFRED H. BARTLETT

The wind cries and the shadow
Broods upon the meadow.

Leisurely, through shrinking skies,
A single, speckled pigeon flies
On comfortable wing
To the green gloom's welcoming.

Oh, hear the waves of night
Encroach upon the light
And break, in empty curves of sound,
On drooping tree and quiet mound,
On farm and inoffensive beast
Dreaming of to-morrow's feast.

The wind sighs and the shadow
Bites into the meadow.

With curious call the owls ride
The hidden crest of eventide;
Beast and building, tree and mound,
In an ebon sea are drowned;
And through the dew-wet grass and deep
Man goes home to his long sleep.

The wind dies, and the shadow
Swallows up the meadow.

The day can pass very gently, turning from the early morning,
through the sunshine of midday, to the quietness of the night.

'SWEET IS THE BREATH OF MORN'
JOHN MILTON

Sweet is the breath of morn, her rising sweet,
With charm of earliest Birds; pleasant the Sun,
When first on this delightful Land he spreads
His orient Beams, on herb, tree, fruit, and flower,
Glist'ring with dew; fragrant the fertile earth
After soft showers; and sweet the coming on
Of grateful Evening mild; then silent night. . . .

If we are troubled by lack of sleep, the next morning cannot
be fully lived.

TO SLEEP
WILLIAM WORDSWORTH

A flock of sheep that leisurely pass by,
One after one; the sound of rain, and bees
Murmuring; the fall of rivers, winds and seas,
Smooth fields, white sheets of water, and pure sky:
By turns have all been thought of; yet I lie
Sleepless, and soon the small birds' melodies
Must hear, first uttered from my orchard trees;
And the first cuckoo's melancholy cry.
Even thus last night, and two nights more, I lay,
And could not win thee, sleep! by any stealth.
So do not let me wear to-night away:
Without thee what is all the morning's wealth?
Come, blessed barrier betwixt day and day,
Dear mother of fresh thoughts and joyous health!

'TIME TO GO HOME'

JAMES REEVES

Time to go home!
  Says the great steeple clock.
Time to go home!
  Says the gold weathercock.
Down sinks the sun
  In the valley to sleep;
Lost are the orchards
  In blue shadows deep.
Soft falls the dew
  On cornfield and grass;
Through the dark trees
  The evening airs pass:
Time to go home,
  They murmur and say;
Birds to their homes
  Have all flown away.
Nothing shines now
  But the gold weathercock.
Time to go home!
  Says the great steeple clock.

'NIGHT IS THE TIME FOR REST'

JAMES MONTGOMERY

Night is the time for rest;
How sweet, when labours close,
To gather round an aching breast
The curtain of repose,
Stretch the tired limbs, and lay the head
Upon our own delightful bed!
Night is the time to pray;
Our Saviour oft withdrew
To desert mountains far away;
So will his followers do;
Steal from the throng to haunts untrod,
And commune there alone with God.

From 'Night'

A Thanksgiving for sleep.

'CREATOR OF THE EARTH AND SKY'
ST. AMBROSE

Creator of the earth and sky,
Ruling the firmament on high,
Clothing the day with robes of light,
Blessing with gracious sleep the night,

That rest may comfort weary men,
And brace to useful toil again,
And soothe awhile the harassed mind,
And sorrow's heavy load unbind:

Day sinks; we thank thee for thy gift;
Night comes; and once again we lift
Our prayers and vows and hymns that we
Against all ills may shielded be.

Translated by Charles Bigg

156

A prayer for strength to be restored through peace and quiet rest.

FOR SLEEP OR DEATH
RUTH PITTER

Cure me with quietness,
Bless me with peace;
Comfort my heaviness,
Stay me with ease.
Stillness in solitude
Send down like dew;
Mine armour of fortitude
Piece and make new:
That when I rise again
I may shine bright
As the sky after rain,
Day after night.

111

I

SPRING

157. Verses
158. Praise . . . . . *Mary Anderson*
159. Written in March . . *William Wordsworth*
160. Spring Prayer . . *Ralph Waldo Emerson*
161. A Spring Magnificat . . . *Teresa Hooley*
162. 'Loveliest of trees, the cherry now' *A. E. Housman*
163 'The year's at the spring' . *Robert Browning*
164. The Embroideress . . . *Sylvia Lynd*

157

VERSES

For, lo, the winter is past,
The rain is over and gone;
The flowers appear on the earth;
The time of the singing of birds is come,
And the voice of the turtle is heard in our land.

The Song of Solomon II. 11, 12

Spring goeth all in white,
  Crowned with milk-white may:
In fleecy flocks of light
  O'er heaven the white clouds stray:

White butterflies in the air:
  White daisies prank the ground:
The cherry and the hoary pear
  Scatter their snow around.

Robert Bridges

For as the earth bringeth forth her bud,
And as the garden causeth the things that are sown in it
    to spring forth;
So the Lord God will cause righteousness and praise to
    spring forth before all the nations.

Isaiah LXI. 11

PRAISE

MARY ANDERSON

Praise the Lord for all the seasons,
    Praise Him for the gentle spring,
Praise the Lord for glorious summer,
    Birds and beasts and everything.
Praise the Lord who sends the harvest,
    Praise Him for the winter snows;
Praise the Lord, all ye who love Him,
    Praise Him, for all things He knows.

159

The Spring appears to bring renewed vigour to everything and everybody. There is general rejoicing at the passing of bad weather.

WRITTEN IN MARCH

WILLIAM WORDSWORTH

The cock is crowing,
The stream is flowing,
The small birds twitter,
The lake doth glitter,
The green field sleeps in the sun;
    The oldest and youngest
    Are at work with the strongest;
The cattle are grazing,
Their heads never raising;
There are forty feeding like one!

Like an army defeated
The snow hath retreated,
And now doth fare ill
On the top of the bare hill;
The ploughboy is whooping—anon—anon:
    There's joy in the mountains;
    There's life in the fountains;
Small clouds are sailing,
Blue sky prevailing;
The rain is over and gone!

*Written whilst resting on the bridge at the foot
of Brother's Water*

A prayer of gratitude for the beauties of Spring.

SPRING PRAYER
RALPH WALDO EMERSON

For flowers that bloom about our feet;
For tender grass, so fresh, so sweet;
For song of bird, and hum of bee;
For all things fair we hear or see,
Father in heaven, we thank Thee!

For blue of stream and blue of sky;
For pleasant shade of branches high;
For fragrant air and cooling breeze;
For beauty of the blooming trees,
Father in heaven, we thank Thee!

A song of praise for the glories of Spring and early Summer.

A SPRING MAGNIFICAT
TERESA HOOLEY

For wild anemones star-shining in the little wood;
For the scent of wet earth and of growing things after
    rain;
For the song of the thrush;
For the mounting sap;
For the unfolding of the little curled ferns and the
    daisies' awakening,
Praise ineffable!

For the dance of the white narcissi in the south wind;
For the feathery emerald fronds of the tossing larch;
For the sulphur butterflies;
For purple shadows on a blossoming mist of bluebells;
For young lambs and little rabbits and all happy new-
    born things at play in the fields,
Praise unutterable!

For the fragrant foam of the wild parsley;
For bees in the clover;
For rainbows and stars and the rosy blossom of the wild
    apple;

For the sense of birth;
For the voice of resurrection;
For all sounds and sights and scents of the eternal
    miracle, Spring,
Praise, praise, and thanks for ever!

162

For the time of cherry blossom, which is so beautiful and enjoyable that all other occupations should be left, just to go to the woods.

'LOVELIEST OF TREES, THE CHERRY NOW'
A. E. HOUSMAN

Loveliest of trees, the cherry now
Is hung with bloom along the bough,
And stands about the woodland ride
Wearing white for Eastertide.

Now, of my threescore years and ten,
Twenty will not come again,
And take from seventy springs a score,
It only leaves me fifty more.

And since to look at things in bloom
Fifty springs are little room,
About the woodlands I will go
To see the cherry hung with snow.

163

'THE YEAR'S AT THE SPRING'
ROBERT BROWNING

The year's at the spring
And day's at the morn;
Morning's at seven;
The hill-side's dew-pearled;
The lark's on the wing;
The snail's on the thorn;
God's in his heaven—
All's right with the world!

From 'Pippa Passes'

The gradual appearance of more and more spring flowers can be compared to the gradual working of the stitches on a piece of fine embroidery.

THE EMBROIDERESS
SYLVIA LYND

Carefully now Spring puts her stitches
Along the hedges and the ditches,
Deciding what shall first appear
On the dark fabric of the year;
To mark the pattern, to define
With delicate, brief line,
Where soon her prodigality will shine
And all her riches.

Of white or gold or crimson red
Or emerald green, she takes a thread;
With here a pearl and here a star
Where the wild plum and blackthorn are;
With here a curl and there a stud,
This for the orchard, this the wood;
With here a spear and there a frond
To fill the garden, edge the pond;—
Tinsel for frog and willow;
For celandine, chrome yellow;
Red sprig for dark green laurel;
Rose-bush, a crest of coral;
White horse-shoe for the small wood-sorrel;
The hazel stave, many a crochet;
For veronica, her watchet;
The strawberry leaf, well notchèd;
And amid the brown
Cross-hatching shown,
The honey-suckle's Attic crown.
Feather-stitch, petit-point and couch,
The season deepens touch by touch,
Till what was little becomes much;
Last, the perfection of her art—
To give to every flower a jewelled heart.

SUMMER

165. Verses
166. Summer Sun   .   .   *Robert Louis Stevenson*
167. Song of Summer Days .   .   .   *J. W. Foley*
168. Symphony .   .   .   .   *. Phoebe Hesketh*
169. Summer   .   .   .   .   *Christina Rossetti*

165

VERSES

Now simmer blinks on flowery braes,
And o'er the crystal streamlet plays.

Robert Burns

Again the summer comes, and all is fair;
A sea of tender blue, the sky o'erhead
Stretches its peace; the roses white and red
Through the deep silence of the tranced air,
In a mute ecstasy of love declare
Their souls in perfume, while their leaves are fed
With dew and sunlight that softly falls, shed
Like slumber on pure eyelids unaware.

Philip Bourke Marston

O summer sun, O moving trees!
O cheerful human noise, O busy glittering street!
What hour shall Fate in all the future find,
Or what delights, ever to equal these:
Only to taste the warmth, the light, the wind,
Only to be alive, and feel that life is sweet?

Laurence Binyon

SUMMER SUN
ROBERT LOUIS STEVENSON

Great is the sun, and wide he goes
Through empty heaven without repose;
And in the blue and glowing days
More thick than rain he showers his rays.

Though closer still the blinds we pull
To keep the shady parlour cool,
Yet he will find a chink or two
To slip his golden fingers through.

The dusty attic, spider-clad,
He, through the keyhole, maketh glad;
And through the broken edge of tiles,
Into the laddered hayloft smiles.

Meantime his golden face around
He bares to all the garden ground,
And sheds a warm and glittering look
Among the ivy's inmost nook.

Above the hills, along the blue,
Round the bright air with footing true,
To please the child, to paint the rose,
The gardener of the world he goes.

167

Perhaps this poet was looking forward to a country holiday.

SONG OF SUMMER DAYS
J. W. FOLEY

Sing a song of hollow logs,
Chirp of cricket, croak of frogs,
Cry of wild bird, hum of bees,
Dancing leaves and whisp'ring trees;
Legs all bare, and dusty toes,
Ruddy cheeks and freckled nose,
Splash of brook and swish of line,
Where the song that's half so fine?

Sing a song of summer days,
Leafy nooks and shady ways,
Nodding roses, apples red,
Clover like a carpet spread;
Sing a song of running brooks,
Cans of bait and fishing hooks,
Dewy hollows, yellow moons,
Birds a-pipe with merry tunes.

Sing a song of skies of blue,
Eden's garden made anew,
Scarlet hedges, leafy lanes,
Vine-embowered sills and panes;
Stretch of meadows, splash'd with dew,
Silver clouds with sunlight through,
Call of thrush and pipe of wren,
Sing and call it home again.

168

Only when there is a general silence can we enjoy the little sounds mentioned in this poem.

SYMPHONY
PHOEBE HESKETH

This symphony of stillness is composed
Of sounds that make the silence yet more still:
The sky-bound tremor of a lark's noon song,
The wind, scarce stirring bracken on the hill.
The heart-drugged burring of a single bee,
And ether-drilling insects spin the air
Around them with innumerable sounds.
The zooming dragon-fly that flashes fair
Across the lead-hot pond where midges swarm
In cacophonic concert of their own,
The grasshopper's dry rattle, paper-parched,
And bird that cracks a snail on burning stone,
The brittle, sun-blacked gorse-pods' sudden snap,
And startled pigeon's clatter on a bough—
All these compose this mid-day symphony,
Conducting silence as I listen now.

In praise of the Summer.

SUMMER
CHRISTINA ROSSETTI

Winter is cold-hearted,
  Spring is yea and nay,
Autumn is a weather-cock
  Blown every way.
Summer days for me
When every leaf is on its tree;

When Robin's not a beggar,
  And Jenny Wren's a bride,
And larks hang singing, singing, singing,
  Over the wheat-fields wide,
  And anchored lilies ride,
And the pendulum spider
Swings from side to side;

And the blue-back beetles transact business
  And gnats fly in a host,
And furry caterpillars hasten
  That no time be lost,
And moths grow fat and thrive,
And ladybirds arrive.

Before green apples blush,
  Before green nuts embrown,
Why one day in the country
  Is worth a month in town;
  Is worth a day and a year
Of the dusty, musty, lag-last fashion
That days drone elsewhere.

AUTUMN AND HARVEST

170. Verses
171. 'Thou visitest the earth, and waterest it'
                                    Psalm LXV. 9–13
172. Autumn . . . . . *Jack Gilbey*
173. Ode to Autumn . . . . *John Keats*
174. Autumn . . . . . *John Clare*
175. An Old Story . . . . *Eden Phillpotts*
176. Digging . . . . *Edward Thomas*
177. Field of Autumn . . . . *Laurie Lee*
178. This Way to Winter . . . *James Stephens*

170

VERSES

(Thou shalt keep) the feast of harvest, the first-fruits of
    thy labours,
Which thou hast sown in the field;
And the feast of ingathering,
Which is in the end of the year,
When thou hast gathered in thy labours out of the field.
                                    Exodus XXIII. 16

If ye walk in my statutes,
And keep my commandments, and do them;
Then I will give you rain in due season,
And the land shall yield her increase,
And the trees of the field shall yield their fruit.
                                    Leviticus XXVI. 3, 4

And ye shall eat in plenty, and be satisfied,
And praise the name of the Lord your God,
That hath dealt wondrously with you.
                                    Joel II. 26

The eyes of all wait upon thee;
And thou givest them their meat in due season.
Thou openest thine hand,
And satisfiest the desire of every living thing.
                                    Psalm CXLV. 15, 16

Yea, the Lord shall give that which is good;
And our land shall yield her increase.
                                    Psalm LXXXV. 12

While the earth remaineth,
Seedtime and harvest,
And cold and heat,
And summer and winter,
And day and night shall not cease.

Genesis VIII. 22

Let us, with a gladsome mind,
Praise the Lord, for he is kind:
For his mercies ay endure,
Ever faithful, ever sure. *John Milton*

READING

171

'THOU VISITEST THE EARTH, AND WATEREST IT'

Psalm LXV. 9–13

An abundant harvest is the climax of God's providence throughout the year.

172

A calm day at the end of Autumn is a reminder that this is not a sad time but merely a period of rest.

AUTUMN

JACK GILBEY

How still the day! No branches stir at all.
Never the slightest quiver seemingly
Disturbs the tree tops now. What makes them fall,
These shrivelled leaves that flutter noiselessly,
To lie a-moulding on the soil below,
But that their course is run, the sap is dry
That once flowed through their veins and made them grow
To tell a waiting world that Spring was nigh?
Yet Autumn does not call for tears, its skies
Show blue among the grey, and though there be
Regret because a part of Nature dies,
There is a feeling of tranquillity
In all this pageantry, for God knows best
The way to put all weary things to rest.

In praise of the fruits, occupations and sounds of Autumn.

ODE TO AUTUMN
JOHN KEATS

Season of mists and mellow fruitfulness!
  Close bosom-friend of the maturing sun;
Conspiring with him how to load and bless
  With fruit the vines that round the thatch-eaves run;
To bend with apples the moss'd cottage-trees,
  And fill all fruit with ripeness to the core;
    To swell the gourd, and plump the hazel shells
With a sweet kernel; to set budding more,
  And still more, later flowers for the bees,
  Until they think warm days will never cease,
    For Summer has o'er-brimm'd their clammy cells.

Who hath not seen thee oft amid thy store?
  Sometimes whoever seeks abroad may find
Thee sitting careless on a granary floor,
  Thy hair soft-lifted by the winnowing wind;
Or on a half-reap'd furrow sound asleep,
  Drows'd with the fume of poppies, while thy hook
    Spares the next swath and all its twined flowers;
And sometime like a gleaner thou doest keep
  Steady thy laden head across a brook;
  Or by a cider-press, with patient look,
    Thou watchest the last oozings, hours by hours.

Where are the songs of Spring? Ay, where are they?
  Think not of them, thou hast thy music too,
While barred clouds bloom the soft-dying day,
  And touch the stubble-plains with rosy hue;
Then in a wailful choir the small gnats mourn
  Among the river sallows, borne aloft
    Or sinking as the light wind lives or dies;
And full-grown lambs loud bleat from hilly bourn;
  Hedge-crickets sing; and now with treble soft
  The redbreast whistles from a garden-croft,
    And gathering swallows twitter in the skies.

AUTUMN
JOHN CLARE

I love the fitful gust that shakes
  The casement all the day,
And from the mossy elm-tree takes
  The faded leaves away,
Twirling them by the window pane
With thousand others down the lane.

I love to see the shaking twig
  Dance till the shut of eve,
The sparrow on the cottage rig,
  Whose chirp would make believe
That spring was just now flirting by
In summer's lap with flowers to lie.

I love to see the cottage smoke
  Curl upwards through the trees,
The pigeons nestled round the cote
  On November days like these;
The cock upon the dunghill crowing,
The mill-sails on the heath a-going.

The feather from the raven's breast
  Falls on the stubble lea,
The acorns near the old crow's nest
  Drop pattering down the tree;
The grunting pigs, that wait for all,
Scramble and hurry where they fall.

175

For a stormy day in late Autumn.

AN OLD STORY
EDEN PHILLPOTTS

The winds of heaven bare their teeth again
And, from his fiery marches upon high,
The sun sinks lower, lower tardily;

On hill and dale their Summer beauties wane;
From hurst and holt the leaves take wing and fly,
And hedge-row berries fall till none remain
Within the treasury of Autumn's reign:
Their pageants pass, their pomp and glory die.

Now harvest's home and mother-naked Earth
Unto the plough her patient bosom yields,
Affirming Winter's transitory dearth,
Dismantled forests and storm-beaten fields.
Through many a stark and steely night forlorn
She plans her next year's gown of golden corn.

176

This poem might well have been called 'Scents'.

DIGGING

EDWARD THOMAS

To-day I think
Only with scents—scents dead leaves yield,
And bracken, and wild carrot's seed,
And the square mustard field;

Odours that rise
When the spade wounds the root of tree,
Rose, currant, raspberry, or goutweed,
Rhubarb or celery;

The smoke's smell, too,
Flowing from where a bonfire burns
The dead, the waste, the dangerous,
And all to sweetness turns.

It is enough
To smell, to crumble the dark earth,
While the robin sings over again
Sad songs of Autumn mirth.

An impression of a calm autumn day in the Cotswold Country.

FIELD OF AUTUMN

LAURIE LEE

Slow moves the acid breath of noon
over the copper-coated hill,
slow from the wild crab's bearded breast
the palsied apples fall.

Like coloured smoke the day hangs fire,
taking the village without sound;
the vulture-headed sun lies low
chained to the violet ground.

The horse upon the rocky height
rolls all the valley in his eye,
but dares not raise his foot or move
his shoulder from the fly.

The sheep, snail-backed against the wall,
lifts her blind face but does not know
the cry her blackened tongue gives forth
is the first bleat of snow.

Each bird and stone, each roof and well,
feels the gold foot of autumn pass;
each spider binds with glittering snare
the splintered bones of grass.

Slow moves the hour that sucks our life,
slow drops the late wasp from the pear,
the rose tree's thread of scent draws thin—
and snaps upon the air.

For the time when the evenings draw in and the weather becomes harder.

THIS WAY TO WINTER

JAMES STEPHENS

Day by day
The sun's broad beam
Fades away
By a golden gleam;
—Hark on the cliff
How the sea-gulls scream!

Eve by eve
The wind, more drear,
Stays to grieve
That the winter's near;
—Hark how the crisp leaves
Dart and fleer!

Night by night
The shade grows dense,
And the cold starlight
Beams more intense;
—Hark how the beggar boy
Asks for pence!

Get you out
Your muffler grey,
Your boots so stout,
And your great-coat, pray,
And put on your gloves,
—'Tis a hardy day!

WINTER

179. Verses
180. Winter . . . . *Alfred Lord Tennyson*
181. Winter's Beauty . . . . *W. H. Davies*
182. Old Winter . . . . . *T. Noel*
183. Winter . . . . . *Anonymous*
184. 'Through the hushed air the whitening shower descends'. . . . *James Thomson*
185. 'Blow, blow, thou winter wind' *William Shakespeare*
186. Snow . . . . . *Alfred Noyes*

179
VERSES

The waters are hid as with a stone,
And the face of the deep is frozen.
Job XXXVIII. 30

He saith to the snow,
  Be thou on the earth;
Likewise to the small rain,
And to the great rain of his strength.
Job XXXVII. 6

He giveth snow like wool;
He scattereth the hoarfrost like ashes.
Psalm CXLVII. 16

180

Here are some of the effects of a hard frost.

WINTER
ALFRED LORD TENNYSON

The frost is here,
And fuel is dear,
And woods are sear,
And fires burn clear,
And frost is here
And has bitten the heel of the going year.

Bite, frost, bite!
You roll away from the light
The blue wood-louse, and the plump dormouse,
And the bees are still'd and the flies are kill'd,
And you bite far into the heart of the house,
But not into mine.

Bite, frost, bite!
The woods are all the searer,
The fuel is all the dearer,
The fires are all the clearer,
My spring is all the nearer,
You have bitten into the heart of the earth,
But not into mine.

181

After a fall of snow.

WINTER'S BEAUTY
W. H. DAVIES

Is it not fine to walk in spring,
When leaves are born, and hear birds sing?
And when they lose their singing powers,
In summer, watch the bees at flowers?
Is it not fine, when summer's past,
To have the leaves, no longer fast,
Biting my heel where'er I go,
Or dancing lightly on my toe?
Now winter's here and rivers freeze;
As I walk out I see the trees,
Wherein the pretty squirrels sleep,
All standing in the snow so deep:
And every twig, however small,
Is blossomed white and beautiful.
Then welcome, winter, with thy power
To make this tree a big white flower;
To make this tree a lovely sight,
With fifty brown arms draped in white,
While thousands of small fingers show
In soft white gloves of purest snow.

How to forget the howling of the cold winter wind.

OLD WINTER

T. NOEL

Old Winter, sad, in snow yclad,
    Is making a doleful din;
But let him howl till he crack his jowl,
    We will not let him in.

Ay, let him lift from the billowy drift
    His hoary, haggard form,
And scowling stand, with his wrinkled hand
    Outstretching to the storm.

And let his weird and sleety beard
    Stream loose upon the blast,
And, rustling, chime to the tinkling rime
    From his bald head falling fast.

Let his baleful breath shed blight and death
    On herb and flower and tree;
And brooks and ponds in crystal bonds
    Bind fast, but what care we?

Let him push at the door, in the chimney roar,
    And rattle the window pane;
Let him in at us spy with his icicle eye,
    But he shall not entrance gain.

Let him gnaw, forsooth, with his freezing tooth,
    On our roof-tiles, till he tire;
But we care not a whit, as we jovial sit
    Before our blazing fire.

Come, lads, let's sing, till the rafters ring;
    Come push the can about—
From our snug fireside this Christmas-tide
    We'll keep old Winter out.

A reminder of better days to come.

WINTER
ANONYMOUS

Winter creeps,
Nature sleeps;
Birds are gone,
Flowers are none,
Fields are bare,
Bleak the air,
Leaves are shed:
All seems dead.

God's alive!
Grow and thrive,
Hidden away,
Bloom of May,
Robe of June!
Very soon
Nought but green
Will be seen!

184

'THROUGH THE HUSHED AIR THE WHITENING SHOWER DESCENDS'
JAMES THOMSON

Through the hushed air the whitening shower descends,
At first thin-wavering; till at last the flakes
Fall broad and wide and fast, dimming the day
With a continual flow. The cherished fields
Put on their winter-robe of purest white.
'Tis brightness all; save where the new snow melts
Along the mazy current.

From 'The Seasons'

*A philosophical sigh at thoughts of ingratitude from friends,
colder than the winter's wind.*

'BLOW, BLOW, THOU WINTER WIND'
WILLIAM SHAKESPEARE

Blow, blow, thou winter wind,
Thou art not so unkind
    As man's ingratitude;
Thy tooth is not so keen,
Because thou art not seen,
    Although thy breath be rude.
Heigh ho! sing, heigh ho! unto the green holly:
Most friendship is feigning, most loving mere folly.
        Then heigh ho, the holly!
        This life is most jolly.

Freeze, freeze, thou bitter sky,
That dost not bite so nigh
    As benefits forgot:
Though thou the waters warp,
Thy sting is not so sharp
    As friend remember'd not.
Heigh ho! sing, heigh ho! unto the green holly:
Most friendship is feigning, most loving mere folly.
        Then heigh ho, the holly!
        This life is most jolly.

From 'As You Like It' II. 7

Verses which emphasize the gentleness of falling snow.

SNOW

ALFRED NOYES

A pure white mantle blotted out
   The world I used to know:
There was no scarlet in the sky
   Or on the hills below,
Gently as mercy out of heaven
   Came down the healing snow.

The trees that were so dark and bare
   Stood up in radiant white,
And the road forgot its furrowed care
   As day forgets the night,
And the new heavens and the new earth
   Lay robed in dazzling light.

And every flake that fell from heaven
   Was like an angel's kiss,
Or a feather fluttering from the wings
   Of some dear soul in bliss
Who gently leaned from that bright world
   To soothe the pain of this.

187. 'My New Year's wish shall be'   *Edmund Gosse*
188. January . . . . *Robert Bridges*
189. February . . . . *Francis Brett Young*
190. 'Hail, Bishop Valentine' . . *John Donne*
191. February Fill-dyke . . . *Alfred Noyes*
192. 'March, blow by' . . . *Eleanor Farjeon*
193. April Fool's Day . . . *Laurence Housman*
194. The Hitchen May-Day Song . . *Anonymous*
195. June . . . . . . *Irene F. Pawsey*
196. Four Sweet Months . . . *Robert Herrick*
197. July . . . . . . *Austin Dobson*
198. September . . . . . *Mary Howitt*
199. October . . . . *Christina Rossetti*
200. November . . . . . *Margaret Rose*
201. Fireworks . . . . . *James Reeves*
202. No! . . . . . . *Thomas Hood*
203. Things to Remember . . . *James Reeves*
204. 'Ring out, wild bells' . . *Alfred Lord Tennyson*

187

'MY NEW YEAR'S WISH SHALL BE'

My New Year's wish shall be
  For love, and love alone;
More hands to hold out joy for me,
  More hearts for me to own;
For more than gold a thousandfold
Is love that's neither bought nor sold.

Edmund Gosse

134

JANUARY
ROBERT BRIDGES

Cold is the winter day, misty and dark:
  The sunless sky with faded gleams is rent:
And patches of thin snow outlying, mark
  The landscape with a drear disfigurement.

The trees their mournful branches lift aloft:
  The oak with knotty twigs is full of trust,
With bud-thronged bough the cherry in the croft;
  The chestnut holds her gluey knops upthrust.

No birds sing, but the starling chaps his bill
  And chatters mockingly; the newborn lambs
Within their strawbuilt fold beneath the hill
  Answer with plaintive cry their bleating dams.

Their voices melt in welcome dreams of spring,
  Green grass and leafy trees and sunny skies:
My fancy decks the woods, the thrushes sing,
  Meadows are gay, bees hum and scents arise.

And God the Maker doth my heart grow bold
  To praise for wintry works not understood,
Who all the worlds and ages doth behold,
  Evil and good as one, and all as good.

189

FEBRUARY

FRANCIS BRETT YOUNG

The robin on my lawn,
He was the first to tell
How, in the frozen dawn,
This miracle befell,
Waking the meadows white
With hoar, the iron road
Agleam with splintered light,
And ice where water flowed:
Till, when the low sun drank
Those milky mists that cloak
Hanger and hollied bank,
The winter world awoke
To hear the feeble bleat
Of lambs on downland farms:
A blackbird whistled sweet:
Old beeches moved their arms
Into a mellow haze
Aerial, newly-born:
And I, alone, agaze,
Stood waiting for the thorn
To break in blossom white,
Or burst in a green flame . . .
So, in a single night,
Fair February came,
Bidding my lips to sing
Or whisper their surprise,
With all the joy of Spring
And morning in her eyes.

190

*St. Valentine's Day is traditionally the day on which the birds
are supposed to pair off for nesting.*

'HAIL, BISHOP VALENTINE'

JOHN DONNE

Hail, Bishop Valentine, whose day this is,
All the air is thy diocese,

136

And all the chirping choristers
And other birds are thy parishioners;
    Thou marriest every year
The lyric Lark, and the grave whispering Dove,
The Sparrow that neglects his life for love,
The household Bird, with the red stomacher;
    Thou mak'st the Blackbird speed as soon
As doth the Goldfinch, or the Halcyon;
The husband cock looks out, and straight is sped,
And meets his wife, which brings her feather-bed.
This day more cheerfully than ever shine,
This day, which might enflame thy self, Old Valentine.

191

FEBRUARY FILL-DYKE
ALFRED NOYES

February Fill-dyke
    Breaks the crusted earth,
Fills the flowing brook with song
    And brings the seed to birth.

Here and there a primrose
    Takes a timid look
Through the fern to see herself
    Trembling in the brook.

Blackbird tries a note or two
    In the boughs above.
February Fill-dyke
    Will bring him to his love.

The light comes, the night comes,
    Tears will come and go.
February Fill-dyke
    Will never cease to flow.

'MARCH, BLOW BY'
ELEANOR FARJEON

March, blow by
With your stormy grey eye!
April, run in
With your pear-blossom skin!
  The catkin is shaking
  A powder of gold,
  The daisy is breaking
  A way through the mould,
  The chaffinch is taking
  Her morsel of moss,
  The wind is making
  The rookery toss.
March, good-bye
To your stormy grey eye!
April, begin
With the bloom on your chin!

APRIL FOOL'S DAY
LAURENCE HOUSMAN

We are getting to the short night,
  And 'summer time' is near;
And now, within a fortnight,
  The cuckoo may be here.

The silences are voicing,
  And song brims loud,
And a rainbow hangs rejoicing
  On a clear April cloud;

And the little loves are meeting
  In field and copse and glen,
As spring comes defeating
  The dark deeds of men.

For wrath can black-out reason,
  And cities it can slay;
But the promise of the season
  It cannot take away.

O Man, what a Hell you
　　Have made of earth and sky—
The wise bird will tell you;
　　And 'cuckoo' he will cry.

THE HITCHEN MAY-DAY SONG
ANONYMOUS

Remember us poor Mayers all,
　　And thus we do begin
To lead our lives in righteousness,
　　Or else we die in sin.

We have been rambling half the night,
　　And almost all the day,
And now returned back again
　　We've brought you a branch of May.

A branch of May we have brought you,
　　And at your door it stands,
It is but a sprout, but it's well budded out
　　By the work of our Lord's hands.

The hedges and trees they are so green,
　　As green as any leek,
Our heavenly Father He watered them
　　With His heavenly dew so sweet.

The heavenly gates are open wide,
　　Our paths are beaten plain,
And if a man be not too far gone,
　　He may return again.

The life of man is but a span,
　　It flourishes like a flower,
We are here to-day and gone to-morrow
　　And we are dead in an hour.

The moon shines bright, and the stars give a light
　　A little before it is day,
So God bless you all, both great and small,
　　And send you a joyful May!

JUNE
IRENE F. PAWSEY

Month of leaves,
Month of roses;
Gardens full
Of dainty posies;
   Skies of blue,
   Hedgerows gay,
   Meadows sweet
   With new-mown hay.

Flowery banks,
A-drone with bees,
Dreaming cattle
Under trees:
   Song-birds pipe
   A merry tune—
   This is summer,
   This is June.

FOUR SWEET MONTHS
ROBERT HERRICK

First, April, she with mellow showers
Opens the way for early flowers;
Then after her comes smiling May
In a more rich and sweet array;
Next enters June, and brings us more
Gems than those two that went before;
Then, lastly, July comes, and she
More wealth brings in than all those three.

JULY

AUSTIN DOBSON

Good-bye to the Town!—good-bye!
Hurrah! for the sea and the sky!

In the street the flower-girls cry;
In the street the water-carts ply;
And a fluter, with features awry,
Plays fitfully 'Scots, wha hae'—
And the throat of that fluter is dry;
Good-bye to the Town!—good-bye!

And over the roof-tops high
Comes a waft like a dream of the May;
And a lady-bird lit on my tie,
And a cock-chafer came with the tray;
And a butterfly (no one knows why)
Mistook my Aunt's cap for a spray;
And 'next door' and 'over the way'
The neighbours take wing and fly;
Hurrah! for the sea and the sky!

To Buxton, the waters to try,
To Buxton goes old Mrs. Bligh;
And the Captain to Homberg and play
Will carry his cane and his eye;
And even Miss Morgan Lefay
Is flitting—to far Peckham Rye;
And my Grocer has gone—in a 'Shay',
And my Tailor has gone—in a 'Fly':
Good-bye to the Town!—good-bye!

So Phyllis, the fawn-footed, hie
For a Hansom. Ere close of the day
Between us a 'world' must lie:
Good-bye to the Town! GOOD-BYE!
Hurrah! for the sea and the sky!

SEPTEMBER
MARY HOWITT

There are twelve months throughout the year,
From January to December—
And the primest month of all the twelve
Is the merry month of September!
Then apples so red
Hang overhead,
And nuts ripe-brown
Come showering down
In the bountiful days of September!
There are flowers enough in the summer-time,
More flowers than I can remember—
But none with the purple, gold and red
That dyes the flowers of September!
The gorgeous flowers of September!
The sun looks through
A clearer blue,
And the moon at night
Sheds a clearer light
On the beautiful flowers of September.

OCTOBER
CHRISTINA ROSSETTI

I've brought you nuts and hops;
And when the leaf drops, why, the walnut drops.
Crack your first nut and light your first fire,
Roast your first chestnut crisp on the bar;
Make the logs sparkle, stir the blaze higher,
Logs are cheery as sun or as star,
Logs we can find wherever we are.
Spring one soft day will open the leaves,
Spring one bright day will lure back the flowers;
Never fancy my whistling wind grieves,
Never fancy I've tears in my showers:
Dance, night and days! and dance on, my hours!
From 'The Months', a Pageant

NOVEMBER

MARGARET ROSE

November is a spinner
　Spinning in the mist,
Weaving such a lovely web
　Of gold and amethyst.
In among the shadows
　She spins till close of day,
Then quietly she folds her hands
　And puts her work away.

FIREWORKS

JAMES REEVES

They rise like sudden fiery flowers
　That burst upon the night,
Then fall to earth in burning showers
　Of crimson, blue, and white.

Like birds too wonderful to name,
　Each miracle unfolds,
And catherine-wheels begin to flame
　Like whirling marigolds.

Rockets and Roman candles make
　An orchard of the sky,
Whence magic trees their petals shake
　Upon each gazing eye.

NO!

THOMAS HOOD

No sun—no moon!
No morn—no noon—
No dawn—no dusk—no proper time of day—
No sky—no earthly view—
No distance looking blue—
No road—no street—no 't'other side the way'—
No end to any Row—
No indications where the Crescents go—
No top to any steeple—
No recognitions of familiar people—
No courtesies for showing 'em—
No knowing 'em!—
No travelling at all—no locomotion,
No inkling of the way—no notion—
'No go'—by land or ocean—
No mail—no post—
No news from any foreign coast—
No Park—no Ring—no afternoon gentility—
No company—no nobility—
No warmth, no cheerfulness, no healthful ease,
No comfortable feel in any member—
No shade, no shine, no butterflies, no bees,
No fruits, no flowers, no leaves, no birds—
November!

THINGS TO REMEMBER

JAMES REEVES

The buttercups in May,
The wild rose on the spray,
The poppy in the hay,
The primrose in the dell,
The freckled foxglove bell,
The honeysuckle's smell

Are things I would remember
When cheerless, raw November
Makes room for dark December.

'RING OUT, WILD BELLS'

ALFRED LORD TENNYSON

Ring out, wild bells, to the wild sky,
  The flying cloud, the frosty light:
  The year is dying in the night;
Ring out, wild bells, and let him die.

Ring out the old, ring in the new,
  Ring, happy bells, across the snow:
  The year is going, let him go;
Ring out the false, ring in the true.

Ring out the grief that saps the mind,
  For those that here we see no more;
  Ring out the feud of rich and poor,
Ring in redress to all mankind.

Ring out a slowly dying cause,
  And ancient forms of party strife;
  Ring in the nobler modes of life,
With sweeter manners, purer laws.

Ring out the want, the care, the sin,
  The faithless coldness of the times;
  Ring out, ring out my mournful rhymes,
But ring the fuller minstrel in.

Ring out false pride in place and blood,
  The civic slander and the spite;
  Ring in the love of truth and right,
Ring in the common love of good.

Ring out old shapes of foul disease;
  Ring out the narrowing lust of gold;
  Ring out the thousand wars of old,
Ring in the thousand years of peace.

Ring in the valiant man and free,
  The larger heart, the kindlier hand;
  Ring out the darkness of the land,
Ring in the Christ that is to be.

From 'In Memoriam'

205. Christmas . . . . . *John Betjeman*
206. The Oxen . . . . . *Thomas Hardy*
207. 'I sing of a maid' . . . *Anonymous*
208. Bethlehem . . . . . *William Canton*
209. A Christmas Carol . . *Christina Rossetti*
210. Royal Presents . . . *Nathaniel Wanley*
211. 'As Joseph was a-walking' . . *Traditional*
212. In the Wilderness . . . *Robert Graves*
213. 'Yet if his majesty our sovereign lord' *Anonymous*
214. 'The world itself keeps Easter Day' *Anonymous*

205

The voice of him that crieth in the wilderness,
Prepare ye the way of the Lord,
Make straight in the desert a highway for our God.
Isaiah XL. 3

CHRISTMAS
JOHN BETJEMAN

The bells of waiting Advent ring,
  The Tortoise stove is lit again
And lamp-oil light across the night
  Has caught the streaks of winter rain
In many a stained-glass window sheen
From Crimson Lake to Hooker's Green.

The holly in the windy hedge
  And round the Manor House the yew
Will soon be stripped to deck the ledge,
  The altar, font and arch and pew,
So that the villagers can say
'The church looks nice' on Christmas Day.

Provincial public houses blaze
  And Corporation tram cars clang,
On lighted tenements I gaze
  Where paper decorations hang,
And bunting in the red Town Hall
Says, 'Merry Christmas to you all'.

And London shops on Christmas Eve
   Are strung with silver bells and flowers
As hurrying clerks the City leave
   To pigeon-haunted classic towers,
And marbled clouds go scudding by
The many-steepled London sky.

And girls in slacks remember Dad,
   And oafish louts remember Mum,
And sleepless children's hearts are glad,
   And Christmas-morning bells say 'Come!'
Even to shining ones who dwell
Safe in the Dorchester Hotel.

And is it true? And is it true,
   This most tremendous tale of all,
Seen in a stained-glass window's hue,
   A Baby in an ox's stall?
The Maker of the stars and sea
Become a Child on earth for me?

And is it true? For if it is,
   No loving fingers tying strings
Around those tissued fripperies,
   The sweet and silly Christmas things,
Bath salts and inexpensive scent
And hideous tie so kindly meant,

No love that in a family dwells,
   No carolling in frosty air,
Nor all the steeple-shaking bells
   Can with this single Truth compare—-
That God was Man in Palestine
And lives to-day in Bread and Wine.

THE OXEN

THOMAS HARDY

Christmas Eve, and twelve of the clock.
  'Now they are all on their knees,'
An elder said as we sat in a flock
  By the embers in hearthside ease.

We pictured the meek mild creatures where
  They dwelt in their strawy pen,
Nor did it occur to one of us there
  To doubt they were kneeling then.

So fair a fancy few would weave
  In these years! Yet, I feel,
If someone said on Christmas Eve,
  'Come; see the oxen kneel

'In the lonely barton by yonder coomb
  Our childhood used to know,'
I should go with him in the gloom,
  Hoping it might be so.

Behold, a virgin shall be with child, and shall bring forth
  a son, and they shall call his name, Emmanuel,
which being interpreted is, God with us.

St. Matthew i. 23

'I SING OF A MAID'

ANONYMOUS

I sing of a maid that is matchless,
King of all Kings to her son she chose.

He came all so still where his mother was,
As dew in April that falleth on the grass.

He came all so still to his mother's bower,
As dew in April that falleth on the flower.

He came all so still where his mother lay,
As dew in April that falleth on the spray.

Mother and maiden was never none but she,
Well may such a Lady God's mother be.

208

BETHLEHEM
WILLIAM CANTON

When the herds were watching
    In the midnight chill,
Came a spotless lambkin
    From the heavenly hill.

Snow was on the mountains,
    And the wind was cold,
When from God's own garden
    Dropped a rose of gold.

When 'twas bitter winter,
    Houseless and forlorn
In a star-lit stable
    Christ the Babe was born.

Welcome, heavenly lambkin;
    Welcome, golden rose;
Alleluia, Baby
    In the swaddling clothes.

A CHRISTMAS CAROL

CHRISTINA ROSSETTI

Before the paling of the stars,
  Before the winter morn,
Before the earliest cock crow,
  Jesus Christ was born:
Born in a stable,
  Cradled in a manger,
In the world His hands had made
  Born a stranger.

Priest and King lay fast asleep
  In Jerusalem,
Young and old lay fast asleep
  In crowded Bethlehem:
Saint and Angel, ox and ass,
  Kept a watch together,
Before the Christmas daybreak
  In the winter weather.

Jesus on His Mother's breast
  In the stable cold,
Spotless Lamb of God was He,
  Shepherd of the fold:
Let us kneel with Mary Maid,
  With Joseph bent and hoary,
With Saint and Angel, ox and ass,
  To hail the King of Glory.

And when they were come into the house, they saw the young child with Mary his mother, and fell down, and worshipped him: and when they had opened their treasures, they presented him gifts; gold, and frankincense, and myrrh.

St. Matthew II. 11

Our prayers, our feelings of repentance, our sharing of sorrow are offerings as acceptable as those of the Magi.

ROYAL PRESENTS

NATHANIEL WANLEY

The off'rings of the Eastern Kings of old
Unto our Lord were Incense, Myrrh and Gold,
Incense because a God; Gold as a king
And Myrrh as to a dying man they bring:
Instead of Incense blessed Lord if we
Can send a Sigh or fervent Prayer to Thee,
Instead of Myrrh if we can but provide
Tears that from penitential eyes do slide,
And though we have no Gold if for our part
We can present Thee with a broken heart
Thou wilt accept, and say those Eastern Kings
Did not present Thee with more precious things.

'AS JOSEPH WAS A-WALKING'

TRADITIONAL

As Joseph was a-walking,
  He heard an angel sing:
'This night there shall be born
  On earth our heavenly King;

'He neither shall be born
  In housen nor in hall,
Nor in the place of Paradise,
  But in an ox's stall.

'He neither shall be clothed
  In purple nor in pall,
But all in fair linen
  As usen babies all.

'He neither shall be rocked
  In silver nor in gold,
But in a wooden cradle
  That rocks upon the mould.

'He neither shall be christened
  In white wine nor in red,
But with fair spring water
  As we were christened.'

Then Mary took her young son,
  And set Him on her knee:
Saying, 'My dear son, tell me,
  Tell how this world shall be.'

'O I shall be as dead, mother,
  As stones are in the wall;
O the stones in the streets, mother,
  Shall sorrow for me all.

'On Easter-day, dear mother,
  My rising up shall be;
O the sun and the moon, mother,
  Shall both arise with me.'

From 'The Cherry Tree' carol

Then was Jesus led up of the Spirit into the wilderness to
be tempted of the devil.
St. Matthew IV. I

*The wild creatures of the wilderness perhaps gained comfort
from the presence of Christ amongst them.*

IN THE WILDERNESS
ROBERT GRAVES

He, of His gentleness,
Thirsting and hungering
Walked in the wilderness;
Soft words of grace He spoke
Unto lost desert-folk
That listened wondering.
He heard the bittern call
From ruined palace-wall,
Answered him brotherly;
He held communion
With the she-pelican
Of lonely piety.
Basilisk, cockatrice,
Flocked to His homilies,
With mail of dread device,
With monstrous barbed stings,
With eager dragon-eyes;
Great bats on leathern wings
And old, blind, broken things
Mean in their miseries.
Then ever with Him went,
Of all His wanderings
Comrade, with ragged coat,
Gaunt ribs—poor innocent—
Bleeding foot, burning throat,
The guileless young scapegoat:
For forty nights and days
Followed in Jesus' ways,
Sure guard behind Him kept,
Tears like a lover wept.

We would make elaborate preparations for the reception of an earthly king, but are still unprepared for the coming of Christ, just as we were when He first came.

'YET IF HIS MAJESTY OUR SOVEREIGN LORD'
ANONYMOUS

Yet if his majesty our sovereign lord
Should of his own accord
Friendly himself invite,
And say, 'I'll be your guest to-morrow night,'
How should we stir ourselves, call and command
All hands to work! 'Let no man idle stand.
Set me fine Spanish tables in the hall;
See they be fitted all;
Let there be room to eat,
And order taken that there want no meat.
See every sconce and candlestick made bright,
That without tapers they may give a light.
Look to the presence; are the carpets spread,
The dais o'er the head,
The cushions in the chairs,
And all the candles lighted on the stairs?
Perfume the chambers, and in any case
Let each man give attendance in his place!'
Thus if the king were coming would we do,
And 'twere good reason too;
For 'tis a duteous thing
To show all honour to an earthly king,
And after all our travail and our cost,
So he be pleased, to think no labour lost.
But at the coming of the King of Heaven
All's set at six and seven:
We wallow in our sin,
Christ cannot find a chamber in the inn.
We entertain Him always like a stranger,
And as at first still lodge Him in the manger.

214

He saith unto them, Be not affrighted: Ye seek Jesus
of Nazareth, which was crucified: he is risen; he is
not here:

St. Mark XVI. 6

'THE WORLD ITSELF KEEPS EASTER DAY'
ANONYMOUS

The world itself keeps Easter Day,
  And Easter larks are singing;
And Easter flowers are blooming gay,
  And Easter buds are springing:
  Alleluya, Alleluya:
The Lord of all things lives anew,
And all His works are rising too:
  Hosanna in excelsis.

There stood three Marys by the tomb,
  On Easter morning early;
When day had scarcely chased the gloom,
  And dew was white and pearly:
  Alleluya, Alleluya:
With loving but with erring mind,
They came the Prince of Life to find:
  Hosanna in excelsis.

The world itself keeps Easter Day,
  Saint Joseph's star is beaming;
Saint Alice has her primrose gay,
  Saint George's bells are gleaming:
  Alleluya, Alleluya:
The Lord has risen, as all things tell:
Good Christians, see ye rise as well!
  Hosanna in excelsis.

Old carol

PART II

MAN'S WORLD

MAN-MAKING

215. Verses
216. 'God spake all these words' .   *Exodus* XX. I–17
217. 'Lay not up for yourselves treasures'
                              St. Matthew VI. 19–21
218. 'Add to your faith virtue' .   2 *St. Peter* I. 5–9
219. My Creed .   .   .   *Howard Arnold Walter*
220. Man-making   .   .   .   *Edwin Markham*
221. 'Souls are built as temples are'   . *Susan Coolidge*
222. 'Make sure of truth'   .   .   . *Horatius Bonar*
223. 'Thou must be true thyself' .   . *Horatius Bonar*
224. 'What asks our Father'   .   . *J. G. Whittier*
225. 'Not on the vulgar mass'   .   . *R. Browning*

215

VERSES

Who shall ascend into the hill of the Lord?
Or who shall stand in his holy place?
He that hath clean hands, and a pure heart;
Who hath not lifted up his soul unto vanity,
      nor sworn deceitfully.
                              Psalm XXIV. 3, 4

Were I so tall to reach the pole
      Or grasp the ocean with my span,
I must be measured by my soul:
      The mind's the standard of the man.
                              Isaac Watts

Four things a man must learn to do
If he would make his record true;
To think without confusion clearly;
To love his fellow-men sincerely;
To act from honest motives purely;
To trust in God and Heaven securely.
                              Henry van Dyke

156

216

'GOD SPAKE ALL THESE WORDS'   Exodus xx. 1–17
The ten commandments.

217

'LAY NOT UP FOR YOURSELVES TREASURES UPON EARTH'
St. Matthew vi. 19–21

218

'ADD TO YOUR FAITH VIRTUE'   2 St. Peter i. 5–9
*A list of the qualities needed by the man who would lead a
worthy life.*

219

MY CREED
HOWARD ARNOLD WALTER

I would be true, for there are those who trust me;
I would be pure, for there are those that care.
I would be strong, for there is much to suffer,
I would be brave, for there is much to dare.
I would be friend to all—the foe, the friendless;
I would be giving, and forget the gift.
I would be humble, for I know my weakness;
I would look up—and laugh—and love—and lift.

220

*The only activities that are worth-while are those which help
to build our characters.*

MAN-MAKING
EDWIN MARKHAM

We all are blind until we see
    That, in the human plan,
Nothing is worth the making, if
    It does not make the man.

Why build these cities glorious
    If man unbuilded goes?
In vain we build the world, unless
    The builder also grows.

The complexity and interest of the human character can be compared to a fine building made up from a wealth of beautiful detail.

'SOULS ARE BUILT AS TEMPLES ARE'
SUSAN COOLIDGE

Souls are built as temples are—
Here a carving rich and quaint,
There the image of a saint,
Here a deep-hued pane to tell
Sacred truth or miracle.
Every little helps the much;
Every careful, careless touch
Adds a charm, or leaves a scar.

222

Good advice from a hardworking Scots parson who points out that the man who keeps to the truth is always sure of himself.

'MAKE SURE OF TRUTH'
HORATIUS BONAR

Make sure of truth,
And truth will make thee sure;
It will not shift nor fade nor die,
But like the heav'ns endure.

Man and his earth
Are varying day by day;
Truth cannot change, nor ever grow
Feeble and old and gray.

God's Thoughts, not man's,
Be these thy heritage;
They, like himself, are ever young,
Untouched by time or age.

With God alone
Is truth, and joy, and light;
Walk thou with him in peace and love,
Hold fast the good and right.

Only the sincere person can hope to influence others.

'THOU MUST BE TRUE THYSELF'
HORATIUS BONAR

Thou must be true thyself,
　If thou the truth wouldst teach;
Thy soul must overflow if thou
　Another's soul would reach.

Think truly, and thy thoughts
　Shall the world's famine feed;
Speak truly, and each word of thine
　Shall be a fruitful seed;
Live truly, and thy life shall be
　A great and noble creed.

The American Quaker poet, so much admired by his own countrymen for his own fine character, places the good, simple life above that of the public hero.

'WHAT ASKS OUR FATHER'
JOHN GREENLEAF WHITTIER

What asks our Father of His children save
Justice and mercy and humility,
　A reasonable service of good deeds,
　Pure living, tenderness to human needs,
Reverence, and trust, and prayer for light to see
The Master's footprints in our daily ways?
　No knotted scourge, nor sacrificial knife,
　But the calm beauty of an ordered life
Whose every breathing is unworded praise.

M

Not only do the visible results of a man's life count but his inner thoughts, too. . . . *All that he hoped to be and hoped to do.*

'NOT ON THE VULGAR MASS CALLED WORK'
ROBERT BROWNING

Not on the vulgar mass
Called 'work' must sentence pass,
Things done, that took the eye and had the price;
O'er which, from level stand,
The low world laid its hand,
Found straightway to its mind, could value in a trice:

But all, the world's coarse thumb
And finger failed to plumb,
So passed in making up the main account;
All instincts immature,
All purposes unsure,
That weighed not as his work, yet swelled the man's
amount:

Thoughts hardly to be packed
Into a narrow act,
Fancies that broke through language and escaped;
All I could never be,
All, man ignored in me,
This, I was worth to God, whose wheel the pitcher
shaped.

From 'Rabbi ben Ezra'

226. Verses
227. 'There is nothing from without a man'
St. Mark VII. 15–23
228. 'Ye shall know them by their fruits'
St. Matthew VII. 16–20
229. 'Hearken; behold, there went out a sower to sow'
St. Mark IV. 3–9
230. 'The sower soweth the word' *St. Mark* IV. 14–20
231. 'Ye are the salt of the earth' *St. Matthew* V. 13–16
232. Myself . . . . . *Edgar A. Guest*
233. Man . . . . . *Sir Ronald Ross*
234. 'Give me a good digestion, Lord' . *Anonymous*
235. 'Good name in man and woman' *William Shakespeare*
236. 'The friends thou hast' . *William Shakespeare*
237. 'I bind unto myself to-day' . *Frances Alexander*

226

VERSES

I beseech you therefore, brethren, by the mercies of God,
That ye present your bodies a living sacrifice, holy,
    acceptable unto God,
Which is your reasonable service.

Romans XII. I

I will praise thee;
For I am fearfully and wonderfully made:
Marvellous are thy works;
And that my soul knoweth right well.

Psalm CXXXIX. 14

Better is the poor, being sound and strong of constitution,
Than a rich man that is afflicted in his body.
Health and good estate of body are above all gold,
And a strong body above infinite wealth.

Ecclesiasticus XXX. 14, 15

Be not slow to visit the sick:
For that shall make thee to be beloved.

Ecclesiasticus VII. 35

Nor love, nor honour, wealth nor power
Can give the heart a cheerful hour
When health is lost. Be timely wise;
With health all taste of pleasure flies.   *John Gay*
Joy and temperance and repose
Slam the door on the doctor's nose.
Henry Wadsworth Longfellow

READINGS

227

'THERE IS NOTHING FROM WITHOUT A MAN'

St. Mark VII. 15–23

More harm is done to a man by evil thoughts inside him than by bad influence from without.

228

'YE SHALL KNOW THEM BY THEIR FRUITS'

St. Matthew VII. 16–20

Every man is known by his actions, as a tree is known by the fruit which it bears.

229

'HEARKEN; BEHOLD, THERE WENT OUT A SOWER TO SOW'
The parable of the sower.   St. Mark IV. 3–9

230

'THE SOWER SOWETH THE WORD' St. Mark IV. 14–20
The meaning of the parable of the sower.

231

'YE ARE THE SALT OF THE EARTH'   St. Matthew V. 13–16
Those who have to set an example cannot hide, so they must be above criticism.

232

MYSELF

EDGAR A. GUEST

I have to live with myself, and so
I want to be fit for myself to know;
I want to be able as days go by
Always to look myself straight in the eye.
I don't want to stand with the setting sun
And hate myself for the things I've done.

Man has solved many mysteries, and no one was more qualified to speak of the difficulties than Sir Ronald Ross, but Man has yet to learn to understand and control mankind itself.

MAN

SIR RONALD ROSS

Man putteth the world to scale
  And weigheth out the stars;
Th'eternal hath lost her veil,
  The infinite her bars;
His balance he hath hung in heaven
  And set the sun therein.

He measures the lords of light
  And fiery orbs that spin;
No riddle of darkest night
  He dares not look within;
Athwart the roaring wrack of stars
  He plumbs the chasm of heaven.

The wings of the wind are his;
  To him the world is given;
His servant the lightning is,
  And slave the ocean even;
He scans the mountains yet unclimb'd
  And sounds the solid sea.

With fingers of thought he holds
  What is or e'er can be;
And, touching it not, unfolds
  The sealed mystery.
The pigmy hands, eyes, head God gave
  A giant's are become.

But tho' to this height sublime
  By labour he hath clomb,
One summit he hath to climb
  One deep the more to plumb—
To rede himself and rule himself,
  And so to reach the sum.

A prayer for the body and the mind.

'GIVE ME A GOOD DIGESTION, LORD'
ANONYMOUS

Give me a good digestion, Lord,
And also something to digest.
Give me a healthy body, Lord,
With sense to keep it at its best.
Give me a healthy mind, good Lord,
To keep the good and pure in sight,
Which seeing sin is not appalled,
But finds a way to set it right.

Give me a mind that is not bored,
That does not whimper, whine or sigh;
Don't let me worry overmuch
About that fussy thing called I.
Give me a sense of humour, Lord,
Give me the grace to see a joke,
To get some happiness from life,
And pass it on to other folk.

From a prayer found in Chester Cathedral

235

To lose one's possessions is as nothing compared with losing one's good name.

'GOOD NAME IN MAN AND WOMAN'
WILLIAM SHAKESPEARE

Good name in man and woman, dear my lord,
Is the immediate jewel of their souls:
Who steals my purse steals trash; 'tis something, nothing;
'Twas mine, 'tis his, and has been slave to thousands:
But he that filches from me my good name
Robs me of that which not enriches him,
And makes me poor indeed.

Othello III. 3

Here is advice on how to treat our friends and how to behave when quarrels come, and the best advice of all . . . if we do what we feel to be right we shall never let anyone down.

'THE FRIENDS THOU HAST'
WILLIAM SHAKESPEARE

The friends thou hast, and their adoption tried,
Grapple them to thy soul with hoops of steel;
But do not dull thy palm with entertainment
Of each new-hatch'd, unfledg'd comrade. Beware
Of entrance to a quarrel, but, being in,
Bear't that th'opposed may beware of thee.
Give every man thine ear, but few thy voice;
Take each man's censure but reserve thy judgment.

 . . . .

Neither a borrower, nor a lender be;
For loan oft loses both itself and friend,
And borrowing dulls the edge of husbandry.
This above all: to thine own self be true,
And it must follow, as the night the day,
Thou canst not then be false to any man.

Hamlet I. 3

237
'I BIND UNTO MYSELF TO-DAY'
FRANCES ALEXANDER

I bind unto myself to-day
 The power of God to hold and lead,
His eye to watch, his might to stay,
 His ear to hearken to my need.
The wisdom of my God to teach,
 His hand to guide, his shield to ward;
The Word of God to give me speech,
 His heavenly host to be my guard.

From 'The Breastplate of St. Patrick'

238. Verses
239. Virtue . . . . . *George Herbert*
240. 'It is not growing like a tree' . *Ben Jonson*
241. Honesty . . . . . *John Clare*
242. 'The loaded bee the lowest flies'
Bishop G. E. L. Cotton
243. 'Father, hear the prayer we offer' . *L. M. Willis*
244. The Gauntlet . . . *Robert Armstrong*
245. 'The quality of mercy' . *William Shakespeare*
246. 'O Man, forgive thy mortal foe' *Alfred Lord Tennyson*

238

VERSES

He that followeth after righteousness and mercy
findeth life, righteousness, and honour.
Proverbs XXI. 21

Do no evil,
So shall no harm come unto thee.
Ecclesiasticus VII. 1

The highway of the upright is to depart from evil:
He that keepeth his way preserveth his soul.
Proverbs XVI. 17

Be swift to hear;
And let thy life be sincere;
And with patience give answer.
Ecclesiasticus V. 11

As for the truth, it endureth, and is always strong;
It liveth and conquereth for evermore.
1 *Esdras* IV. 38

All the earth calleth upon the truth,
And the heaven blesseth it:
All works shake and tremble at it,
And with it is no unrighteous thing.
1 *Esdras* IV. 36

Wherefore putting away lying,
  speak every man truth with his neighbour:
For we are members one of another.

Ephesians IV. 25

Let thine eyes look right on,
And let thine eyelids look straight before thee.

Proverbs IV. 25

Mark the perfect man,
  and behold the upright:
For the end of that man is peace.

Psalm XXXVII. 37

Do good, O Lord, unto those that be good,
And to them that are upright in their hearts.

Psalm CXXV. 4

He hath shewed thee, O man, what is good;
And what doth the Lord require of thee,
But to do justly,
And to love mercy,
And to walk humbly with thy God?

Micah VI. 8

Prove all things;
Hold fast that which is good.

I Thessalonians V. 21

Be not overcome of evil,
But overcome evil with good.

Romans XII. 21

A truth that's told with bad intent
Beats all the lies you can invent.

Those beauties which give us most pleasure all fade in their turn, but the good-living person never gives up and is at his best when things are at their worst.

VIRTUE
GEORGE HERBERT

Sweet day, so cool, so calm, so bright,
The bridal of the earth and sky:
The dew shall weep thy fall to-night;
    For thou must die.

Sweet rose, whose hue angry and brave
Bids the rash gazer wipe his eye:
Thy root is ever in its grave,
    And thou must die.

Sweet spring, full of sweet days and roses,
A box where sweets compacted lie;
My music shows ye have your closes,
    And all must die.

Only a sweet and virtuous soul,
Like season'd timber, never gives;
But though the whole world turn to coal,
    Then chiefly lives.

240

As small things can be beautiful so can a short life be perfect.

'IT IS NOT GROWING LIKE A TREE'
BEN JONSON

It is not growing like a tree
    In bulk, doth make man better be;
Or standing long an oak, three hundred year,
To fall a log at last, dry, bald, and sear:
    A lily of a day
    Is fairer far in May,
    Although it fall and die that night;
    It was the plant and flower of light.
In small proportions we just beauties see:
And in short measures life may perfect be.

Honesty is compared first to a rare plant which defies all attempts to destroy it and, finally, to a gem still shining after being hidden for years.

HONESTY

JOHN CLARE

There is a valued though a stubborn weed,
    That blooms but seldom, and is found, but rare,
In sunless places where it cannot seed—
    Would earth, for truth's sake, had more room to spare!
Cant hates it, hypocrites condemn, the herd,
    Seeking self-interest, frown and pass it by;
'Tis trampled on, 'tis bantered and deterred,
    It is scoffed at, mocked at, yet it will not die;
But like a diamond for a century lost,
    Buried in darkness and obscurity,
When found again, it loses not in cost,
    But keeps its value and its purity,
By time unsullied, still the prince of gems,
    And first of jewels in all diadems.

242

The more gifted we are, the humbler we should be.

'THE LOADED BEE THE LOWEST FLIES'
BISHOP G. E. L. COTTON

The loaded bee the lowest flies;
The richest pearl the deepest lies;
The stalk the most replenished
Doth bow the most its modest head.
Thus deep humility we find
The mark of every master-mind;
The highest-gifted lowliest bends,
And merit meekest condescends,
And shuns the fame that fools adore,
That puff that bids the feather soar.

*A prayer asking that we should be helped to show courage and
determination in overcoming difficulties.*

'FATHER, HEAR THE PRAYER WE OFFER'
L. M. WILLIS

Father, hear the prayer we offer:
  Not for ease that prayer shall be,
But for strength that we may ever
  Live our lives courageously.

Not for ever in green pastures
  Do we ask our way to be;
But the steep and rugged pathway
  May we tread rejoicingly.

Not for ever by still waters
  Would we idly rest and stay;
But would smite the living fountains
  From the rocks along our way.

Be our strength in hours of weakness,
  In our wanderings be our guide;
Through endeavour, failure, danger,
  Father, be thou at our side.

*Refuse to quarrel at trivial provocations. Prefer to keep your
strength for greater causes, of the justice of which you are
convinced.*

THE GAUNTLET
ROBERT ARMSTRONG

Take up your glove again, I shall not fight.
  I will not be provoked to feign a hate.
Let action rest until to-morrow's light
  Casts cooling shadows on our present state.
Did I offend? It was in thoughtless jest.
  I count a life as worth a greater cost;
A grander principle, a rarer test
  Than paid as forfeit for a temper lost.

Say what you will; coward or faint of heart.
  Pick up your glove; replace it on your hand.
Though we who loved upon this issue part
  Now all the past shall, to my comfort, stand.
I do but fight only as when I must;
  The cause imperative, my purpose just.

245

The addition of mercy to the administration of justice makes those in authority almost God-like.

'THE QUALITY OF MERCY'
WILLIAM SHAKESPEARE

The quality of mercy is not strain'd,
It droppeth as the gentle rain from heaven
Upon the place beneath: it is twice bless'd;
It blesseth him that gives and him that takes:
'Tis mightiest in the mightiest; it becomes
The throned monarch better than his crown;
His sceptre shows the force of temporal power,
The attribute to awe and majesty,
Wherein doth sit the dread and fear of kings;
But mercy is above this sceptred sway,
It is enthroned in the hearts of kings,
It is an attribute to God himself,
And earthly power doth then show likest God's
When mercy seasons justice.

From 'The Merchant of Venice' IV. I

246

'O MAN, FORGIVE THY MORTAL FOE'
ALFRED LORD TENNYSON

O Man, forgive thy mortal foe,
Nor ever strike him blow for blow.
For all the souls on earth that live
To be forgiven must forgive.
Forgive him seventy times and seven:
For all the blessed souls in Heaven
Are both forgivers and forgiven.

OUR FELLOW MEN

247. Verses: On Relationships
     On Kindliness
     On Generosity
     On Neighbourliness
     On Our Enemies
     On Speech
     On Mischief-making
     On Anger
248. 'One of them which was a lawyer'
     St. Matthew xxii. 35–40
249. 'Though I speak with the tongues of men and of
     angels' . . . 1 *Corinthians* xiii. 1–13
250. 'Finally be ye all of one mind' 1 *St. Peter* iii. 8–12
251. 'Be kindly affectioned one to another'
     Romans xii. 10–18
252. 'These six things doth the Lord hate'
     Proverbs vi. 16–19
253. 'Ye have heard that it hath been said'
     St. Matthew v. 43–48
254. 'Judge not, that ye be not judged'
     St. Matthew vii. 1–5
255. 'Then came Peter to him' *St. Matthew* xviii. 21–35
256. 'Wherefore putting away lying' *Ephesians* iv. 25–32
257. 'If any man offend not in word' *St. James* iii. 2–8
258. 'Jesus sat over against the treasury'
     St. Mark xii. 41–44
259. 'To every thing there is a season' *Ecclesiastes* iii. 1–8
260. 'He opened his mouth, and taught them, saying'
     St. Matthew v. 2–12
261. Abou Ben Adhem . . . *Leigh Hunt*
262. The House by the Side of the Road *Sam Walter Foss*
263. 'Question not, but live and labour'
     Adam Lindsay Gordon
264. Solitude . . . . *Ella Wheeler Wilcox*
265. No Enemies . . . *Anastasius Grün*
266. 'Let me to-day do something' *Ella Wheeler Wilcox*
267. How to Live . . . . *Jack Gilbey*
268. The Priest and the Mulberry Tree
     Thomas Love Peacock

VERSES

ON RELATIONSHIPS

Behold, how good and how pleasant it is for brethren
to dwell together in unity!

Psalm CXXXIII. 1

See that none render evil for evil unto any man;
But ever follow that which is good,
Both among yourselves,
And to all men.

1 *Thessalonians* V. 15

A good name is rather to be chosen than great riches,
And loving favour rather than silver and gold.

Proverbs XXII. 1

ON KINDLINESS:

This is my commandment,
That ye love one another,
As I have loved you.

St. John XV. 12–13

Render therefore to all their dues:
Tribute to whom tribute is due;
Custom to whom custom;
Fear to whom fear;
Honour to whom honour.
Owe no man any thing, but to love one another:
For he that loveth another hath fulfilled the law.

Romans XIII. 7–8

He that ruleth over men must be just, ruling in the
fear of God.

2 *Samuel* XXIII. 3

Thus speaketh the Lord of hosts, saying,
Execute true judgment,
And shew mercy and compassions every man to his
brother.

Zechariah VII. 9

Let none of you imagine evil against his brother in
your heart.

Zechariah VII. 10

ON GENEROSITY

If thou hast abundance,
  Give alms accordingly:
If thou have but a little,
  Be not afraid to give according to that little.

Tobit IV. 8

Let not thine hand be stretched out to receive,
And shut when thou shouldest repay.

Ecclesiasticus IV. 31

The poor man's farthing is worth more
Than all the gold on Afric's shore.

William Blake

ON NEIGHBOURLINESS

The chief thing for life is water,
  And bread, and clothing,
  And an house to cover shame.
Better is the life of a poor man in a mean cottage,
  Than delicate fare in another man's house.

Ecclesiasticus XXIX. 21, 22

A fool will peep in at the door into the house:
But he that is well nurtured will stand without.

Ecclesiasticus XXI. 23

It is the rudeness of a man to hearken at the door:
But a wise man will be grieved with the disgrace.

Ecclesiasticus XXI. 24

Be faithful to thy neighbour in his poverty,
That thou mayest rejoice in his prosperity:
Abide steadfast unto him in the time of his trouble,
That thou mayest be heir with him in his heritage:
For a mean estate is not always to be contemned:
Nor the rich that is foolish to be held in admiration.

Ecclesiasticus XXII. 23

Therefore if thine enemy hunger, feed him;
If he thirst, give him drink;
For in so doing thou shalt heap coals of fire on his head.

Romans XII. 20

Take heed to yourselves:
If thy brother trespass against thee,
   rebuke him:
And if he repent,
   forgive him.
And if he trespass against thee seven times in a day,
And seven times in a day turn again to thee,
   saying, I repent;
Thou shalt forgive him.

St. Luke XVII. 3, 4

He doeth well who doeth good
To those of his own brotherhood;
He doeth better who doth bless
The stranger in his wretchedness;
Yet best, oh! best of all doth he
Who helps a fallen enemy.

Anonymous

ON SPEECH

A word fitly spoken is like apples of gold in pictures of
   silver.

Proverbs XXV. 11

Keep thy tongue from evil,
And thy lips from speaking guile.
Depart from evil, and do good;
Seek peace, and pursue it.

Psalm XXXIV. 13, 14

Let your speech be alway with grace,
   seasoned with salt,
That ye may know how ye ought to answer every man.

Colossians IV. 6

175

N

Pleasant words are as an honeycomb,
Sweet to the soul,
And health to the bones.

Proverbs XVI. 24

A fool uttereth all his mind:
But a wise man keepeth it in till afterwards.

Proverbs XXIX. 11

ON MISCHIEF-MAKING

A talebearer revealeth secrets:
But he that is of a faithful spirit concealeth the matter.

Proverbs XI. 13

A whisperer defileth his own soul,
And is hated wheresoever he dwelleth.

Ecclesiasticus XXI. 28

Where no wood is,
there the fire goeth out:
So where there is no talebearer,
the strife ceaseth.

Proverbs XXVI. 20

Let all bitterness, and wrath, and anger,
And clamour, and evil speaking,
Be put away from you, with all malice:
And be ye kind one to another,
tender-hearted, forgiving one another,
Even as God for Christ's sake hath forgiven you.

Ephesians IV. 31, 32

ON ANGER

It is much better to reprove, than to be angry secretly:
And he that confesseth his fault shall be preserved
from hurt.

Ecclesiasticus XX. 2

A soft answer turneth away wrath:
But grievous words stir up anger.

Proverbs XV. 1

176

He that is slow to anger is better than the mighty;
And he that ruleth his spirit than he that taketh a city.

Proverbs XVI. 32

Seest thou a man that is hasty in his words?
There is more hope of a fool than of him.

Proverbs XXIX. 20

Do nothing without advice;
And when thou hast once done, repent not.

Ecclesiasticus XXXII. 19

Do all the good you can,
By all the means you can,
In all the ways you can,
In all the places you can,
At all the times you can,
To all the people you can,
As long as ever you can.

John Wesley

As Thou, Lord, hast lived for others
So may we for others live;
Freely have thy gifts been granted,
Freely may thy servants give.
Thine the gold and thine the silver,
Thine the wealth of land and sea,
We but stewards of thy bounty,
Held in solemn trust for thee.

S. C. Lowry

I was angry with my friend;
I told my wrath, my wrath did end:
I was angry with my foe;
I told it not, my wrath did grow.

William Blake

Anger in its time and place
May assume a kind of grace;
It must have some reason in it,
And not last beyond a minute.

Charles and Mary Lamb

248

'ONE OF THEM WHICH WAS A LAWYER'

St. Matthew XXII. 35–40

Christ's reply to the question 'Which is the greatest commandment?'

249

'THOUGH I SPEAK WITH THE TONGUES OF MEN AND OF ANGELS' 1 Corinthians XIII. 1–13

On Faith, Hope and Charity.

250

'FINALLY BE YE ALL OF ONE MIND' 1 St. Peter III. 8–12

We are entreated to be kindly and to do good to others.

251

'BE KINDLY AFFECTIONED ONE TO ANOTHER'

Romans XII. 10–18

St. Paul tells his readers how to treat others . . . with kindness and sympathy, without feelings of revenge, and in peacefulness.

252

'THESE SIX THINGS DOTH THE LORD HATE'

Six of the worst social offences are listed. Proverbs VI. 16–19

253

'YE HAVE HEARD THAT IT HATH BEEN SAID'

St. Matthew V. 43–48

We should not return the animosity of our enemies.

254

'JUDGE NOT, THAT YE BE NOT JUDGED'

St. Matthew VII. 1–5

Do not judge others, in case worse faults lie within you.

255

'THEN CAME PETER TO HIM' St. Matthew XVIII. 21–35

The parable of the unforgiving servant.

256

'WHEREFORE PUTTING AWAY LYING' Ephesians IV. 25–32

Advice on how to treat one another.

257
'IF ANY MAN OFFEND NOT IN WORD'   St. James III. 2–8
Tongues must be controlled, for an unruly tongue can do much harm.

258
'JESUS SAT OVER AGAINST THE TREASURY'
The incident of the widow's mite.   St. Mark XII. 41–44

259
'TO EVERY THING THERE IS A SEASON'
Ecclesiastes III. 1–8

260
'HE OPENED HIS MOUTH, AND TAUGHT THEM, SAYING'
St. Matthew V. 2–12
The Beatitudes.

261
Those who love their fellow men thereby show their love for God.

ABOU BEN ADHEM
LEIGH HUNT

Abou Ben Adhem (may his tribe increase!)
Awoke one night from a deep dream of peace,
And saw, within the moonlight in his room,
Making it rich, and like a lily in bloom,
An angel writing in a book of gold:—
Exceeding peace had made Ben Adhem bold,
And to the presence in the room he said,
'What writest thou?'—The vision raised its head,
And with a look made of all sweet accord,
Answered, 'The names of those who love the Lord.'
'And is mine one?' said Abou. 'Nay, not so,'
Replied the angel. Abou spoke more low,
But cheerly still; and said, 'I pray thee, then,
Write me as one that loves his fellow-men.'

The angel wrote, and vanished. The next night
It came again with a great wakening light,
And showed the names whom love of God had blessed,
And lo! Ben Adhem's name led all the rest.

It is only by living amongst men that one can show friendliness towards them.

THE HOUSE BY THE SIDE OF THE ROAD
SAM WALTER FOSS

There are hermit souls that live withdrawn
  In the peace of their self-content;
There are souls like stars that dwell apart,
  In a fellowless firmament;
There are pioneer souls that blaze their paths
  Where highways never ran—
But let me live by the side of the road,
  And be a friend to man.

A well-known verse with a clear message.

'QUESTION NOT, BUT LIVE AND LABOUR'
ADAM LINDSAY GORDON

Question not, but live and labour
  Till yon goal be won,
Helping every feeble neighbour,
  Seeking help from none;
Life is mostly froth and bubble,
  Two things stand like stone,
Kindness in another's trouble,
  Courage in your own.

This popular American poet was only partly right, for she leaves out of account the help of intimate friends.

SOLITUDE
ELLA WHEELER WILCOX

Laugh, and the world laughs with you;
  Weep, and you weep alone;
For sad old earth must borrow its mirth,
  But has trouble enough of its own.

Sing, and the hills will answer;
  Sigh, it is lost on the air;
The echoes bound to a joyful sound,
  But shrink from voicing care.

Rejoice, and men will seek you;
  Grieve, and they turn and go:
They want full measure of all your pleasure,
  But they do not need your woe.
Be glad, and your friends are many;
  Be sad, and you lose them all—
There are none to decline your nectared wine,
  But alone you must drink life's gall.

Feast, and your halls are crowded;
  Fast, and the world goes by.
Succeed and give, and it helps you live,
  But no man can help you die.
There is room in the halls of pleasure
  For a large and lordly train:
But one by one we must all file on
  Through the narrow aisles of pain.

265

*If we try to right wrongs we are sure to make enemies.
Perhaps the man who has made none has not had the courage to
do so.*

NO ENEMIES

ANASTASIUS GRÜN

He has no enemy, you say;
My friend, your boast is poor.
He who hath mingled in the fray
Of duty that the brave endure
Must have made foes. If he has none
Small is the work that he has done.
He has hit no traitor on the hip;
Has cast no cup from perjured lip;
Has never turned the wrong to right;
Has been a coward in the fight.

A prayer that the evening shall find the world a better place because of what we have done during the day.

'LET ME TO-DAY DO SOMETHING'
ELLA WHEELER WILCOX

Let me to-day do something that shall take
A little sadness from the world's vast store,
And may I be so favoured as to make
Of Joy's too scanty sum a little more.

Let me not hurt by any selfish deed
Or thoughtless word, the heart of foe or friend,
Nor would I pass, unseeing, worthy need,
Or sin by silence where I should defend;

Let me to-night look back across the span
Twixt dawn and dark, and to my conscience say,
'Because of some good act to beast or man,
The world is better that I lived to-day.'

Advice on what will make up a satisfying life.

HOW TO LIVE
JACK GILBEY

Someone had asked a poet how to live
Because he thought a poet best would know.
'Give,' said the poet, 'every time you give,
With graciousness nor count the cost. Bestow
An alms to help the poor or those in need
As often as you can. With gentle word
Soothe those in pain, no matter what their creed,
Yet let them not so much be felt or heard,
Your little cares, nor speak of self because
Of fear of boastfulness. Repeat not all
The idle gossip that you hear. God's laws
Obey: no sin that wounds His love is small.
Count every gain that leads from God a loss,
And Charity the password of the Cross.'

Sometimes it is better to keep one's thoughts to oneself.

THE PRIEST AND THE MULBERRY TREE
THOMAS LOVE PEACOCK

Did you hear of the curate who mounted his mare,
And merrily trotted along to the fair?
Of creature more tractable none ever heard;
In the height of her speed she would stop at a word:
But again with a word, when the curate said, Hey,
She put forth her mettle, and galloped away.

As near to the gates of the city he rode,
While the sun of September all brilliantly glowed,
The good priest discovered, with eyes of desire,
A mulberry tree in a hedge of wild briar;
On boughs long and lofty, in many a green shoot,
Hung large, black, and glossy, the beautiful fruit.

The curate was hungry and thirsty to boot;
He shrank from the thorns, though he longed for the
        fruit;
With a word he arrested his courser's keen speed,
And he stood up erect on the back of his steed;
On the saddle he stood, while the creature stood still,
And he gathered the fruit, till he took his good fill.

'Sure never,' he thought, 'was a creature so rare,
So docile, so true, as my excellent mare.
Lo, here, now I stand' (and he gazed all around)
'As safe and as steady as if on the ground;
Yet how had it been, if some traveller this way,
Had, dreaming no mischief, but chanced to cry Hey?'

He stood with his head in the mulberry tree,
And he spoke out aloud in his fond reverie:
At the sound of the word, the good mare made a push,
And down went the priest in the wild briar bush.
He remembered too late, on his thorny green bed,
Much that well may be thought, cannot wisely be said.

FRIENDS

269. Verses
270. 'Then she arose with her daughters in law'
                                      Ruth I. 6–18
271. 'Saul and Jonathan were lovely and pleasant in
     their lives'   .   .   .   *2 Samuel* I. 23–27
272. 'Father of men, in whom are one'   *H. C. Shuttleworth*
273. 'Fame is a food that dead men eat'   *Austin Dobson*
274. 'Every friend that flatters thee'   *Richard Barnfield*
275. 'It is my joy in life to find'   *Frank Dempster Sherman*
276. The Thousandth Man   .   *Rudyard Kipling*
277. 'When to the sessions of sweet silent thought'
                                  William Shakespeare
278. 'Like as the waves make towards the pebbled shore'
                                  William Shakespeare

269

VERSES

A friend loveth at all times,
And a brother is born for adversity.
                                  Proverbs XVII. 17

A man that hath friends must shew himself friendly:
And there is a friend that sticketh closer than a brother.
                                  Proverbs XVIII. 24

Love thy friend, and be faithful unto him:
But if thou bewrayest his secrets,
   follow no more after him.   *Ecclesiasticus* XXVII. 17

Two are better than one;
Because they have a good reward for their labour.
For if they fall, the one will lift up his fellow:
But woe to him that is alone when he falleth;
For he hath not another to help him up.
                                  Ecclesiastes IV. 9, 10

Forsake not an old friend;
For the new is not comparable to him.
                                  Ecclesiasticus IX. 10

Thine own friend, and thy father's friend, forsake not;
Neither go into thy brother's house in the day of thy
  calamity:
For better is a neighbour that is near than a brother far
  off.

Proverbs XXVII. 10

If thou hast opened thy mouth against thy friend, fear
  not;
  for there may be a reconciliation:
Except for upbraiding, or pride, or disclosing of secrets,
  or a treacherous wound:
For, for these things every friend will depart.

Ecclesiasticus XXII. 22

Devise not a lie against thy brother;
Neither do the like to thy friend.
Use not to make any manner of lie:
For the custom thereof is not good.

Ecclesiasticus VII. 12, 13

Greater love hath no man than this,
That a man lay down his life for his friends.

St. John XV. 13

From quiet homes and first beginning,
  Out to the undiscovered ends,
There's nothing worth the wear of winning,
  But laughter and the love of friends.

Hilaire Belloc

READINGS

270

'THEN SHE AROSE WITH HER DAUGHTERS IN LAW'

Ruth I. 6–18

The story of the love of Ruth for her mother-in-law, Naomi.

271

'SAUL AND JONATHAN WERE LOVELY AND PLEASANT IN
  THEIR LIVES' 2 Samuel I. 23–27

David's lament for Jonathan.

The best is brought out of one when trying to do good to others.

'FATHER OF MEN, IN WHOM ARE ONE'

H. C. SHUTTLEWORTH

Father of men, in whom are one
All humankind beneath thy sun,
Stablish our work in thee begun.
Except the house be built of thee,
In vain the builder's toil must be:
O strengthen our infirmity!

Man lives not for himself alone;
In others' good he finds his own;
Life's worth in fellowship is known.
We, friends and comrades on life's way,
Gather within these walls to pray:
Bless thou our fellowship to-day.

273

'FAME IS A FOOD THAT DEAD MEN EAT'

AUSTIN DOBSON

Fame is a food that dead men eat—
I have no stomach for such meat.
In little light and narrow room,
They eat it in the silent tomb,
With no kind voice of comrade near
To bid the feaster be of cheer.

But Friendship is a nobler thing—
Of Friendship it is good to sing.
For truly, when a man shall end,
He lives in memory of his friend,
Who doth his better part recall
And of his fault make funeral.

True friends are those who help in times of need.

'EVERY FRIEND THAT FLATTERS THEE'
RICHARD BARNFIELD

Every friend that flatters thee
Is no friend in misery.
Words are easy, like the wind;
Faithful friends are hard to find.
Every man will be thy friend
Whilst thou hast wherewith to spend:
But, if score of crowns be scant,
No man will supply thy want.

.   .   .   .   .   .

He that is thy friend indeed,
He will help thee in thy need.
If thou sorrow, he will weep;
If thou wake, he cannot sleep;
Thus of every grief in heart
He with thee will bear a part.
These are certain things to show
Faithful friend from faltering foe.

275

'IT IS MY JOY IN LIFE TO FIND'
FRANK DEMPSTER SHERMAN

It is my joy in life to find
At every turning of the road
The strong arm of a comrade kind
To help me onward with my load.
And since I have no gold to give
And love alone must make amends,
My only prayer is, while I live,
God make me worthy of my friends.

A true friend stands by you through thick and thin.

THE THOUSANDTH MAN
RUDYARD KIPLING

One man in a thousand, Solomon says,
Will stick more close than a brother.
And it's worth while seeking him half your days
If you find him before the other.
Nine hundred and ninety-nine depend
On what the world sees in you,
But the Thousandth Man will stand your friend
With the whole round world agin you.

'Tis neither promise nor prayer nor show
Will settle the finding for 'ee.
Nine hundred and ninety nine of 'em go
By your looks, or your acts, or your glory.
But if he finds you and you find him,
The rest of the world don't matter;
For the Thousandth Man will sink or swim
With you in any water.

You can use his purse with no more talk
Than he uses yours for his spendings,
And laugh and meet in your daily walk
As though there had been no lendings.
Nine hundred and ninety-nine of 'em call
For silver and gold in their dealings;
But the Thousandth Man he's worth 'em all,
Because you can show him your feelings.

His wrong's your wrong, and his right's your right,
In season or out of season.
Stand up and back it in all men's sight—
With *that* for your only reason!
Nine hundred and ninety-nine can't bide
The shame or mocking or laughter,
But the Thousandth Man will stand by your side
To the gallows-foot—and after!

The sorrows of the past can be forgotten in the thought of friends.

'WHEN TO THE SESSIONS OF SWEET SILENT THOUGHT'

WILLIAM SHAKESPEARE

When to the sessions of sweet silent thought
I summon up remembrance of things past,
I sigh the lack of many a thing I sought,
And with old woes new wail my dear times' waste;
Then can I drown an eye, unus'd to flow,
For precious friends hid in death's dateless night,
And weep afresh love's long since cancell'd woe,
And moan the expense of many a vanish'd sight:
Then can I grieve at grievances foregone,
And heavily from woe to woe tell o'er
The sad account of fore-bemoaned moan,
Which I new pay as if not paid before.
　　But if the while I think on thee, dear friend,
　　All losses are restor'd and sorrows end.

In spite of the changes that Time brings about, the worth of a friend can be perpetuated in the record of verse.

'LIKE AS THE WAVES MAKE TOWARDS THE PEBBLED SHORE'

WILLIAM SHAKESPEARE

Like as the waves make towards the pebbled shore,
So do our minutes hasten to their end;
Each changing place with that which goes before,
In sequent toil all forwards do contend.
Nativity, once in the main of light,
Crawls to maturity, wherewith being crown'd,
Crooked eclipses 'gainst his glory fight,
And Time that gave doth now his gift confound.
Time doth transfix the flourish set on youth
And delves the parallels in beauty's brow,
Feeds on the rarities of nature's truth,
And nothing stands but for his scythe to mow:
　　And yet to times in hope my verse shall stand,
　　Praising thy worth, despite his cruel hand.

279. Vale of Evesham . . . *Wilfrid Gibson*
280. 'I remember, I remember' . . *Thomas Hood*
281. The Old Vicarage, Grantchester . *Rupert Brooke*
282. 'Wherever smoke wreaths Heavenward curl'
Stephen Chalmers
283. Going Home . . . . *Patrick MacGill*
284. The Lake Isle of Innisfree . . *W. B. Yeats*
285. A Thanksgiving . . . . *Robert Herrick*
286. An Old Woman of the Roads . *Padraic Colum*

279

*Perhaps when one has searched the world for legendary
treasure, it has after all been left at home, unrecognized as such.*

VALE OF EVESHAM
WILFRID GIBSON

The sailor plucked an apple from an orchard as he
passed,
On the bright October morning that brought him home
at last,
And, as he munched, he muttered—Why can't I always
be
Where a lad can pluck an apple from an overhanging
tree?

For long and sore he'd tossed about upon the windy seas;
And never had he come to port in the Hesperides,
The islands they had told him of, where any lad can see
The golden apples hang like lamps from every emerald
tree.

But now that he was back again in Evesham's goodly
Vale,
With October orchards glowing the colour of rare ale,
It seemed to him the home he'd left was the Hesperides,
Where gold and ruby apples hang from all the amber
trees.

A rather sad list of the pleasant and regretted memories of boyhood retained by a friendly poet who had suffered many personal misfortunes.

'I REMEMBER, I REMEMBER'

THOMAS HOOD

I remember, I remember,
The house where I was born,
The little window where the sun
Came peeping in at morn;
He never came a wink too soon,
Nor brought too long a day,
But now, I often wish the night
Had borne my breath away.

I remember, I remember,
The roses, red and white,
The violets, and the lily-cups,
Those flowers made of light!
The lilacs where the robin built,
And where my brother set
The laburnum on his birthday—
The tree is living yet!

I remember, I remember,
Where I was used to swing,
And thought the air must rush as fresh
To swallows on the wing;
My spirit flew in feathers then,
That is so heavy now,
The summer pools could hardly cool
The fever on my brow!

I remember, I remember,
The fir trees dark and high;
I used to think their slender tops
Were close against the sky;
It was a childish ignorance,
But now 'tis little joy
To know I'm farther off from heav'n
Than when I was a boy.

O

An unwilling traveller thinks longingly of the old house where he had spent many quiet days seeking better health. To him the peace of this particular house and village seemed near perfection.

THE OLD VICARAGE, GRANTCHESTER
RUPERT BROOKE

God! I will pack, and take a train,
And get me to England once again!
For England's the one land, I know,
Where men with Splendid Hearts may go;
And Cambridgeshire, of all England,
The shire for Men who Understand;
And of *that* district I prefer
The lovely hamlet Grantchester.

But Grantchester! ah, Grantchester!
There's peace and holy quiet there,
Great clouds along pacific skies,
And men and women with straight eyes,
Lithe children lovelier than a dream,
A bosky wood, a slumbrous stream,
And little kindly winds that creep
Round twilight corners, half asleep.
In Grantchester their skins are white,
They bathe by day, they bathe by night;
The women there do all they ought;
The men observe the Rules of Thought.
They love the Good; they worship Truth;
They laugh uproariously in youth.

Ah God! to see the branches stir
Across the moon at Grantchester!
To smell the thrilling-sweet and rotten
Unforgettable, unforgotten
River-smell, and hear the breeze
Sobbing in the little trees.
Say, do the elm-clumps greatly stand,
Still guardians of that holy land?

The chestnuts shade, in reverend dream,
The yet unacademic stream?
Is dawn a secret shy and cold
Anadyomene, silver-gold?
And sunset still a golden sea
From Haslingfield to Madingley?
And after, ere the night is born,
Do hares come out about the corn?
Oh, is the water sweet and cool,
Gentle and brown, above the pool?
And laughs the immortal river still
Under the mill, under the mill?
Say, is there Beauty yet to find?
And Certainty? and Quiet kind?
Deep meadows yet, for to forget
The lies, and truths, and pain? . . . oh! yet
Stands the Church clock at ten to three?
And is there honey still for tea?

282

'WHEREVER SMOKE WREATHS HEAVENWARD CURL'

STEPHEN CHALMERS

Wherever smoke wreaths Heavenward curl—
  Cave of a hermit, hovel of churl,
Mansion of merchant, princely dome—
  Out of the dreariness,
  Into its cheeriness,
  Come we in weariness
    Home.

The call of a wild part of Ireland.

GOING HOME

PATRICK MacGILL

I'm going back to Glenties when the harvest fields are
    brown,
And the Autumn sunset lingers on my little Irish town,
When the gossamer is shining where the moorland
    blossoms blow
I'll take the road across the hills I tramped so long ago—
'Tis far I am beyond the seas, but yearning voices call,
'Will you not come back to Glenties, and your wave-
    washed Donegal?'

I've seen the hopes of childhood stifled by the hand of
    time,
I've seen the smile of innocence become the frown of
    crime,
I've seen the wrong rise high and strong, I've seen the
    fair betrayed,
Until the faltering heart fell low the brave became
    afraid—
But still the cry comes out to me, the homely voices call,
From the Glen among the highlands of my ancient
    Donegal.

Sure, I think I see them often, when the night is on the
    town,
The Braes of old Strasala, and the homes of
    Carrigdoun—
There's a light in Jimmy Lynch's house, a shadow on
    the blind,
I often watched the shadow, for 'twas Mary in behind,
And often in the darkness, 'tis myself that sees it all,
For I cannot help but dreaming of the folk in Donegal.

So I'll hie me back to Glenties when the harvest comes
    again,
And the kine are in the pasture and the berries in the lane,
Then they'll give me such a welcome that my heart will
    leap with joy,
When a father and a mother welcome back their way-
    ward boy.
So I'm going back to Glenties when the Autumn showers
    fall,
And the harvest home is cheery in my dear old Donegal.

284

*Most townsmen hope to find a home in the country when they
are older. This poet has his ideal spot already picked, and
thinks of it continually in the middle of the turmoil of town life.*

THE LAKE ISLE OF INNISFREE
W. B. YEATS

I will arise and go now, and go to Innisfree,
And a small cabin build there, of clay and wattles
    made:
Nine bean rows will I have there, a hive for the honey-
    bee,
And live alone in the bee-loud glade.

And I shall have some peace there, for peace comes
    dropping slow,
Dropping from the veils of the morning to where the
    cricket sings;
There midnight's all a glimmer, and noon a purple
    glow,
And evening full of the linnet's wings.

I will arise and go now, for always night and day
I hear the lake water lapping with low sounds by the
    shore;
While I stand on the roadway, or on the pavements
    grey,
I hear it in the deep heart's core.

A THANKSGIVING
ROBERT HERRICK

To God for His House.

Lord, Thou hast given me a cell
   Wherein to dwell,
A little house, whose humble Roof
   Is weather-proof;
Under the spars of which I lie
   Both soft and dry;
Where Thou my chamber for to ward
   Has set a Guard
Of harmless thoughts, to watch and keep
   Me, while I sleep.
Low is my porch, as is my Fate,
   Both void of state;
And yet the threshold of my door
   Is worn by the poor,
Who thither come, and freely get
   Good words, or meat:
Like as my Parlour, so my Hall
   And Kitchen's small;
A little Buttery, and therein
   A little bin,
Which keeps my little loaf of Bread
   Unchipt, unflead.
Some brittle sticks of Thorn or Briar
   Make me a fire,
Close by whose living coal I sit,
   And glow like it.
Lord, I confess too, when I dine,
   The Pulse is Thine,
And all those other bits, that be
   There placed by Thee;
The Worts, the Purslain, and the Mess
   Of Water-cress,

Which of Thy kindness Thou hast sent;
    And my content
Makes those, and my beloved Beet
    To be more sweet.
'Tis Thou that crown'st my glittering Hearth
    With guiltless mirth;
And giv'st me Wassail Bowls to drink,
    Spiced to the brink.
Lord, 'tis Thy plenty-dropping hand,
    That soils my land;
And giv'st me, for my bushel sown
    Twice ten for one:
Thou mak'st my teeming Hen to lay
    Her egg each day:
Besides my healthful ewes to bear
    Me twins each year:
The while the conduits of my Kine
    Run Cream (for Wine).
All these, and better Thou dost send
    Me, to this end,
That I should render, for my part,
    A thankful heart;
Which, fired with incense, I resign,
    As wholly Thine;
But the acceptance, that must be,
    My Christ, by Thee.

The prayer of an old woman, who after a life of wandering, longed for a place of her own in which to rest, and for the comforts of a home.

AN OLD WOMAN OF THE ROADS

PADRAIC COLUM

Oh, to have a little house!
    To own the hearth and stool and all!
The heaped-up sods upon the fire,
    The pile of turf against the wall!

To have a clock with weights and chains
    And pendulum swinging up and down!
A dresser filled with shining delph,
    Speckled and white and blue and brown!

I could be busy all the day
    Clearing and sweeping hearth and floor,
And fixing on their shelf again
    My white and blue and speckled store!

I could be quiet there at night
    Beside the fire and by myself,
Sure of a bed, and loth to leave
    The ticking clock and the shining delph!

Och! but I'm weary of mist and dark,
    And roads where there's never a house or bush,
And tired I am of bog and road
    And the crying wind and the lonesome hush!

And I am praying to God on high,
    And I am praying Him night and day,
For a little house, a house of my own—
    Out of the wind's and the rain's way.

THE TOWN

287. Verse
288. London Spring . . . *Frances Cornford*
289. The Common Street . . *Helen Gray Cone*
290. Blue Stars and Gold . . . *James Stephens*
291. 'Earth has not anything to show more fair'
William Wordsworth
292. 'Come, let us remember the joys of the town'
Doris M. Gill
293. Snow in the Suburbs . . . *Thomas Hardy*
294. A Townsman's Prayer . . . *Eiluned Lewis*

287

VERSE

Except the Lord build the house,
   they labour in vain that build it.
Except the Lord keep the city,
   the watchman waketh but in vain.

Psalm CXXVII. I

288

Even in the city the cheering effect of the spring is felt.

LONDON SPRING
FRANCES CORNFORD

The rounded buses loom through softest blue,
The pavement smells of dust and of narcissus too,
The awnings stretch like petals in the sun,
And even the oldest taxis glitter as they run.

Over the sooted secret garden walls
As in another Eden cherry-blossom falls,
Lithe under shadowing lilacs steal the cats,
And even the oldest ladies tilt their summery hats.

*The dreariness of the city street and the weariness of the
people can be transformed by the glow of a splendid sunset.*

THE COMMON STREET

HELEN GRAY CONE

The common street climbed up against the sky,
Gray meeting gray; and wearily to and fro
I saw the patient, common people go,
Each with his sordid burden trudging by.
And the rain dropped; there was not any sigh
Or stir of a live wind; dull, dull and slow
All motion; as a tale told long ago
The faded world; and creeping night drew nigh.
Then burst the sunset, flooding far and fleet,
Leavening the whole of life with magic leaven.
Suddenly down the long wet glistening hill
Pure splendour poured—and lo! the common street,
A golden highway into golden heaven,
With the dark shapes of men ascending still.

*A quaint poem by one who paused in rather a dangerous place
to admire the sky at night.*

BLUE STARS AND GOLD

JAMES STEPHENS

While walking through the trams and cars
I chanced to look up at the sky,
And saw that it was full of stars!

So starry sown! A man could not,
With any care, have stuck a pin
Through any single vacant spot.

And some were shining furiously;
And some were big and some were small;
But all were beautiful to see.

Blue stars and gold! A sky of grey!
The air between a velvet pall!
I could not take my eyes away!

And there I sang this little psalm
Most awkwardly! Because I was
Standing between a car and tram!

291

A deep peace seems to lie over a great city before the work of the day begins.

'EARTH HAS NOT ANYTHING TO SHOW MORE FAIR'

WILLIAM WORDSWORTH

Composed upon Westminster Bridge, September 3rd, 1803

Earth has not anything to show more fair:
Dull would he be of soul who could pass by
A sight so touching in its majesty:
This city now doth like a garment wear
The beauty of the morning; silent, bare,
Ships, towers, domes, theatres, and temples lie
Open unto the fields, and to the sky;
All bright and glittering in the smokeless air.
Never did sun more beautifully steep
In his first splendour valley, rock, or hill;
Ne'er saw I, never felt, a calm so deep:
The river glideth at his own sweet will:
Dear God! the very houses seem asleep;
And all that mighty heart is lying still!

Perhaps we tend to forget that there are many pleasures and beautiful things to be found in towns and for these we should be grateful. There are also many unpleasing sights which should give us no peace of mind until they are swept away.

'COME, LET US REMEMBER THE JOYS OF THE TOWN'

DORIS M. GILL

Come, let us remember the joys of the town:
Gay vans and bright buses that roar up and down,
Shop windows and playgrounds and swings in the park,
And street-lamps that twinkle in rows after dark.

And let us remember the chorus that swells
From hooters and hammers and whistles and bells,
From fierce-panting engines and clear-striking clocks,
And sirens of vessels afloat in the docks.

And let us remember the life in the street:
The horses that pass us, the dogs that we meet;
Grey pigeons, brown sparrows, and gulls from the sea,
And folk who are friendly to you and to me.

Come, let us now lift up our voices in praise,
And to the Creator a thanksgiving raise,
For towns with their buildings of stone, steel and wood,
For people who love them and work for their good.

We thank Thee, O God, for the numberless things
And friends and adventures which every day brings.
O may we not rest until all that we see
In towns and in cities is pleasing to Thee.

SNOW IN THE SUBURBS
THOMAS HARDY

Every branch big with it,
  Bent every twig with it;
 Every fork like a white web-foot;
 Every street and pavement mute:
Some flakes have lost their way, and grope back upward,
  when
Meeting those meandering down they turn and descend
  again.
 The palings are glued together like a wall,
 And there is no waft of wind with the fleecy fall.

 A sparrow enters the tree,
  Whereon immediately
A snow-lump thrice his own slight size
Descends on him and showers his head and eyes,
  And overturns him,
  And near inurns him,
And lights on a nether twig, when its brush
Starts off a volley of other lodging lumps with a rush.

 The steps are a blanched slope,
  Up which, with feeble hope,
A black cat comes, wide-eyed and thin;
  And we take him in.

In the midst of a busy life in town, too busy to find time to wonder if she is doing right and too busy to find the time to be thankful, the writer prays that she may never forget her countryside.

A TOWNSMAN'S PRAYER
EILUNED LEWIS

Lord, though among this city's press
I squander nights and days
And find no moment to confess
My faults, nor sing Your praise,
Yet grant that I may not forget
The oak tree's coat of brown;
Dark, quiet beds where bulbs are set;
The way the leaves drift down;
A moon above the hill new-born;
The taste of winter-pears,
And how the sheep at misty morn
Wear haloes unawares.
The last-left apple's wrinkled cheek
Where high and free it swings;
The way the country people speak;
A magpie's mottled wings.
Take my wild heart and strip it bare
And teach me to be wise
Who have loved nothing, Lord, more fair
Than wintry skies.

THE COUNTRYSIDE

295. Verse
296. The Country Faith . . . *Norman Gale*
297. 'What are they thinking' . . *Bryan Guinness*
298. The Birthright . . . *Eiluned Lewis*
299. Mountain Air . . . *John Galsworthy*
300. The Vagabond . . *Robert Louis Stevenson*
301. The Vagabond . . *John Drinkwater*
302. Glad in Heart . . . *Nicholas Breton*
303. 'For the comforting warmth of the sun'
         Henry Van Dyke

295
VERSE

I planted me vineyards.
I made me gardens and orchards,
 and I planted trees in them of all kind of fruits:
I made me pools of water, to water therewith the wood
  that bringeth forth trees.
       Ecclesiastes II. 4–6

296
THE COUNTRY FAITH
NORMAN GALE

Here in the country's heart,
Where the grass is green,
Life is the same sweet life
As it e'er hath been.

Trust in a God still lives,
And the bell at morn
Floats with a thought of God
O'er the rising corn.

God comes down in the rain,
And the crop grows tall—
This is the country faith
And the best of all!

Some suggestions for answers to a question about the wor-shippers, the animals and the birds of a quiet village.

'WHAT ARE THEY THINKING'

BRYAN GUINNESS

What are they thinking, the people in churches,
Closing their eyelids and kneeling to pray,
Touching their faces and sniffing their fingers,
Folding their knuckles over one another?
What are they thinking? Do they remember
This is the church: and this is the steeple:
Open the door: and here are the people?
Do they still see the parson climbing upstairs,
Opening the window and saying his prayers?
Do they perceive in the pit of their palms
The way of the walls and the spin of the spire,
The turmoil of tombstones tossed in the grass,
Under the yawning billows of yew?
Can they discover, drooping beyond them,
The chestnuts' fountains of flowers and frills,
And the huge fields folded into the hills?

What are they thinking, the sheep on the hills,
Bobbing and bending to nibble the grass,
Kissing the crisp green coat of the combes?
What are they thinking, lying contented
What vacant regard in long rumination?
Do they consider the sky as a cage,
Their fleeces as fetters, their bones as their bonds?
Or do they rejoice at the thyme on their tongues,
The dome of the sky, the slope of the downs,
The village below, the church and the steeple,
With shepherd and ploughman and parson and people?

And what is he feeling, the lark as he flies,
Does he consider the span of his days,
Does he dissever himself from his spirit,
His flight from his feathers, his song from his singing?
Is he cast down at the thought of his brevity?

Or does he look forward to fond immortality?
He stitches the sky with the thread of his breath
To all the bright pattern of living beneath,
To ploughman and shepherd and parson and people,
To the sheep on the hills and the church and the steeple.

298

*The country-born have a birthright . . . the enjoyment of the
unchanging sights, sounds and smells of their surroundings.*

THE BIRTHRIGHT

EILUNED LEWIS

We who were born
In country places,
Far from cities
And shifting faces,
We have a birthright
No man can sell,
And a secret joy
No man can tell.

For we are kindred
To lordly things,
The wild duck's flight
And the white owl's wings;
To pike and salmon,
To bull and horse,
The curlew's cry
And the smell of gorse.

Pride of trees,
Swiftness of streams,
Magic of frost
Have shaped our dreams:
No baser vision
Their spirit fills
Who walk by right
On the naked hills.

207

If we must have progress, may it belong to the towns, leaving the countryside unchanged.

MOUNTAIN AIR
JOHN GALSWORTHY

Tell me of Progress if you will,
But give me sunshine on a hill—
The grey rocks spiring to the blue,
The scent of larches, pinks, and dew,
And summer sighing to the trees,
And snowy breath on every breeze.
    Take towns and all that you'll find there,
    And leave me sun and mountain air!

The thoughts of a great traveller who valued the joys of the open road more than those of friendship or wealth, for they compensated him for misfortunes.

THE VAGABOND
ROBERT LOUIS STEVENSON

Give to me the life I love,
    Let the lave go by me,
Give the jolly heaven above
    And the byway nigh me.
Bed in the bush with stars to see,
    Bread I dip in the river—
There's the life for a man like me,
    There's the life for ever.

Let the blow fall soon or late,
    Let what will be o'er me;
Give the face of earth around
    And the road before me.
Wealth I seek not, hope nor love,
    Nor a friend to know me;
All I seek, the heaven above
    And the road below me.

Or let autumn fall on me
    Where afield I linger,
Silencing the bird on tree,
    Biting the blue finger.
White as meal the frosty field—
    Warm the fireside haven—
Not to autumn will I yield,
    Not to winter even!

Let the blow fall soon or late,
    Let what will be o'er me;
Give the face of earth around
    And the road before me.
Wealth I ask not, hope nor love,
    Nor a friend to know me;
All I ask, the heaven above
    And the road below me.

301

THE VAGABOND

JOHN DRINKWATER

I know the pools where the grayling rise,
    I know the trees where the filberts fall,
I know the woods where the red fox lies,
    The twisted elms where the brown owls call.
And I've seldom a shilling to call my own,
    And there's never a girl I'd marry,
I thank the Lord I'm a rolling stone
    With never a care to carry.

I talk to the stars as they come and go
    On every night from July to June,
I'm free of the speech of the winds that blow,
    And I know what weather will sing what tune.
I sow no seed and I pay no rent,
    And I thank no man for his bounties,
But I've a treasure that's never spent,
    I'm lord of a dozen counties.

The pleasures of being a boy in the countryside.

GLAD IN HEART

NICHOLAS BRETON

Who can live in heart so glad
As the merry country lad?
Who upon a fair green baulk
May at pleasure sit and walk;
And amidst the azure skies
See the morning sun arise,
While he hears in every spring
How the birds do chirp and sing;
Or, before the hounds in cry,
See the hare go stealing by;
Or along the shallow brook
Angling with a baited hook,
See the fishes leap and play
In a blessed sunny day;
Or to hear the partridge call
Till she have her covey all;
Or to see the subtle fox,
How the villain plays the box,
After feeding on his prey
How he closely sneaks away,
Through the hedge and down the furrow
Till he gets into his burrow;
Then the bee to gather honey,
And the little black-haired coney
On a bank for sunny place
With her fore-feet wash her face:
Are not these with thousands moe
Than the court of kings do know?

A thanksgiving for life in the open air.

'FOR THE COMFORTING WARMTH OF THE SUN'

HENRY VAN DYKE

For the comforting warmth of the sun that my body
    embraces,
For the cool of the waters that run thro' the shadowy
    places,
For the balm of the breezes that brush my face with their
    fingers,
For the vesper hymn of the thrush when the twilight
    lingers,
Now with a breath that is deep-drawn, breath of a
    heart without care,
I will give thanks and adore thee, God of the open air!

304. 'Now pray we for our country' . *Eliza Fowler*
305. 'This royal throne of kings' . *William Shakespeare*
306. 'Breathes there the man' . *Sir Walter Scott*
307. England . . . . . *Walter Meade*
308. On England . . . . *John Masefield*
309. For the Fallen . . . *Laurence Binyon*
310. The Soldier . . . . *Rupert Brooke*

304

'NOW PRAY WE FOR OUR COUNTRY'
ELIZA FOWLER

Now pray we for our country
That England long may be
The holy and the happy,
And the gloriously free.
Who blesseth her is blessed;
So peace be in her walls:
And joy in all her palaces,
Her cottages and halls.

305

*Shakespeare, enumerating all the qualities that make up the
splendour of his native land, finally summarizes the list with the
phrase, 'this England', for these words signify all that he has
said previously.*

'THIS ROYAL THRONE OF KINGS'
WILLIAM SHAKESPEARE

This royal throne of kings, this sceptered isle,
This earth of majesty, this seat of Mars,
This other Eden, demi-paradise,
This fortress built by Nature for herself
Against infection and the hand of war,
This happy breed of men, this little world,
This precious stone set in the silver sea,
Which serves it in the office of a wall,
Or as a moat defensive to a house,
Against the envy of less happier lands;
This blessed plot, this earth, this realm, this **England**.

Richard II, II. I

212

A man who is not proud of his native land is totally unworthy,
no matter what his wealth and position.

'BREATHES THERE THE MAN'
SIR WALTER SCOTT

Breathes there the man with soul so dead,
Who never to himself hath said,
   This is my own, my native land!
Whose heart hath n'er within him burn'd,
As home his footsteps he hath turn'd,
   From wandering on a foreign strand!
If such there breathe, go, mark him well;
For him no minstrel raptures swell;
High though his titles, proud his name,
Boundless his wealth as wish can claim;
Despite those titles, power, and pelf,
The wretch, concentred all in self,
Living, shall forfeit fair renown,
And, doubly dying, shall go down
To the vile dust from whence he sprung,
Unwept, unhonour'd, and unsung.
   From 'The Lay of the Last Minstrel', Canto VI

307

A list which summarizes the meaning of the word, 'England',
in the mind of the writer.

ENGLAND
WALTER MEADE

A cottage garden, speck'd with London pride,
A mansion'd lily, arrogantly tall,
A well at dusk for hesitating love,
A wander'd path, a field where cowslips grow,
A wood, a pillar-box in Parson's wall,
A chancel, dim with long-remember'd prayer,
A tiny school where sun-drows'd voices chant,
A pond, an apple orchard, and a dove.

It is the people of England that give her character.

ON ENGLAND
JOHN MASEFIELD

England with mucky arms, and cheer, and spanner
Kneels at your car to help you in distress;
On many a bridge in many a crazy ship,
England in oilskins keeps a stiffened lip;
In burnt or freezing lands beyond the sea
England will welcome you to England's banner
(The chances of the football cup, and tea)
England comes nearer when the troubles press.

No man can praise her, she is full of fault;
No man can blame her, she is full of good,
Kindness, stupidity and hardihood,
Wisdom and gentleness, the sweet and salt.
She grows more wise and gentle, growing old,
New stars arise, to light her to exalt
The Life within her borders above gold;
New buds are springing from the ancient wood.

From 'England'

FOR THE FALLEN
LAURENCE BINYON

With proud thanksgiving, a mother for her children,
England mourns for her dead across the sea.
Flesh of her flesh they were, spirit of her spirit,
Fallen in the cause of the free.

Solemn the drums thrill: Death august and royal
Sings sorrow up into immortal spheres.
There is music in the midst of desolation
And a glory that shines upon our tears.

They went with songs to the battle, they were young,
Straight of limb, true of eye, steady and aglow.
They were staunch to the end against odds uncounted,
They fell with their faces to the foe.

They shall not grow old, as we that are left grow old:
Age shall not weary them, nor the years condemn.
At the going down of the sun and in the morning
We will remember them.

They mingle not with their laughing comrades again;
They sit no more at familiar tables of home;
They have no lot in our labour of the day-time;
They sleep beyond England's foam.

But where our desires are and our hopes profound,
Felt as a well-spring that is hidden from sight,
To the innermost heart of their own land they are known
As the stars are known to the Night;

As the stars that shall be bright when we are dust
Moving in marches upon the heavenly plain,
As the stars that are starry in the time of our darkness,
To the end, to the end, they remain.

310

*In the grave of every English soldier buried abroad there lies
the essence of all that England taught.*

THE SOLDIER
RUPERT BROOKE

If I should die, think only this of me:
    That there's some corner of a foreign field
That is for ever England. There shall be
    In that rich earth a richer dust concealed;
A dust whom England bore, shaped, made aware,
    Gave, once, her flowers to love, her ways to roam,
A body of England's, breathing English air,
    Washed by the rivers, blest by suns of home.

And think, this heart, all evil shed away,
    A pulse in the eternal mind, no less
        Gives somewhere back the thoughts by England
            given;
Her sights and sounds; dreams happy as her day;
    And laughter, learnt of friends; and gentleness,
        In hearts at peace, under an English heaven.

311. Verses
312. 'And many nations shall come' . *Micah* IV. 2–5
313. Then As Now . . . *Walter de la Mare*
314. Refugees . . . . . *Thomas Moult*
315. 'For the brave of every race' . *G. W. Briggs*
316. Stanzas on Freedom . . *J. Russell Lowell*
317. The Little Black Boy . . . *William Blake*

311

VERSES

The Lord looketh from heaven:
He beholdeth all the sons of men.
From the place of his habitation he looketh upon all the
　　inhabitants of the earth.
He fashioneth their hearts alike:
He considereth all their works.

Psalm XXXIII. 13–15

I will praise thee, O Lord, among the people:
And I will sing praises unto thee among the nations.
For thy mercy is great above the heavens:
And thy truth reacheth unto the clouds.

Psalm CVIII. 3, 4

All nations whom thou hast made shall come and
　　worship before thee, O Lord:
And shall glorify thy name.
For thou art great and doest wondrous things:
Thou art God alone.

Psalm LXXXVI. 9, 10

Other sheep I have, which are not of this fold:
Them also I must bring, and they shall hear my voice;
And there shall be one fold, and one shepherd.

St. John x. 16

I exhort therefore, that, first of all, supplications, prayers, intercessions, and giving of thanks, be made for all men;

For kings, and all that are in authority;

That we may lead a quiet and peaceable life in all godliness and honesty.   I *Timothy* II. 1, 2

> From all that dwell below the skies
> Let the Creator's praise arise:
> Let the Redeemer's name be sung
> Through every land, by every tongue.
>
> *Isaac Watts*

READING

312

'AND MANY NATIONS SHALL COME'   .   Micah IV. 2–5
A vision of the peaceful days that will come to the nations that follow God's laws.

313

Each of our innumerable predecessors, whatever his colour, has played his part.

THEN AS NOW

WALTER DE LA MARE

Then as Now; and Now as Then,
Spins on this World of Men.
White—Black—Yellow—Red:
They wake, work, eat, play, go to bed.
Black—Yellow—Red—White:
They talk, laugh, weep, dance, morn to night.
Yellow—Red—White—Black:
Sun shines, moon rides, clouds come back.
Red—White—Black—Yellow:
Count your hardest, who could tell o'
The myriads that have come and gone,
Stayed their stay this earth upon,
And vanished then, their labour done?
Sands of the wilderness, stars in heaven,
Solomon could not sum them even:
Then as Now; Now as Then
Stills spins on this World of Men.

We should welcome men and women refugees for the gifts of intellect that their minds bring, and we should try to help them to forget as their children have already forgotten.

REFUGEES
THOMAS MOULT

Now praised be God for all these unfamiliar faces
That I behold when I walk through our English streets.
This motley people exiled from far, ravaged places—
Not East and West alone, but South here also meets!
Ever to England's refuge have the dispossessed
Brought their vast wealth of mind: to-day a grander gift
Enriches our Garden Land already by Nature blest.
I see defeated, silent-dragging men (Ah, lift
Your heads, my ill-starred brothers, lose the old despair!)
Women I see, heavy with memories . . . I mark,
Hidden behind their eyes, a heartbreak past repair
(Women, be your hearts eased: your children from a dark
Blacker than frightening night are safe). These too I see—
The children here, of their own lands bereft, and yet
Laughing again, new flowers in our proud garden,
    growing free.
Now praised be God that children, laughing, can forget.

We should praise God for all those who have helped the world on its way, for their work was in itself an act of praise.

'FOR THE BRAVE OF EVERY RACE'
G. W. BRIGGS

For the brave of every race,
    All who served and fell on sleep,
Whose forgotten resting-place
    Rolling years have buried deep—
Brotherhood and sisterhood
    Of earth's age-long chivalry—
Source and giver of all good,
    Lord, we praise, we worship thee.

Prince and peasant, bond and free,
   Warriors wielding freedom's sword,
Bold adventurers on the sea,
   Faithful stewards of the word,
Toilers in the mine and mill,
   Toilers at the furnace-blaze,
Long forgotten, living still,
   All thy servants tell thy praise.

316

Personal freedom is not enough. We are still slaves if we are afraid to fight in the minority for what we believe to be right.

STANZAS ON FREEDOM
J. RUSSELL LOWELL

Men! whose boast it is that ye
Come of fathers brave and free,
If there breathe on earth a slave,
Are ye truly free and brave?
If ye do not feel the chain,
When it works a brother's pain,
Are ye not base slaves indeed,
Slaves unworthy to be freed?
Is true Freedom but to break

Fetters for our own dear sake,
And, with leathern hearts, forget
That we owe mankind a debt?
No! true freedom is to share
All the chains our brothers wear,
And, with heart and hand, to be
Earnest to make others free!

They are slaves who fear to speak
For the fallen and the weak;
They are slaves who will not choose
Hatred, scoffing, and abuse,
Rather than in silence shrink
From the truth they needs must think;
They are slaves who dare not be
In the right with two or three.

In the sight of God black and white people are of equal importance.

THE LITTLE BLACK BOY

WILLIAM BLAKE

My mother bore me in the southern wild,
And I am black, but O! my soul is white;
White as an angel is the English child,
But I am black, as if bereaved of light.

My mother taught me underneath a tree,
And, sitting down before the heat of day,
She took me on her lap and kissed me,
And, pointing to the east, began to say:

'Look on the rising sun—there God does live,
And gives His light, and gives His heat away;
And flowers and trees and beasts and men receive
Comfort in morning, joy in the noonday.

'And we are put on earth a little space,
That we may learn to bear the beams of love;
And these black bodies and this sunburnt face
Is but a cloud, and like a shady grove.

'For when our souls have learn'd the heat to bear,
The cloud will vanish; we shall hear His voice,
Saying: "Come out from the grove, My love and care,
And round My golden tent like lambs rejoice." '

Thus did my mother say, and kissed me;
And thus I say to little English boy.
When I from black and he from white cloud free,
And round the tent of God like lambs we joy,

I'll shade him from the heat, till he can bear
To lean in joy upon our Father's knee;
And then I'll stand and stroke his silver hair,
And be like him, and he will then love me.

318. 'Rebuke not an elder' . . 1 *Timothy* v. 1–4
319. 'Lord, thou hast been our dwelling place' *Psalm* xc
320. Lines on a Clock in Chester Cathedral *Henry Twells*
321. 'Before the beginning of years'
          Algernon Charles Swinburne
322. The Song of All Creation . . *Anonymous*
323. When— . . . . . *Lord Gorell*
324. Prayers . . . . *Henry Charles Beeching*
325. 'All the world's a stage' . *William Shakespeare*
326. 'My heart leaps up' . . *William Wordsworth*

READINGS

318

'REBUKE NOT AN ELDER' . . 1 Timothy v. 1–4
Advice on the treatment of both the young and the elderly.

319

'LORD, THOU HAST BEEN OUR DWELLING PLACE' Psalm xc
*The psalm of which the hymn, 'O God, our help in ages past',
is a paraphrase.*

320

*The speed with which time passes increases as we get older,
until, suddenly, life has ended, perhaps too soon for us to make
amends.*

LINES ON A CLOCK IN CHESTER CATHEDRAL
HENRY TWELLS

When as a child, I laughed and wept,
    Time crept.
When as a youth, I dreamt and talked,
    Time walked.
When I became a full-grown man,
    Time ran.
When older still I daily grew,
    Time flew.
Soon I shall find on travelling on—
    Time gone.
O Christ, wilt Thou have saved me then?
    Amen.

A recital of the many diverse factors which constitute the complex human soul.

'BEFORE THE BEGINNING OF YEARS'

ALGERNON CHARLES SWINBURNE

Before the beginning of years,
   There came to the making of man
Time, with a gift of tears;
   Grief, with a glass that ran;
Pleasure, with pain for leaven;
   Summer, with flowers that fell;
Remembrance fallen from heaven;
   And madness risen from hell;
Strength without hands to smite;
   Love that endures for a breath;
Night, the shadow of light,
   And life, the shadow of death.

.   .   .   .

From the winds of the north and the south
   They gathered as unto strife;
They breathed upon his mouth,
   They filled his body with life;
Eyesight and speech they wrought
   For the veils of the soul therein,
A time for labour and thought,
   A time to serve and to sin;
They gave him light in his ways,
   And love, and a space for delight,
And beauty and length of days,
   And night, and sleep in the night.
His speech is a burning fire;
   With his lips he travaileth;
In his heart is a blind desire,
   In his eyes foreknowledge of death;
He weaves, and is clothed with derision;
   Sows, and he shall not reap;
His life is a watch or a vision
   Between a sleep and a sleep.

From 'Atalanta in Calydon'

A hope for a full and satisfying life.

THE SONG OF ALL CREATION
ANONYMOUS

And I, too, sing the song of all creation—
  A brave sky and a glad wind flowing by,
A clear trail, and an hour for meditation,
  A long day, and the joy to make it fly:
A hard task, and the muscle to achieve it,
  A fierce noon, and a well-contented gloam,
A good strife, and no regret to leave it,
  A still night, and the far red lights of home.

323

We are told how the attitude of men towards life changes as they pass from Youth to Old Age.

WHEN—
LORD GORELL

When we are young, we are so clever,
Our thoughts a free, quick-silver ball:
Care comes—but briefly; visions call.
We think that Youth will last for ever—
Or do not think of it at all:
It is a wealth past evil powers,
Vastly, inevitably ours.

When we are in the midst of living,
We surge against the shifting tides;
We stand erect, we choose our sides,
Loving, rebuffing, getting, giving:
High on the mast our lantern rides.
We labour, and, like sunshine, zest
Lights up the waters of our quest.

When we are old, we see Time's finger
Steadily beckon to the great beyond:
Life's book lies open as a lesson conned;
Things past and present strangely linger
Fastened together in a single bond.
Regrets, fulfilments jostle Pain—
And we must smile and start again.

*Three offerings to the Trinity from the beginning, the middle
and the end of a lifetime.*

PRAYERS
HENRY CHARLES BEECHING

God who created me
  Nimble and light of limb,
In three elements free,
  To run, to ride, to swim:
Not when the sense is dim,
  But now from the heart of joy,
I would remember Him:
  Take the thanks of a boy.

Jesu, King and Lord,
  Whose are my foes to fight,
Gird me with Thy sword,
  Swift and sharp and bright.
Thee would I serve if I might;
  And conquer if I can,
From day-dawn till night,
  Take the strength of a man.

Spirit of Love and Truth,
  Breathing in grosser clay,
The light and flame of youth,
  Delight of men in the fray,
Wisdom in strength's decay;
  From pain, strife, wrong to be free,
This best gift I pray,
  Take my spirit to Thee.

325

'ALL THE WORLD'S A STAGE'
WILLIAM SHAKESPEARE

All the world's a stage,
And all the men and women merely players:
They have their exits and their entrances;
And one man is his time plays many parts,
His acts being seven ages. At first the infant,
Mewling and puking in the nurse's arms.

And then the whining schoolboy, with his satchel,
And shining morning face, creeping like snail
Unwillingly to school. And then the lover,
Sighing like furnace, with a woful ballad
Made to his mistress' eyebrow. Then a soldier,
Full of strange oaths, and bearded like the pard,
Jealous in honour, sudden and quick in quarrel,
Seeking the bubble reputation
Even in the cannon's mouth. And then the justice,
In fair round belly with good capon lin'd,
With eyes severe, and beard of formal cut,
Full of wise saws and modern instances;
And so he plays his part. The sixth age shifts
Into the lean and slipper'd pantaloon,
With spectacles on nose and pouch on side,
His youthful hose well sav'd, a world too wide
For his shrunk shank; and his big manly voice,
Turning again toward childish treble, pipes
And whistles in his sound. Last scene of all,
That ends this strange eventful history,
Is second childishness and mere oblivion,
Sans teeth, sans eyes, sans taste, sans everything.

'As You Like It' II. 7

326

As the rainbow appears to be a link so may godliness be the bond which joins old age to childhood.

'MY HEART LEAPS UP'
WILLIAM WORDSWORTH

My heart leaps up when I behold
   A rainbow in the sky:
So was it when my life began;
So is it now I am a man:
So be it when I shall grow old,
   Or let me die!
The child is father of the man;
And I could wish my days to be
Bound each to each by natural piety.

CHILDHOOD

327. Verses
328. 'And they brought young children to him'
St. Mark x. 13–16
329. 'Who is the greatest in the kingdom of heaven?'
St. Matthew xviii. 1–6
330. The Toys . . . . *Coventry Patmore*
331. The Storke . . . *Old English Carol*
332. To a Child on Leaving School . *Jack Gilbey*
333. 'Born of a Monday' . . . *Anonymous*
334. The Blind Boy . . . . *Colley Cibber*

327

VERSES

Even a child is known by his doings,
Whether his work be pure,
And whether it be right.   *Proverbs* xx. 11

Train up a child in the way he should go:
And when he is old, he will not depart from it.
    Proverbs xxii. 6

Children, obey your parents in the Lord: for this is right.
Honour thy father and mother; which is the first
    commandment with promise.
    Ephesians vi. 1, 2

READINGS

328

'AND THEY BROUGHT YOUNG CHILDREN TO HIM'
St. Mark x. 13–16
Christ receives and blesses small children.

329

'WHO IS THE GREATEST IN THE KINGDOM OF HEAVEN?'
St. Matthew xviii. 1–6

*We, like small children who when in disgrace seek comfort
from their toys, find in trivial pleasures relief from misfortunes
which we cannot understand.*

THE TOYS
COVENTRY PATMORE

My little Son, who look'd from thoughtful eyes
And moved and spoke in quiet grown-up wise,
Having my law the seventh time disobey'd,
I struck him, and dismiss'd
With hard words and unkiss'd,
His Mother, who was patient, being dead.
Then, fearing lest his grief should hinder sleep,
I visited his bed,
But found him slumbering deep,
With darken'd eyelids, and their lashes yet
From his late sobbing wet.
And I, with moan,
Kissing away his tears, left others of my own;
For, on a table drawn beside his head,
He had put, within his reach,
A box of counters and a red-vein'd stone,
A piece of glass abraded by the beach
And six or seven shells,
A bottle with bluebells
And two French copper coins, ranged there with careful art,
To comfort his sad heart.
So when that night I pray'd
To God, I wept, and said:
Ah, when at last we lie with tranced breath
Not vexing Thee in death,
And Thou rememberest of what toys
We made our joys,
How weakly understood
Thy great commanded good,
Then, fatherly not less
Than I whom Thou has moulded from the clay,
Thou'lt leave Thy wrath and say,
'I will be sorry for their childishness.'

How the stork came to be associated with small children.

THE STORKE
OLD ENGLISH CAROL

The storke she rose on Christmas eve,
    And sayed unto her broode,

'I must now fare to Bethleem,
    To vieue the Sonne of God.'

She gave to each his dole of mete,
    She stowed them fayrlie in,

And farre she flewe and fast she flewe,
    And came to Bethleem.

'Now where is He of David's line?' shee
    asked at house and hall,

'He is not here', they spake hardlye, 'but
    in the Maungier stalle.'

She found Hym in the Maungier stalle, with
    that most holy Mayde,

The gentyle storke she wept to see the
    Lord so rudely layde.

Then from her pauntynge brest she plucked
    The fethers whyte and warm;

She strawed them in the Maungier bed to
    Keep the Lorde from harm.

'Now blessed bee the gentyle storke for
    evermore,' quoth Hee,

'For that shee saw My sadde estate and
    showed such Pitye.

'Ful welkum shal shee ever bee in
hamlet and in halle,

'And hight henceforth the Blessed Byrd and
Friend of Babyes all.'

332

TO A CHILD ON LEAVING SCHOOL
JACK GILBEY

When you have gone from school into the world
Will you remember what I told you once,
Between these very walls, about a Child
Who came to dwell awhile upon this earth?
A tender little child like you, and yet
'Twas God the Son Who came to teach mankind
The way to live. Such simple things He taught,
So often very hard for us to learn
Because our faith is weak; because our thoughts
Are centred on ourselves and not on God;
Because we plan and build as if our home
Were here below for all eternity.
When you are grown and gone into the world
Will you remember Christ and what He came to teach?

333

'BORN OF A MONDAY'
ANONYMOUS

Born of a Monday, fair in the face,
Born of a Tuesday, full of God's grace,
Born of a Wednesday, merry and glad,
Born of a Thursday, sour and sad,
Born of a Friday, Godly given,
Born of a Saturday, work for your living,
Born of a Sunday, n'er shall you want,
So ends the week, and there's an end on't.

229

The boy who has never seen the light does not notice the absence of the day. To him 'day' is the time when he is awake and playing. He does not need our pity.

THE BLIND BOY
COLLEY CIBBER

O say! what is that Thing called Light,
   Which I can ne'er enjoy;
What is the blessing of the sight,
   O tell your poor Blind Boy!

You talk of wondrous things you see,
   You say the sun shines bright;
I feel him warm, but how can he
   Then make it Day or Night?

My Day or Night myself I make,
   Whene'er I wake or play;
And could I ever keep awake
   It would be always Day.

With heavy sighs, I often hear,
   You mourn my hopeless woe;
But sure, with patience I may bear
   A loss I ne'er can know.

Then let not what I cannot have
   My cheer of mind destroy;
Whilst thus I sing, I am a king,
   Although a poor blind boy.

YOUTH

335. Verses

336. To My Son . . . . *Siegfried Sassoon*

337. For Any Boy . . . *Geoffrey W. Young*

338. A Boy's Thanksgiving *Richard Molesworth Dennis*

339. Wool-gathering . . . . *Wilfrid Gibson*

340. A Farewell . . . . *Charles Kingsley*

341. To Vincent Corbet, His Son *Bishop Richard Corbet*

342. 'This is our Lord and Elder Brother' *John Oxenham*

343. 'Oh, the wild joys of living' . *Robert Browning*

335

VERSES

Wherewithal shall a young man cleanse his way?
By taking heed thereto according to thy word.
With my whole heart have I sought thee:
O let me not wander from thy commandments.

Psalm CXIX. 9, 10

It is good for a man that he bear the yoke in his youth.

Lamentations III. 27

Remember now thy Creator in the days of thy youth,
While the evil days come not,
Nor the years draw nigh. *Ecclesiastes* XII. 1

The glory of young men is their strength:
And the beauty of old men is the gray head.

Proverbs XX. 29

Rejoice, O young man, in thy youth;
And let thy heart cheer thee in the days of thy youth,
And walk in the ways of thine heart,
And in the sight of thine eyes:
But know thou, that for all these things God will bring
thee into judgment. *Ecclesiastes* XI. 9

HEROISM

So nigh is grandeur to our dust,
So near to God is man,
When Duty whispers low, Thou must,
The youth replies, I can.

Ralph Waldo Emerson

In books, or work, or healthful play,
Let my first years be past,
That I may give for every day
Some good account at last.

Isaac Watts

336

Four wise instructions, with the reasons for them.

TO MY SON

SIEGFRIED SASSOON

Go, and be gay;
You are born into the dazzling light of day.
Go, and be wise;
You are born upon an earth which needs new eyes.
Go, and be strong;
You are born into a world where love rights wrong.
Go, and be brave;
Possess your soul; that you alone can save.

337

A wish that every boy should possess those qualities which will enable him to enjoy such a full and happy life that he will not be reluctant to leave it.

FOR ANY BOY

GEOFFREY W. YOUNG

I wish for him
strength; that he may be strong in every limb,
stubborn and fearless, with no cover to thank,
fighting for men with men in the front rank.

I wish for him kind;
that he may have the weak always in mind:
such kindness as first treads the path of fear,
not tendance on the wounded in the rear.

I'd have him grow
deep-breathed, deep-hearted, cherished of wind and
       snow;
loving delightful laughter, and harsh thrills
in summer rivers and on perilous hills.

I wish him sight;
that he may read the world's real beauties right:
and for himself, wit and a laughing heart,
lest he may rage to bear so small a part.

I wish him thought;
that he may fashion faith even to a nought,
rather than take another's creed on trust,
and pass a fool and profitless to dust.

I'd have him range
a rebel, loving change only for change;
till he can forge a yoke for his broad back
and drag his kind one step up some new track.

Let him know men,
and have all acts, all passions in his ken:
they win no wars who peep on life askance
and shoot wise saws from sheltered ignorance.

Let him be flame,
quenchless and vital, in all winds the same;
fuse soul and body, and refine through years
judgment from passion, joy from his burning tears.

So let him live:
love work, love rest, love all that life can give;
and when he grows too weary to feel joy,
leave life, with laughter, to some other boy.

A catalogue of the many good things for which a boy should be grateful, with the hope that familiarity will not have removed that gratitude by the time he is grown up.

A BOY'S THANKSGIVING
RICHARD MOLESWORTH DENNIS

God's gifts so many a pleasure bring
That I may make a thanksgiving.

For eyes whereby I clearly see
The many lovely things there be;
For lungs to breathe the morning air,
For nose to smell its fragrance rare;
For tongue to taste the fruits that grow,
For birds that sing and flowers that blow;
For limbs to climb, and swim, and run,
And skin to feel the cheerful sun;
For sun and moon and stars in heaven,
Whose gracious light is freely given;
The river where the green weed floats,
And where I sail my little boats;
The sea, where I can bathe and play,
The sands where I can race all day;
The pigeons wheeling in the sun,
Who fly more quick than I can run;
The winds that sing as they rush by,
The clouds that race across the sky;
The pony that I sometimes ride,
The curly dog that runs beside;
The shelter of the shady woods,
Where I may spend my lonely moods;
The gabled house that is my home,
The garden where I love to roam;
And bless my parents, every day,
Though they be very far away.
Take Thou my thanks, O God above,
For all these tokens of Thy love.
And when I am a man, do Thou
Make me as grateful then as now.

*The youth who appears to be day-dreaming may be gathering
ideas for a life of action or one of writing words or music.*

WOOL-GATHERING

WILFRID GIBSON

Youth that goes wool-gathering,
Mooning and star-gazing,
Always finds everything
Full of fresh amazing,
Best can meet the moment's need
When the dream brings forth the deed.

He who keeps through all his days
Open eyes of wonder
Is the lord of skyey ways
And the earth thereunder,
For the heart to do and sing
Comes of youth's wool-gathering.

340

Simple advice to a girl.

A FAREWELL

CHARLES KINGSLEY

My fairest child, I have no song to give you;
  No lark could pipe in skies so dull and grey;
Yet, if you will, one quiet hint I'll leave you,
  For every day.

I'll tell you how to sing a clearer carol
  Than lark who hails the dawn or breezy down;
To earn yourself a purer poet's laurel
  Than Shakespeare's crown.

Be good, sweet maid, and let who can be clever;
  Do lovely things, not dream them, all day long,
And so make Life, and Death and that For Ever
  One grand sweet song.

*A poem of good wishes for a three-year-old son, from a
father who loved to lead a gay life.*

TO VINCENT CORBET, HIS SON
RICHARD CORBET, BISHOP OF OXFORD

What I shall leave thee, none can tell,
But all shall say I wish thee well;
I wish thee, Vin, before all wealth,
Both bodily and ghostly health:
Nor too much wealth, nor wit, come to thee,
So much of either may undoe thee.
I wish thee learning, not for show,
Enough for to instruct, and know;
Not such as Gentlemen require,
To prate at Table, or at Fire.

I wish thee all thy mother's graces,
Thy father's fortunes, and his places.
I wish thee friends, and one at Court,
Not to build on, but support;
To keep thee, not in doing many
Oppressions, but from suffering any.
I wish thee peace in all thy ways,
Nor lazy nor contentious days;
And when thy soul and body part,
As innocent as now thou art.

342

Thoughts on the boyhood of Christ.

'THIS IS OUR LORD AND ELDER BROTHER'
JOHN OXENHAM

This is our Lord and Elder Brother:
   He loved all birds and beasts and flowers,
     And in the hills spent happy days
     Lying unseen in cunning bowers
   Where He could watch their curious ways.

He was great-hearted, tender, true,
   And brave as any boy could be,
And very gentle, for He knew
   That Love is God's own chivalry.

He was a boy—like you—and you—,
   As full of jokes, as full of fun,
But always He was bravely true,
   And did no wrong to anyone.

And one thing I am sure about—
   He never stumbled into sin,
But kept Himself, within, without,
   As God had made Him, sweet and clean.
From 'Gentlemen, The King!'

343

*When we are young the sheer enjoyment of life can occupy all
our powers.*

'OH, THE WILD JOYS OF LIVING'
ROBERT BROWNING

Oh, the wild joys of living! the leaping from rock up to
   rock,
The strong rending of boughs from the fir tree, the cool
   silver shock
Of the plunge in a pool's living water, the hunt of the
   bear,
And the sultriness showing the lion is couched in his
   lair.
And the meal, rich dates yellowed over with gold dust
   divine,
And the locust-flesh steeped in the pitcher, the full
   draught of wine,
And the sleep in the dried river-channel where bulrushes
   tell
That the water was wont to go warbling so softly and
   well.
How good is man's life, the mere living! how fit to
   employ
All the heart and the soul and the senses for ever in joy!
Part of David's song to Saul from 'Saul'

WISDOM AND LEARNING

344. Verses: On Wisdom
345. Verses: On Learning
346. 'But where shall wisdom be found?'
                                  Job XXVIII. 12–28
347. 'The Lord appeared to Solomon in a dream'
                                  I *Kings* III. 5–13
348. 'This, books can do' .   .   .   *George Crabbe*
349. 'O Thou whose feet have climbed life's hill'
                                  L. F. Benson
350. An Arabian Proverb .   .   .   *Anonymous*

344

VERSES

ON WISDOM

The fear of the Lord is the beginning of wisdom:
A good understanding have all they that do his
    commandments:
His praise endureth for ever.   *Psalm* CXI. 10

Wise men lay up knowledge,
But the mouth of the foolish is near destruction.
                                  Proverbs X. 14

A wise man is strong;
Yea, a man of knowledge increaseth strength.
                                  Proverbs XXIV. 5

If any of you lack wisdom, let him ask of God,
That giveth to all men liberally, and upbraideth not;
And it shall be given him.   *St. James* I. 5

Even a fool, when he holdeth his peace, is counted
    wise:
And he that shutteth his lips is esteemed a man of
    understanding.   *Proverbs* XVII. 28

238

He that walketh with wise men shall be wise:
But a companion of fools shall be destroyed.

Proverbs XIII. 20

Give instruction to a wise man,
    and he will be yet wiser:
Teach a just man,
    and he will increase in learning.

Proverbs IX. 9

For whoso despiseth wisdom and nurture,
    he is miserable,
    and their hope is vain,
    their labours unfruitful,
    and their works unprofitable.

The Wisdom of Solomon III. 11

345

ON LEARNING

Draw near unto me, ye unlearned,
    and dwell in the house of learning.
Wherefore are ye slow,
    and what say ye of these things, seeing your souls are
        very thirsty?
Put your neck under the yoke,
    and let your soul receive instruction:
She is hard at hand to find.

Ecclesiasticus LI. 23, 24, 26

Whoso loveth instruction loveth knowledge:
But he that hateth reproof is brutish.

Proverbs XII. 1

Take fast hold of instruction;
Let her not go:
Keep her;
For she is thy life.   *Proverbs* IV. 13

239

R

346

'BUT WHERE SHALL WISDOM BE FOUND?'

Job XXVIII. 12–28

Job tries both to assess the value of wisdom and to determine its highest form. He concludes that its possession cannot be valued and that the expression of its highest form lies in doing what is right.

347

'THE LORD APPEARED TO SOLOMON IN A DREAM'

1 Kings III. 5–13

Solomon chooses wisdom.

348

On the many benefits to be obtained from books.

'THIS, BOOKS CAN DO'

GEORGE CRABBE

This, books can do—nor this alone: they give
New views to life, and teach us how to live;
They soothe the grieved, the stubborn they chastise;
Fools they admonish, and confirm the wise.
Their aid they yield to all: they never shun
The man of sorrow, nor the wretch undone;
Unlike the hard, the selfish, and the proud,
They fly not sullen from the suppliant crowd;
Nor tell to various people various things,
But show to subjects, what they show to kings.

From 'The Library'

A prayer that the example of Christ's life shall be our guide.

'O THOU WHOSE FEET HAVE CLIMBED LIFE'S HILL'

LOUIS FITZGERALD BENSON

O Thou whose feet have climbed life's hill,
 And trod the path of youth,
Our Saviour and our Brother still,
 Now lead us into truth.

Who learn of Thee the truth shall find,
 Who follow, gain the goal;
With reverence crown the earnest mind,
 And speak within the soul.

Awake the purpose high which strives,
 And, falling, strives again;
Confirm the will of eager lives
 To quit ourselves like men;

Thy life the bond of fellowship,
 Thy love the law that rules,
Thy Name, proclaimed by every lip,
 The Master of our schools.

350

AN ARABIAN PROVERB

Who knows not, and knows not that he knows not, is
 foolish;
 shun him.
Who knows not, and knows that he knows not, is humble;
 teach him.
Who knows, but knows not that he knows, is asleep;
 wake him.
Who knows, and knows that he knows, is wise;
 follow him.

351. Verses

352. 'He hath filled him with the spirit of God'
Exodus XXXV. 31–35

353. 'They helped every one his neighbour'
Isaiah XLI. 6, 7

354. 'Behold us, Lord, a little space' . *John Ellerton*

355. The Elixir . . . . *George Herbert*

356. Domestic Economy . . . *Anna Wickham*

357. The Divine Office of the Kitchen *Cecily R. Hallack*

358. 'Snug in my easy chair' . . *Wilfrid Gibson*

359. Gardeners . . . . *Gerald Bullett*

360. The Journeyman . . . *Dorothy Sayers*

361. 'The men who work in wood' . *Douglas Malloch*

362. Toil Away . . . *John Jay Chapman*

363. They work who dream . *Kennedy Williamson*

351

VERSES

There is nothing better for a man, than that he should
make his soul enjoy good in his labour.
This also I saw, that it was from the hand of God.
Ecclesiastes II. 24

Thou shalt eat the labour of thine hands:
Happy shalt thou be,
And it shall be well with thee. *Psalm* CXXVIII. 2

Great is the dignity of labour; it honours man.
Beautiful is the intellectual occupation if combined with
some practical work. *The Talmud*

It is good and comely for one to eat and to drink,
And to enjoy the good of all his labour
that he taketh under the sun all the days of his life,
which God giveth him:
For it is his portion. *Ecclesiastes* V. 18

242

For the want of a nail, the shoe was lost,
For the want of a shoe, the horse was lost,
For the want of a horse, the rider was lost,
For the want of the rider, the battle was lost,
For want of the battle, the kingdom was lost,
And all for the loss of a horseshoe nail.

Old rhyme

Shew thy servants thy work and their children thy glory,
And the glorious Majesty of the Lord our God be upon us:
Prosper thou the work of our hands upon us,
O prosper thou our handy-work.

Psalm xc. 16, 17
From the Book of Common Prayer

Unto thee, O Lord, belongeth mercy:
For thou renderest to every man according to his work.

Psalm lxii. 12

Seest thou a man diligent in his business?
He shall stand before Kings.

Proverbs xxii. 29

The trivial round, the common task,
Will furnish all we need to ask;
Room to deny ourselves, a road
To bring us daily nearer God.

John Keble

READINGS

352

'HE HATH FILLED HIM WITH THE SPIRIT OF GOD'

Exodus xxxv. 31–35

The spirit of God is in the work of all good craftsmen.

353

'THEY HELPED EVERY ONE HIS NEIGHBOUR'

Isaiah xli. 6, 7

A great work can be produced only if craftsmen work together well and encourage one another.

Work, bestowed and blessed by God, becomes, when performed with patience and sincerity, an offering to Him.

'BEHOLD US, LORD, A LITTLE SPACE'
JOHN ELLERTON

Behold us, Lord, a little space
    From daily tasks set free,
And met within Thy holy place
    To rest awhile with Thee.

Yet these are not the only walls
    Wherein Thou may'st be sought;
On homeliest work Thy blessing falls,
    In truth and patience wrought.

Thine is the loom, the forge, the mart,
    The wealth of land and sea;
The worlds of science and of art,
    Revealed and ruled by Thee.

All work is prayer, if it be wrought
    As Thou wouldst have it done,
And prayer, by Thee inspired and taught,
    Itself with work is one.

Some perform their work merely as an act of drudgery; others, in doing their best, however lowly the task, make their labour a fulfilment of God's wishes.

THE ELIXIR
GEORGE HERBERT

Teach me, my God and King,
    In all things Thee to see,
And what I do in anything,
    To do it as for Thee:

Not rudely, as a beast,
    To runne into an action;
But still to make Thee prepossest,
    And give it his perfection.

A man that looks on glasse,
On it may stay his eye;
Or if he pleaseth, through it passe,
And then the heav'n espie.

All may of Thee partake:
Nothing can be so mean,
Which with his tincture (for Thy sake)
Will not grow bright and clean.

A servant with this clause
Makes drudgerie divine:
Who sweeps a room, as for Thy laws,
Makes that and th' action fine.

This is the famous stone
That turneth all to gold:
For that which God doth touch and own
Cannot for lesse be told.

356

Even those who are engaged in simple work can achieve perfection; and by living sincerely and frugally will have a little to give away, as well as possessing the right to give good advice.

DOMESTIC ECONOMY

ANNA WICKHAM

I will have few cooking-pots,
They shall be bright;
They shall reflect to blinding
God's straight light.
I will have four garments,
They shall be clean;
My service shall be good,
Though my diet be mean,
Then I shall have excess to give to the poor,
And right to counsel beggars at my door.

As the sun when it ariseth in the high heaven;
So is the beauty of a good wife in the ordering of her
    house.   *Ecclesiasticus* xxvi. 16

THE DIVINE OFFICE OF THE KITCHEN
CECILY R. HALLACK

Lord of the pots and pipkins, since I have no time to be
A saint by doing lovely things and Vigilling with Thee,
By watching in the twilight dawn, and storming Heaven's
    gates,
Make me a saint by getting meals and washing up the
    plates.

358

*This poet saw such dazzling pictures in the fire that he was
forced to close his eyes. Then he remembered the working
conditions of the miner who gave him his coal.*

'SNUG IN MY EASY CHAIR'
WILFRID GIBSON

Snug in my easy chair,
I stirred the fire to flame.
Fantastically fair
The flickering fancies came,
Born of heart's desire—
Amber woodlands streaming;
Topaz islands dreaming,
Sunset-cities gleaming,
Spire on burning spire;
Ruddy-windowed taverns;
Sunshine-spilling wines;
Crystal-lighted caverns
Of Golconda's mines;
Summers, unreturning;
Passion's crater yearning;
Troy, the ever-burning;
Shelley's lustral pyre;
Dragon-eyes unsleeping:
Witches' cauldrons leaping;

Golden galleys sweeping
Out of sea-walled Tyre—
Fancies fugitive and fair
Flashed with singing through the air
Till, dazzled by the drowsy glare,
I shut my eyes to heat and light,
And saw in sudden night,
Crouched in the dripping dark
With steaming shoulders stark,
The man who hews the coal to feed my fire.

359

An appreciation of the cunning and skill of gardeners.

GARDENERS

GERALD BULLETT

Gardeners are good. Such vices as they have
Are like the warts and bosses in the wood
Of an old oak. They're patient, stubborn folk,
As needs must be whose busyness it is
To tutor wildness, making war on weeds.
With slow, sagacious words and knowing glance
They scan the sky, do all that mortals may
To learn civility to pesty birds
Come after new green peas, cosset and prune
Roses, wash with lime the orchard trees,
Make sun-parlours for seedlings.
                                        Patient, stubborn.
Add cunning next, unless you'd put it first;
For while to dig and delve is all their text
There's cunning in their fingers to persuade
Beauty to bloom and riot to run right,
Mattock and spade, trowel and rake and hoe
Being not tools to learn by learning rules
But extra limbs these husbands of the earth
Had from their birth. Of malice they've no more
Than snaring slugs and wireworms will appease,
Or may with ease be drowned in mugs of mild.
Wherefore I say again, whether or no
It is their occupation makes them so,
Gardeners are good, in grain.

A legend telling of a craftsman who, badly in arrears with his work, received help from a fellow-craftsman, whom, for a time, he did not recognize.

THE JOURNEYMAN
DOROTHY SAYERS

'Make haste, good Master Carpenter,
To carve the beams for Saint Saviour's shrine,
For the Bishop cometh at Holy Rood feast
To break the wafer and bless the wine.

'Set up the pillars of golden oak,
For Trinity-tide wanes out right late;
In three days' time cometh Holy Rood mass,
When Saint Saviour's Church shall be consecrate.'

John the Carver looked to the west,
And saw how the sun went plunging down,
And all night long, while men were at rest,
His candle shone in the dusky town.

John the Carver looked to the East,
And saw how the sun sprang upward soon,
His hammer and chisel rang out all day,
Till the bells of the city rang down at noon,
And his hammer and chisel rang up the moon.

John the Carver toils in the Church,
The time draws nigh, and the night draws in,
The salt sweat runs over his face,
The salt tears run over his chin.

There are five little devils in the organ loft,
They wriggle and laugh to see him cry;
He planes the wood and he trims it oft,
But ever those pillars stand awry.

And woe for the Bishop in his pomp and pride,
In his gloves and mitre and broidered hood,
If the shrine still stand so wrenched aside
When he singeth High Mass at Holy Rood.

The Carver carves by the lanthorn's light,
As the last ray leaps from the distant hill,

When he was aware of a strong young man
That leaned in over the window sill.

'How goeth thy work, good John?' quoth he;
'How goeth thy work here all alone?
They sing the Mass on to-morrow's morn,
And why is thy labour not yet done?'

'Who may'st thou be, my lusty lad,
That hast my name so pat to the tongue?'
'Oh, I am a man of strength and skill,
And I am come with a right good will
To finish thy work by the matin's song.'

John the Carver looked at his head,
John the Carver looked at his feet;
'If thou be the devil as I think,' he said,
'Go, get thee back to thy burning seat.

'I never will trade with the devil of hell
To save my neck from the hempen cord,
And if thou be but a mortal man
'Tis but little wage that I can afford.'

He crossed himself on the breast and brow:
'Thou seest I be no devil,' quoth he;
'I will work for thee till break of day,
And all for Sweet Saint Charity.'

He set the chisel into his hand;
'Let see,' quoth John, 'how well ye can,'
But all amazed must he stare and stand,
There was never a carver in wide England
Could handle his tools like that strange man.

John and the stranger toiled all night,
Till the loud bells rang to the matin's-call,
And the five little devils took angry flight,
And under the rose-red, eastern light
The shrine stood seemly and straight and tall.

'What mighty master art thou,' said John,
'Thou art so gracious to give me aid?'
'My name is God, but in years long gone
I was a Carpenter by trade.'

Those who have experienced the smell which English oak gives as it is being worked will appreciate this poem, which is a reminder of our dependence upon timber.

'THE MEN WHO WORK IN WOOD'

DOUGLAS MALLOCH

The men who work in wood!—here is a clan
That other workers well may envy—these
Who serve so much, so well, their fellow-men,
Who turn to use the tall and sheltering trees.
The roof of green becomes a roof of gray,
The sturdy trunk the pillars of a home,
They fashion us the infant's cradle, they
Are part of every threshold, every room.
The chair we dream in by the cheery fire,
The board at which we gather for the meal,
The bed to which our weary limbs retire,
And everything we know and love and feel
They shape from fallen forests for our need—
Yea! even that last room in which we rest,
When we lie down to rest at last indeed,
The woodlands' sainted lily on our breast.
Theirs not the dust of mines, the grime of toil
In sweaty shops of steel and molten brass,
Theirs is the scent of sawdust and of soil,
The song of waters, wind across the grass,
In everything they make for us they leave
The wooden upland and the quiet shores,
Yea! into every article they weave
Some memory of God's great out-of-doors.

TOIL AWAY

JOHN JAY CHAPMAN

Toil away and set the stone
That shall stand when you are gone,
   Ask not that another see
   The meaning of your masonry.

Grind the gem and dig the well,
For what? for whom?—I cannot tell.
   The stone may mark a boundary line,
   The well may flow, the gem may shine.

Be it wage enough for you
To shape them well and set them true.
   Of the future who can tell?
   Work, my friend, and so farewell.

363

Those who think and plan are as essential as those who carry out the plans. They also deserve praise for their work.

THEY WORK WHO DREAM

KENNEDY WILLIAMSON

The vast cathedral, now sublimely wrought,
   Was once a vision in a builder's heart.
   The sculpture that enthrals us with its art
Once had its being as a misty thought.

The poem that has shape in word and line
   Was formless once within the poet's soul.
   The journey's end that is the pilgrim's goal
Was first seen dimly at an inner shrine.

The beacon light was once an inward gleam,
   Discovery a glimmer in the brain.
   Give honour to the heroes who attain,
But Heaven give us heroes who can dream!

CRAFTSMANSHIP

364. 'O you gotta get a Glory' . . *Anonymous*
365. 'They who tread the path of labour' *Henry Van Dyke*
366. Laus Deo . . . . *Robert Bridges*
367. A Craftsman's Creed . . *James Parton Haney*
368. 'Praise God! Praise God! Give me my tools again!'
A. R. Wells

369. The Balanced Mind . . . *Harry Waine*
370. A Boy's Hymn . . . . *Lesbia Scott*
371. The Carpenter . . . . *Phyllis Hartnoll*

364

If we cannot enjoy our work, life is scarcely worth living is the theme of this negro spiritual from America.

'O YOU GOTTA GET A GLORY IN THE WORK YOU DO'

ANONYMOUS

O you gotta get a Glory in the work you do,
A Hallelujah Chorus in the heart of you.
Paint, or tell a story, sing, or shovel coal,
O you gotta get a Glory, or the job lacks soul.
O Lord, give me a Glory—is it much to give?
For you gotta get a Glory, or you just don't live.

The great, whose shining labours make our pulses throb,
Were men who got a Glory in their daily job.
The battle might be gory, and the odds unfair,
But the men who got a Glory never knew despair.
O Lord, give me a Glory—when all else is done,
If you've only got a Glory, you can still go on.

For those who get a Glory, it is like the sun,
And you can see it glowing through the work they've
done.
O fame is transitory—riches fade away—
But when you've got a Glory, it is there to stay.
O Lord, give me a Glory, and a workman's pride,
For you gotta get a Glory, or you're dead inside.

Christ, Himself, laboured for a living. Wherever work is going on the will of God is being fulfilled.

'THEY WHO TREAD THE PATH OF LABOUR'
HENRY VAN DYKE

They who tread the path of labour follow where My
    feet have trod;
They who work without complaining do the holy will of
    God;
Nevermore thou needest seek Me; I am with thee
    ev'rywhere;
Raise the stone, and thou shalt find Me; cleave the
    wood and I am there.

Where the many toil together, there am I among My
    own;
Where the tired workman sleepeth, there am I with him
    alone.
I, the Peace which passeth knowledge, dwell amid the
    daily strife;
I, the Bread of heaven, am broken in the sacrament of
    life.

Every task, however simple, sets the soul that does it
    free;
Every deed of love and mercy done to man, is done to
    Me.
Nevermore thou needest seek Me; I am with thee
    ev'rywhere;
Raise the stone, and thou shalt find Me; cleave the wood
    and I am there.

A craftsman is proud of work into which he has enjoyed putting all his skill. Such work is a form of praise to God.

LAUS DEO
ROBERT BRIDGES

Let praise devote thy work, and skill employ
Thy whole mind, and thy heart be lost in joy.
Well-doing bringeth pride, this constant thought
Humility, that thy best done is nought.
Man doeth nothing well, be it great or small,
Save to praise God; but that hath saved all:
For God requires no more than thou hast done,
And takes thy work to bless it for his own.

Our work should be an offering to our fellows; our skill, which is a gift from our ancestors, should be used and then passed on to those who follow us.

A CRAFTSMAN'S CREED
JAMES PARTON HANEY

I hold with none who think not work a boon,
Vouchsafed to man that he may aid his kind
With offerings from his chisel, wheel or loom,
Fashioned with loving hand and loving mind.
All of the fine traditions and the skill,
Come from my elders through the long line down,
Are mine to use, to raise our craft's renown,
And mine to teach again with reverent will.
Thus do I live to serve, tho' least for pay,
With fingers that are masters of the tool,
And eyes which light to see the pattern's play,
As it unfolds, obedient to each rule
Of our dear Art. So all my craft is praise
To God—at once part homage and part song.
My work's my prayer, I sing the whole day long,
As faith and beauty shape the forms I raise.

An expression of the joy which a craftsman must have felt on having his powers restored by Christ.

'PRAISE GOD! PRAISE GOD! GIVE ME MY TOOLS AGAIN!'

A. R. WELLS

Praise God! Praise God! Give me my tools again!
Oh! Let me grasp a hammer and a saw!
Bring me a nail, and any piece of wood,
Come, see me shut my hand and open it,
And watch my nimble fingers twirl a ring.
How good are solids!—oak and stone and iron,
And rough and smooth, and curved and straight and
      round!
. . . Come, wife, and see:
I am a man again, a man for work,
A man for earning bread and clothes and home;
A man, and not a useless hold-the-hand;
A man, no more a bandaged cumberer.
Oh, blessed Sabbath of all Sabbath days!
And did you hear them muttering at Him?
And did you see them looking sour at me?
They'll cast me from the synagogue, perchance;
But let them; I've a hand, a hand, a hand!
And ah, dear wife, to think He goes about
So quietly, and does such things as this,
Making poor half-men whole, in hand and foot,
In eye and ear, and witless maniac mind,
To get such praise as that! Well, here's a hand,
A strong, true hand that now is wholly His,
To work or fight for Him, or what He will;
For He has been the Hand of God to me.

We should not allow machines to become our masters, but use them to noble ends.

THE BALANCED MIND
HARRY WAINE

Happy is he who, in this Robot Age,
Keeps reasoned balance between fast and slow,
Who lets the mighty engines jar and rage,
So makes them serve him and then bids them go.
He is their master, and his servants they;
He sees them in perspective, knows their worth,
And reckons well their limits. He can weigh
Their value to man's destiny on earth.
He rates them but as means to nobler ends,
Handmaids to culture, vassals to man's mind;
So keeps serenity of soul, nor bends
His loftier instincts from their course designed:
The simple virtues of the human heart
The base from which his valuations start.

370

We should praise God for the wonders of modern industry, for He gave us the ability to create.

A BOY'S HYMN
LESBIA SCOTT

God had filled the mountains with metals hard and
  bright;
Man has learned to mine them and bring them to the
  light;
Man has made them into tools, great machines and
  cranes—
But who made man? Why God made man, and God
  gave man his brains.

God had filled with wonders the earth on which we
    dwell;
Man has learnt their powers and usefulness to tell:
Man has made his telephones, cars and aeroplanes—
But who made man? Why God made man, and God
    gave man his brains.

So let us praise the Father for mines beneath the rocks,
The whirring power-stations, the steamships and the
    docks,
The magic of the wireless, the thunder of the trains,
For man made these, but God made man, and God
    gave man his brains.

371

*A prayer asking for the same contentment to be gained from
making simple things that Christ gained whilst working in His
father's workshop.*

THE CARPENTER

PHYLLIS HARTNOLL

Silent at Joseph's side He stood,
And smoothed and trimmed the shapeless wood,
And with firm hand, assured and slow,
Drove in each nail with measured blow.

Absorbed, He planned a wooden cask,
Nor asked for any greater task,
Content to make, with humble tools,
Tables and little children's stools.

Lord, give me careful hands to make
Such simple things as for Thy sake,
Happy within Thine house to dwell
If I may make one table well.

SERVICE

372. Verses
373. 'For the kingdom of heaven is as a man'
St. Matthew xxv. 14–29
374. Io Victis . . . . *William Wetmore Story*
375. Wanted . . . . . *J. G. Holland*
376. 'When I consider how my Light is spent'
John Milton
377. Lifting and Leaning . . *Ella Wheeler Wilcox*
378. 'Let the lowliest task be mine' *John Greenleaf Whittier*
379. Indian Fevers . . . . *Sir Ronald Ross*

372
VERSES

Know thou the God of thy father,
And serve him with a perfect heart and with a willing
mind:
For the Lord searcheth all hearts,
And understandeth all the imaginations of the thoughts:
1 *Chronicles* xxviii. 9

Wherefore seeing we also are compassed about with so
great a cloud of witnesses,
Let us lay aside every weight,
And the sin which doth so easily beset us,
And let us run with patience the race that is set before us.
Hebrews xii. 1

No servant can serve two masters:
For either he will hate the one, and love the other;
Or else he will hold to the one, and despise the other.
Ye cannot serve God and mammon.
St. Luke xvi. 13

We live in deeds, not years; in thoughts, not breaths,
In feelings, not in figures on a dial.
We should count time by heart throbs. He most lives
Who thinks most, feels the noblest, acts the best.
Philip J. Bailey

I am only one
But I am one.
I cannot do everything,
But I can do something.
What I can do
I ought to do;
And what I ought to do
By the grace of God I will do.

Frederick William Farrar

That man may last, but never lives,
Who much receives but nothing gives;
Whom none can love, whom none can thank—
Creation's blot, creation's blank.

Thomas Gibbons

Teach us, Good Lord, to serve Thee as Thou deservest:
To give and not to count the cost;
To fight and not to heed the wounds;
To toil and not to seek for rest;
To labour and not to ask for any reward
Save that of knowing that we do Thy will.

St. Ignatius Loyola

Be useful where thou livest, that they may
   Both want and wish thy pleasing presence still.
Kindness, good parts, great places, are the way
   To compass this. Find out men's wants and will,
      And meet them there. All worldly joys go less
      To the one joy of doing kindnesses.

George Herbert

When Duty comes a-knocking at your gate,
Welcome him in; for if you bid him wait,
He will depart only to come once more
And bring seven other duties to your door.

Edwin Markham

373

'FOR THE KINGDOM OF HEAVEN IS AS A MAN'

St. Matthew xxv. 14–29

The parable of the talents.

374

A commemoration of those who have tried hard but have failed.

IO VICTIS

WILLIAM WETMORE STORY

I sing the hymn of the conquered, who fell in
    the battle of life,
The hymn of the wounded, the beaten who died
    overwhelmed in the strife;
Not the jubilant song of the victors for whom
    the resounding acclaim
Of nations was lifted in chorus, whose brows
    wore the chaplet of fame,
But the hymn of the low and the humble, the weary,
    the broken in heart,
Who strove and who failed, acting bravely a silent
    and desperate part.

375

A plea for the advent of sincere, disinterested men capable of tackling the problems of the times.

WANTED

J. G. HOLLAND

God give us men. A time like this demands
Strong minds, great hearts, true faith and ready hands!
Men whom the lust of office does not kill,
Men whom the spoils of office cannot buy,
Men who possess opinions and a will,
Men who love honour, men who cannot lie.

Milton himself produced his greatest works after becoming blind. He overcame his difficulties by composing his lines in his head and dictating them. He can scarcely be included with those who 'stand and wait'.

'WHEN I CONSIDER HOW MY LIGHT IS SPENT'

JOHN MILTON

When I consider how my Light is spent,
Ere half my days, in this dark world and wide,
And that one Talent which is death to hide,
Lodg'd with me useless, though my Soul more bent
To serve therewith my Maker, and present
My true account, lest he returning chide,
Doth God exact day-labour, light deny'd,
I fondly ask; but patience to prevent
That murmur, soon replies, God doth not need
Either man's work or his own gifts; who best
Bear his mild yoke, they serve him best; his State
Is Kingly. Thousands at his bidding speed
And post o'er Land and Ocean without rest:
They also serve who only stand and wait.

377

LIFTING AND LEANING

ELLA WHEELER WILCOX

There are two kinds of people on earth to-day,
Just two kinds of people, no more, I say.
Not the good and the bad, for 'tis well understood
That the good are half bad and the bad are half good . . .
No! the two kinds of people on earth I mean
Are the people who lift and the people who lean.

Andrew Rykman was a Dutchman. Whittier wrote these lines after seeing his tombstone.

'LET THE LOWLIEST TASK BE MINE'

JOHN GREENLEAF WHITTIER

Let the lowliest task be mine,
Grateful, so the task be Thine;

. . . . .

If there be some weaker one,
Give me strength to help him on;
If a blinder soul there be,
Let me guide him nearer Thee.
Make my mortal dreams come true,
With the work I fain would do;
Clothe with life the weak intent,
Let me be the thing I meant;
Let me find in Thy employ
Peace that dearer is than joy;
Out of self to love be led
And to heaven acclimated,
Until all things sweet and good
Seem my natural habitude.

. . . . .

Thus did Andrew Rykman pray;
Are we wiser, better grown,
That we may not, in our day,
Make his prayer our own?

From 'Andrew Rykman's Prayer'

Sir Ronald Ross spent many years trying to verify the theory that mosquitoes were the means of distribution of malaria. In this poem he reveals his earnest prayers for his success and, later, his deep gratitude when he eventually succeeded.

INDIAN FEVERS

SIR RONALD ROSS

The Petition.

In this, O Nature, yield, I pray, to me.
  I pace and pace, and think, and think, and take
The fever's hands, and note down all I see,
  That some dim distant light may haply break.

The painful faces ask, Can we not cure?
  We answer, No, not yet: we seek the laws.
O God, reveal through all this thing obscure
  The unseen, small but million-murdering cause.

(Bangalore 1890–3.)

The Reply.

This day, relenting God
  Has placed within my hand
A wondrous thing: and God
  Be praised. At His command,

Seeking His secret deeds
  With tears and toiling breath,
I find thy cunning seeds,
  O million-murdering Death.

I know this little thing
  A myriad men will save:
O Death, where is thy sting?
  Thy victory, O grave?

ENDEAVOUR

380. Verses
381. 'An emerald is as green' . . *Christina Rossetti*
382. The Will .   .   .   . *John Masefield*
383. For those who fail .   . . *Joaquin Miller*
384. 'Listen! I will be honest with you' *Walt Whitman*
385. Uphill .   .   . . *Christina Rossetti*
386. 'Lord, make us strong' *William Vaughan Jenkins*
387. The Pilgrim's Valour . . *John Bunyan*

380
VERSES

Whatsoever thy hand findeth to do,
Do it with thy might.

Ecclesiastes IX. 10

Know ye not that they which run in a race run all,
But one receiveth the prize?
So run, that ye may obtain.
And every man that striveth for the mastery is temperate
in all things.

I *Corinthians* IX. 24–25

Be not deceived;
God is not mocked:
For whatsoever a man soweth,
That shall he also reap.

Galatians VI. 7

Let us not be weary in well doing:
For in due season we shall reap, if we faint not.

Galatians VI. 9

Be strong and of a good courage,
Fear not, nor be afraid of them:
For the Lord thy God, he it is that doth go with thee;
He will not fail thee, nor forsake thee.

Deuteronomy XXXI. 6

Though I do my best I shall scarce succeed.
But what if I fail of my purpose here?
It is but to keep the nerves at strain,
    To dry one's eyes and laugh at a fall,
And, baffled, get up and begin again—
    So the chace takes up one's life, that's all.
Robert Browning

'Twixt failure and success the point's so fine
Men sometimes know not when they touch the line.
Just when the pearl is waiting one more plunge,
How many a struggler has thrown up the sponge!...
Then take this honey from the bitterest cup:
'There is no failure save in giving up!'
From 'Perseverance Conquers All'
Henry Austin

Behold, we live through all things—famine, thirst,
Bereavement, pain; all grief and misery,
All woe and sorrow; life inflicts its worst
On soul and body—but we can not die,
Though we be sick and tired and faint and worn—
Lo, all things can be borne!
Elizabeth Akers Allen

381

*Precious stones have great beauty but fire can be struck from a
lustreless flint. Perhaps men and women have such varying
and hidden qualities too.*

'AN EMERALD IS AS GREEN AS GRASS'
CHRISTINA ROSSETTI

An emerald is as green as grass,
    A ruby red as blood;
A sapphire shines as blue as heaven;
    A flint lies in the mud.

A diamond is a brilliant stone,
    To catch the world's desire;
An opal holds a fiery spark,
    But a flint holds fire.

265

Surely if man has shown sufficient determination to find ways of subduing Nature and to produce inventions for his benefit, he can find ways in which to overcome poverty, ignorance and hatred.

THE WILL
JOHN MASEFIELD

By Will, Man dared in den and heath
The dagger-claws and sabre-teeth
And brought their savageries beneath.

By Will, he beat the flint to fire
And burned the jungle in his ire
And lit the dark to his desire.

By Will, his spirit tamed the force
Of the wild bull and the wild horse
And the wild river in her course.

By Will, he quarried and made bright
Stone spires lifting into light
With visions of the infinite.

By Will, he made his eyes to see
The Death that kills in secrecy
From fly and louse and gnat and flea.

By Will, he made him slaves with hands
That without words do his commands
In air, in oceans and in lands.

Earth, water, air and brute and fool,
And crazy rebel against rule
By Will, he made each one his tool.

And shall he not, by Will attack
The country's shame, the people's lack,
The rags upon the nation's back?

The blots upon the nation's mind,
The ignorance that makes us blind,
The hate that shuts us from our Kind?

Surely, by Will, he will blow clear
His trumpets that all ears shall hear,
And helping angels shall sweep near,

And the banners of the soul advance,
Up, out of hate and ignorance,
Into a new inheritance.

383

An expression of admiration for the triers who do not succeed.

FOR THOSE WHO FAIL
JOAQUIN MILLER

'All honour to him who shall win the prize,'
The world has cried for a thousand years;
But to him who tries and who fails and dies,
I give great honour and glory and tears.

O great is the hero who wins a name,
But greater many and many a time
Some pale-faced fellow who dies in shame,
And lets God finish the thought sublime.

And great is the man with a sword undrawn,
And good is the man who refrains from wine;
But the man who fails and yet fights on,
Lo he is the twin-born brother of mine!

A call to follow the example of the Great, although there can be expected little rest and few rewards.

'LISTEN! I WILL BE HONEST WITH YOU'
WALT WHITMAN

Listen! I will be honest with you,
I do not offer the old smooth prizes, but offer rough new
    prizes,
These are the days that must happen to you:
You shall not heap up what is call'd riches,
You shall scatter with lavish hand all that you earn or
    achieve,
You but arrive at the city to which you are destin'd,
    you hardly settle yourself to satisfaction before you
    are call'd by an irresistible call to depart,
You shall be treated to the ironical smiles and mockings
    of those who remain behind you. . . .
You shall not allow the hold of those who spread their
    reach'd hands toward you.

Allons! after the great Companions, and to belong to
    them!
They too are on the road—they are the swift and majestic
    men—
They are the greatest women.

From 'Song of the Open Road'

Life is similar to a journey, with fellow travellers, brief rests on the way, and a long final rest when the journey has been completed.

UPHILL
CHRISTINA ROSSETTI

Does the road wind uphill all the way?
    Yes, to the very end.
Will the day's journey take the whole long day?
    From morn to night, my friend.

But is there for the night a resting place?
A roof for when the slow dark hours begin.
May not the darkness hide it from my face?
You cannot miss that inn.

Shall I meet other wayfarers at night?
Those who have gone before.
Then must I knock, or call when just in sight?
They will not keep you standing at that door.

Shall I find comfort, travel-sore and weak?
Of labour you shall find the sum.
Will there be beds for me and all who seek?
Yea, beds for all who come.

386

A prayer for courage in the face of difficulties.

'LORD, MAKE US STRONG'
WILLIAM VAUGHAN JENKINS

Lord, make us strong, for Thou alone dost know
How oft we turn our faces from the foe;
How oft, when claimed by dark temptation's hour,
We lose our hold of Thee, and of Thy power.

Go with us, Lord, from hence: we only ask
That Thou be sharer in our daily task;
So, side by side, with Thee, shall each one know
The blessedness of heaven begun below.

*The determined pilgrim, following what he believes to be right,
labours on regardless of all opposition and discouragement.*

THE PILGRIM'S VALOUR

JOHN BUNYAN

Who would true valour see,
Let him come hither;
One here will constant be,
Come wind, come weather.
There's no discouragement
Shall make him once relent
His first avowed intent,
To be a pilgrim.

Whoso beset him round
With dismal stories
Do but themselves confound;
His strength the more is.
No lion can him fright,
He'll with a giant fight,
But he will have a right
To be a pilgrim.

Hobgoblin, nor foul fiend,
Can daunt his spirit;
He knows he at the end
Shall life inherit.
Then fancies fly away;
He'll fear not what men say;
He'll labour night and day
To be a pilgrim.

PIONEERS

388. 'And he sent them to preach the kingdom of God'
 St. Luke IX. 2–6
389. 'Oh may I join the choir invisible' *George Eliot*
390. Pioneers .   .   .   . *Gertrude B. Gunderson*
391. All Saints   .   .   .   . *Anonymous*

READING

388

'AND HE SENT THEM TO PREACH THE KINGDOM OF GOD'
 St. Luke IX. 2–6

The first disciples were pioneers for Christ.

389

A wish to join those who, by their example, have inspired succeeding generations.

'OH MAY I JOIN THE CHOIR INVISIBLE'
GEORGE ELIOT

Oh may I join the choir invisible
Of those immortal dead who live again
In minds made better by their presence; live
In pulses stirred to generosity,
In deeds of daring rectitude, in scorn
For miserable aims that end with self,
In thoughts sublime that pierce the night like stars,
And with their mild persistence urge man's search
To vaster issues.

271

T

390

A prayer beseeching support for those who have had the courage to be different from the rest.

PIONEERS

GERTRUDE B. GUNDERSON

As mountain peaks that tower above the plain,
  With solitude their only diadem;
As oaks made strong in blinding storms and rain,
  That ivy may the better cling to them;
As rivers flowing seaward never lag
  In quest of goal with swiftly rushing might;
As eagles meeting on the mountain crag,
  Waiting, unweary, through the lonely night—
So the intrepid ones of earth, apart,
  Unfriended, blaze our paths and write our creeds.

O God of lonely ones, fling wide Your heart
  And grant sufficiency to meet their needs!
Sustain—forgiving where they may have erred—
  The Pioneers, who run not with the herd.

391

A declaration of respect for those who made our country a God-fearing land.

ALL SAINTS

ANONYMOUS

Lord, we hold in veneration
  All the saints our land has known,
Bishops, Doctors, Priests, Confessors,
  Martyrs standing round Thy throne;
Alban, Anselm, Bede, Augustine—
  Sing the great and glorious band!
Who of old by prayer and labour
  Hallowed this our fatherland.

392. Verses
393. The Incoming Tide . . *Arthur Hugh Clough*
394. 'Every night and every morn' . *William Blake*
395. For the Records . *Joseph Easton McDougall*
396. The Way . . . . . *Edwin Muir*
397. 'Sweet is the Rose' . . . *Edmund Spenser*

392

VERSES

ON GOOD AND BAD FORTUNE

Whatsoever is brought upon thee take cheerfully,
And be patient when thou art changed to a low estate.
For gold is tried in the fire,
And acceptable men in the furnace of adversity.

Ecclesiasticus II. 4, 5

If thou faint in the day of adversity,
Thy strength is small.

Proverbs XXIV. 10

I returned, and saw under the sun,
That the race is not to the swift,
Nor the battle to the strong,
Neither yet bread to the wise,
Nor yet riches to men of understanding,
Nor yet favour to men of skill;
But time and chance happeneth to them all.

Ecclesiastes IX. 11

And this for comfort thou must know:
Times that are ill won't still be so;
Clouds will not ever pour down rain;
A sullen dawn will clear again.

Robert Herrick

273

Behind the cloud the starlight lurks,
    Through showers the sunbeams fall;
For God, who loveth all His works,
    Has left His hope with all!

John G. Whittier

He sendeth sun, He sendeth shower,
Alike they're needful to the flower;
And joys and tears alike are sent
To give the soul fit nourishment.
As comes to me or cloud or sun,
Father! Thy will, not mine, be done.

Sarah Flower Adams

Under the storm and the cloud to-day,
And to-day the hard peril and pain—
To morrow the stone shall be rolled away,
For the sunshine shall follow the rain.
Merciful Father, I will not complain,
I know that the sunshine shall follow the rain.

Joaquin Miller

393

Often, when in spite of all our efforts we seem to make no progress, unexpected relief is waiting.

THE INCOMING TIDE
ARTHUR HUGH CLOUGH

Say not the struggle naught availeth,
    The labour and the wounds are vain,
The enemy faints not, nor faileth,
    And as things have been they remain.

If hopes were dupes, fears may be liars;
    It may be, in yon smoke concealed,
Your comrades chase e'en now the fliers,
    And, but for you, possess the field.

274

For while the tired waves, vainly breaking,
　Seem here no painful inch to gain,
Far back, through creeks and inlets making,
　Comes silent, flooding in, the main.

And not by eastern windows only,
　When daylight comes, comes in the light;
In front the sun climbs slow, how slowly!
　But westward, look, the land is bright!

394

*One of the most difficult lessons that we have to learn is that
life is a mixture of happiness and sadness.*

'EVERY NIGHT AND EVERY MORN'

WILLIAM BLAKE

Every night and every morn
Some to misery are born.
Every morn and every night
Some are born to sweet delight.
Some are born to sweet delight,
Some are born to endless night.
Joy and woe are woven fine.
A clothing for the soul divine;
Under every grief and pine
Runs a joy with silken twine.
It is right it should be so;
Man was made for joy and woe;
And when this we rightly know,
Thro' the world we safely go.

From 'Auguries of Innocence'

Sorrows and misfortunes give a stimulus to Life.

FOR THE RECORDS

JOSEPH EASTON McDOUGALL

I'd liefer be nothing,
I'd liefer be dead
And a white shroud over
My empty head,

Than walking about
With an empty heart,
With never a hurt
To make it start,

To make me be wishing
That I could be dead
With a white shroud over
My empty head.

396

However tired or afraid we might be, we have to go on without knowing what the future holds in store.

THE WAY

EDWIN MUIR

Friend, I have lost the way.
    The way leads on.
Is there another way?
    The way is one.
I must retrace the track.
    It's lost and gone.
Back, I must travel back!
    None goes there, none.
Then I'll make here my place,
    (*The road runs on*),

Stand still and set my face,
  (*The road leaps on*),
Stay here, for ever stay.
  None stays here, none.
I cannot find the way.
  The way leads on.
Oh places I have passed!
  That journey's done.
And what will come at last?
  The road leaps on.

397

We value most those delights that we gain after some suffering.

'SWEET IS THE ROSE'

EDMUND SPENSER

Sweet is the Rose, but grows upon a brere;
  sweet is the Juniper, but sharp his bough;
  sweet is the Eglantine, but pricketh near;
  sweet is the firbloom, but his branches rough.
Sweet is the Cyprus, but his rind is tough,
  sweet is the nut, but bitter is his pill;
  sweet is the broomflower, but yet sour enough;
  and sweet is Moly, but his root is ill;
So every sweet with sour is tempered still,
  that maketh it be coveted the more:
  for easy things that may be got at will,
  most sorts of men do set but little store.
Why then should I account of little pain,
  that endless pleasure shall unto me gain?

398. Verses: On Being Cheerful
399.　　　　　On Music
400. 'O come, let us sing unto the Lord'　*Psalm* XCV. 1–7
401. 'Praise ye the Lord. Praise God in his sanctuary'
　　　　　　　　　　　　　　　　　Psalm CL
402. 'The man that hath no music in himself'
　　　　　　　　　　　　　　William Shakespeare
403. Laugh and Be Merry　　　.　　.　*John Masefield*
404. 'Let me go where'er I will'.　*Ralph Waldo Emerson*
405. 'There is sweet music here that softer falls'
　　　　　　　　　　　　　　　Alfred Lord Tennyson
406. ''Twas a jolly old pedagogue'　.　*George Arnold*
407. 'There lived a King, as I've been told'
　　　　　　　　　　　　　　　　Sir W. S. Gilbert
408. Angler's Song　.　　.　　.　　.　*Anonymous*
409. The Piper　　.　　.　　.　*Seumas O'Sullivan*

398

VERSES

ON BEING CHEERFUL

The heart of a man changeth his countenance,
　whether it be for good or evil:
And a merry heart maketh a cheerful countenance.
　　　　　　　　　　　　Ecclesiasticus XIII. 25

A merry heart maketh a cheerful countenance:
But by sorrow of the heart the spirit is broken.
　　　　　　　　　　　　Proverbs XV. 13

Some have much, and some have more,
Some are rich, and some are poor,
Some have little, some have less,
Some have not a cent to bless
Their empty pockets, yet possess
True riches in true happiness.

John Oxenham

Jog on, jog on, the footpath way,
  And merrily hent the stile-a:
A merry heart goes all the day,
  Your sad tires in a mile-a.

From 'The Winter's Tale'
William Shakespeare

Read in old books, and you shall find
  How all the ages through,
Men have made wars: but bear in mind
  How they made gardens, too.

Oh, all our tears and all our sighs
  Will never right the wrong.
Perhaps the way of healing lies
  In laughter and a song.

From 'Midsummer Madness'
Clifford Bax

Let the word of Christ dwell in you richly in all wisdom;
Teaching and admonishing one another in psalms and
     hymns and spiritual songs,
Singing with grace in your hearts.

Colossians III. 16

I will sing unto the Lord as long as I live:
I will sing praise to my God while I have my being.

Psalm CIV. 33

Serve the Lord with gladness:
Come before his presence with singing.
Know ye that the Lord he is God:
It is he that hath made us, and not we ourselves;
We are his people, and the sheep of his pasture.

Psalm C. 2, 3

I will praise the name of God with a song,
And will magnify him with thanksgiving.

Psalm LXIX. 30

Sing praises to God, sing praises:
Sing praises unto our King, sing praises.
For God is the King of all the earth.
Sing ye praises with understanding.

Psalm XLVII. 6, 7

Praise ye the Lord:
For it is good to sing praises unto our God;
For it is pleasant;
And praise is comely.   *Psalm* CXLVII. 1

Make a joyful noise unto the Lord, all the earth:
Make a loud noise, and rejoice, and sing praise.
With trumpets and sound of cornet make a joyful noise
     before the Lord, the King.

Psalm XCVIII. 4, 6

Make a joyful noise unto God, all ye lands:
Sing forth the honour of his name:
Make his praise glorious.

Psalm LXVI. 1, 2

Wherefore be ye not unwise,
But understanding what the will of the Lord is.
Speaking to yourselves in psalms and hymns and spiritual
    songs,
Singing and making melody in your heart to the Lord;
Giving thanks always for all things.

Ephesians v. 17–20

Sing to the Lord a joyful song,
    Lift up your hearts, your voices raise:
To us His gracious gifts belong,
    To Him our songs of love and praise.

J. S. B. Monsell

READINGS

400

'O COME, LET US SING UNTO THE LORD' Psalm xcv. 1–7
The call to worship God as the Creator.

401

'PRAISE YE THE LORD. PRAISE GOD IN HIS SANCTUARY'
Psalm CL.
The call to praise God with the help of all musical instruments.

402

*The man who has no liking for music is not to be trusted as
a friend.*

'THE MAN THAT HATH NO MUSIC IN HIMSELF

WILLIAM SHAKESPEARE

The man that hath no music in himself,
Nor is not mov'd with concord of sweet sounds,
Is fit for treasons, stratagems, and spoils;
The motions of his spirit are dull as night,
And his affections dark as Erebus:
Let no such man be trusted.

From 'The Merchant of Venice', v. i

281

LAUGH AND BE MERRY
JOHN MASEFIELD

Laugh and be merry, remember, better the world with
  a song,
Better the world with a blow in the teeth of a wrong.
Laugh, for the time is brief, a thread the length of a
  span.
Laugh and be proud to belong to the old proud pageant
  of man.

Laugh and be merry: remember, in olden time,
God made Heaven and Earth for joy He took in a rhyme,
Made them, and filled them full with the strong red
  wine of His mirth,
The splendid joy of the stars: the joy of the earth.

So we must laugh and drink from the deep blue cup of
  the sky,
Join the jubilant song of the great stars sweeping by,
Laugh, and battle, and work, and drink of the wine
  outpoured
In the dear green earth, the sign of the joy of the Lord.

Laugh and be merry together, like brothers akin,
Guesting awhile in the rooms of a beautiful inn,
Glad till the dancing stops, and the lilt of the music ends.
Laugh till the game is played; and be you merry, my
  friends.

404

*Even the most humble and simple things have some music to
add to the great song of praise.*

'LET ME GO WHERE'ER I WILL'
RALPH WALDO EMERSON

Let me go where'er I will
I hear a sky-born music still;
It sounds from all things old,

It sounds from all things young,
From all that's fair, from all that's foul,
Peals out a cheerful song.
It is not only in the rose,
It is not only in the bird,
Not only where the rainbow glows,
Nor in the song of woman heard,
But in the darkest, meanest things
There alway, alway something sings.
'Tis not in the high stars alone,
Nor in the cups of budding flowers,
Nor in the redbreast's mellow tone,
Nor in the bow that smiles in showers,
But in the mud and scum of things
There alway, alway something sings.

From 'Music'

405

*A vision of the peaceful drowsiness caused by the beauty of
soft music.*

'THERE IS SWEET MUSIC HERE THAT SOFTER FALLS'

ALFRED LORD TENNYSON

There is sweet music here that softer falls
Than petals from blown roses on the grass,
Or night-dews on still waters between walls
Of shadowy granite, in a gleaming pass;
Music that gentlier on the spirit lies,
Than tir'd eyelids upon tir'd eyes;
Music that brings sweet sleep down from the blissful skies.
Here are cool mosses deep,
And thro' the moss the ivies creep,
And in the stream the long-leaved flowers weep,
And from the craggy ledge the poppy hangs in sleep.

From 'The Lotus Eaters'

''TWAS A JOLLY OLD PEDAGOGUE'
GEORGE ARNOLD

'Twas a jolly old pedagogue, long ago,
  Tall and slender, and sallow and dry;
His form was bent, and his gait was slow,
His long thin hair was white as snow,
  But a wonderful twinkle shone in his eye.
And he sang every night as he went to bed,
  'Let us be happy down here below;
The living should live, though the dead be dead,'
  Said the jolly old pedagogue long ago.

407

'When every one is somebodee, then no one's anybody!'

'THERE LIVED A KING, AS I'VE BEEN TOLD'
SIR W. S. GILBERT

There lived a King, as I've been told,
  In the wonder-working days of old,
When hearts were twice as good as gold,
  And twenty times as mellow.
Good-temper triumphed in his face,
And in his heart he found a place
For all the erring human race
  And ev'ry wretched fellow.
When he had Rhenish wine to drink
It made him very sad to think
That some, at junket or at jink,
  Must be content with toddy.

He wished all men as rich as he
(And he was rich as rich could be),
So to the top of ev'ry tree
   Promoted ev'rybody.

Lord Chancellors were cheap as sprats,
And Bishops in their shovel hats
Were plentiful as tabby-cats—
   In point of fact, too many.
Ambassadors cropped up like hay,
Prime Ministers and such as they
Grew like asparagus in May,
   And Dukes were three a penny.
On ev'ry side Field-Marshals gleam'd,
Small beer were Lords Lieutenant deem'd,
With Admirals the ocean teem'd
   All round his wide dominions.
And Party Leaders you might meet
In twos and threes in ev'ry street,
Maintaining, with no little heat,
   Their various opinions.

That King, although no one denies
His heart was of abnormal size,
Yet he'd have acted otherwise
   If he had been acuter.
The end is easily fore-told,
When ev'ry blessed thing you hold
Is made of silver, or of gold,
   You long for simple pewter.
When you have nothing else to wear
But cloth of gold and satins rare,
For cloth of gold you cease to care—
   Up goes the price of shoddy.
In short, who-ever you may be,
To this conclusion you'll agree,
When every one is somebodee,
   Then no one's anybody!
          From 'The Gondoliers'

Here is a hobby that has made many men forget their anxieties.

ANGLER'S SONG
ANONYMOUS

Man's life is but vain; for 'tis subject to pain,
  And sorrow, and short as a bubble;
'Tis a hodge-podge of business, and money, and care,
  And care, and money, and trouble.

But we'll take no care when the weather proves fair;
  Nor will we vex now though it rain;
We'll banish all sorrow, and sing till to-morrow,
  And angle, and angle again.

409

In the gaiety of a tune all worries can be forgotten.

THE PIPER
SEUMAS O'SULLIVAN

A piper in the streets to-day
Set up and tuned, and started to play,
And away, away, away on the tide
Of his music we started; on every side
Doors and windows were opened wide,
And men left their work and came,
And women with petticots coloured like flame,
And little bare feet that were blue with cold,
Went dancing back to the age of gold,
And all the world went gay, went gay,
For half an hour in the street to-day.

410. Verses: On Old Age
411.   On Our Forbears
412. 'My son, keep thy father's commandments'
                              Proverbs VI. 20–23
413. Danny Murphy   .   .   .   *James Stephens*
414. Old Shepherd's Prayer   .   .   *Charlotte Mew*
415. The Coach of Time .   .   *Alexander Pushkin*
                              (*Translated C. N. Bowra*)
416. 'Here lies an old woman'   .   .   *Anonymous*
417. Forefathers   .   .   .   .   *Edmund Blunden*
418. Young and Old   .   .   .   *Charles Kingsley*
419. 'Perhaps in this neglected spot'   .   *Thomas Gray*
420. Relieving Guard   .   .   *Francis Bret Harte*
421. Those Older Men   .   .   .   *Harry Waine*
422. Requiem .   .   .   .   *Robert Louis Stevenson*

410

VERSES

ON OLD AGE

I have been young, and now am old;
Yet have I not seen the righteous forsaken,
Nor his seed begging bread.   *Psalm* XXXVII. 25

My son, help thy father in his age,
And grieve him not as long as he liveth.
And if his understanding fail, have patience with him;
And despise him not when thou art in thy full strength.
                              Ecclesiasticus III. 12, 13

Dishonour not a man in his old age:
For even some of us wax old.   *Ecclesiasticus* VIII. 6

As the clear light is upon the holy candlestick;
So is the beauty of the face in ripe age.
                              Ecclesiasticus XXVI. 17

A fool despiseth his father's instruction:
But he that regardeth reproof is prudent.
                              Proverbs XV. 5

287

U

As a white candle
In a holy place,
So is the beauty
Of an aged face.

From 'An Old Woman'
Joseph Campbell

Grow old along with me!
The best is yet to be,
The last of life, for which the first was made:
Our times are in His hand
Who saith 'A whole I planned,
Youth shows but half; trust God: see all nor be afraid!'

From 'Rabbi Ben Ezra'
Robert Browning

411

ON OUR FORBEARS

Honour thy father and thy mother:
That thy days may be long upon the land which the
Lord thy God giveth thee.

Exodus XX. 12

Children, obey your parents in the Lord:
for this is right.
Honour thy father and mother;
which is the first commandment with promise;
That it may be well with thee,
And thou mayest live long on the earth.

Ephesians VI. 1–3

Honour thy father with thy whole heart,
And forget not the sorrows of thy mother.
Remember that thou wast begotten of them;
And how canst thou recompense them the things that
they have done for thee?

Ecclesiasticus VII. 27, 28

A wise son maketh a glad father:
But a foolish son is the heaviness of his mother.

Proverbs X. 1

412

'MY SON, KEEP THY FATHER'S COMMANDMENTS'

Proverbs VI. 20–23

An exhortation to obey the instructions of one's parents.

413

Although people might appear to grow old, the spirit inside them often remains young and gay.

DANNY MURPHY

JAMES STEPHENS

He was as old as old could be,
His little eye could scarcely see,
His mouth was sunken in between
His nose and chin, and he was lean
And twisted up and withered quite,
So that he couldn't walk aright.

His pipe was always going out,
And then he'd have to search about
In all his pockets, and he'd mow
—O, deary me! and, musha now!—
And then he'd light his pipe, and then
He'd let it go clean out again.

He couldn't dance or jump or run,
Or ever have a bit of fun
Like me and Susan, when we shout
And jump and throw ourselves about:
—But when he laughed, then you could see
He was as young as young could be!

The prayer of an ailing, old shepherd that, when he died, he might still have the familiar surroundings that he loved.

OLD SHEPHERD'S PRAYER
CHARLOTTE MEW

Up to the bed by the window, where I be lyin',
Comes bells and bleat of the flock wi' they two
    children's clack.
Over, from under the eaves there's the starlings flyin',
And down in yard, fit to burst his chain, yapping out
    at Sue I do hear young Mac.

Turning around like a falled-over sack
I can see team ploughin' in Whithy-bush field and
    meal carts startin' up road to Church-Town;
Saturday arternoon the men goin' back
And the women from market, trapin' home over the
    down.

Heavenly Master, I wud like to wake to they same
    green places
Where I be know'd for breakin' dogs and follerin'
    sheep.
And if I may not walk in th' old ways and look on
    th' old faces
I wud sooner sleep.

In this poem, translated from the Russian, Life is compared to a coach journey.

THE COACH OF TIME
ALEXANDER PUSHKIN

Often with heavy burdens freighted,
The coach rolls on with easy pace.
The driver on the box is seated,
Grey Time, who never leaves his place.

We take our seats at early morning,
And by the coachman start the trip;
Our indolence and comfort scorning,
We cry: 'Now let the horses rip!'

When noon comes we have lost our daring.
We're shaken up: we fear and doubt,
And down steep slopes and gullies faring
We cry, 'Go slow, you fool! look out!'

The coach rolls as before unshaken.
We're used to it ere day is done.
At last, by slumber overtaken,
We reach the inn—but Time drives on.

Translated C. N. Bowra

416

The last words of a weary old lady who had had a life of monotonous drudgery and was joyfully looking forward to rest and freedom.

'HERE LIES AN OLD WOMAN WHO ALWAYS WAS TIRED'

ANONYMOUS

Here lies an old woman who always was tired;
She lived in a house where help never was hired;
Her last words on earth were, 'Dear friends, I am going
To where there's no cooking, or washing, or sewing,
But everything there is exact to my wishes,
For where they don't eat there's no washing of dishes;
I'll be where loud anthems will always be ringing,
But having no voice I'll be clear of the singing.
Don't mourn for me now; don't mourn for me never,
I'm going to do nothing for ever and ever.'

Many of our ancestors left no record other than that which is found in the cottages and barns which they built, and in the survival of their familiar surroundings.

FOREFATHERS

EDMUND BLUNDEN

Here they went with smock and crook,
    Toiled in the sun, lolled in the shade,
Here they mudded out the brook
    And here their hatchet cleared the glade:
Harvest-supper woke their wit,
Huntsman's moon their wooings lit.

From this church they led their brides,
    From this church themselves were led
Shoulder-high; on these waysides
    Sat to take their beer and bread.
Names are gone—what men they were
These their cottages declare.

Names are vanished, save the few
    In the old brown Bible scrawled;
These were men of pith and thew,
    Whom the city never called;
Scarce could read or hold a quill,
Built the barn, the forge, the mill.

On the green they watched their sons
    Playing till too dark to see,
As their fathers watched them once,
    As my father once watched me;
While the bat and beetle flew
On the warm air webbed with dew.

Unrecorded, unrenowned,
    Men from whom my ways begin,
Here I know you by your ground
    But I know you not within—
There is silence, there survives
Not a moment of your lives.

Like the bee that now is blown
    Honey-heavy on my hand,
From his toppling tansy-throne
    In the green tempestuous land—
I'm in clover now, you know
Who made honey long ago.

418

Here Youth and Age are contrasted.

YOUNG AND OLD
CHARLES KINGSLEY

When all the world is young, lad,
    And all the trees are green;
And every goose a swan, lad,
    And every lass a queen;
Then hey for boot and horse, lad,
    And round the world away;
Young blood must have its course, lad,
    And every dog his day.

When all the world is old, lad,
    And all the trees are brown;
And all the sport is stale, lad,
    And all the wheels run down;
Creep home, and take your place there,
    The spent and maimed among;
God grant you find one face there,
    You loved when all was young.

293

How many humble folk have qualities which would give them
greatness and fame if their circumstances were different?

'PERHAPS IN THIS NEGLECTED SPOT'
THOMAS GRAY

Perhaps in this neglected spot is laid
Some heart, once pregnant with celestial fire,
Hands, that the reins of empire might have sway'd,
Or waked to ecstasy the living lyre:

But Knowledge to their eyes her ample page,
Rich with the spoils of time, did ne'er unroll:
Chill Penury had damp'd their noble rage,
And froze the genial current of the soul.

Full many a gem of purest ray serene
The dark unfathom'd caves of ocean bear:
Full many a flower is born to blush unseen,
And waste its sweetness on the desert air.

Some village Hampden that, with dauntless breast,
The little tyrant of his fields withstood;
Some mute inglorious Milton here may rest;
Some Cromwell guiltless of his country's blood.

Th' applause of listening senates to command,
The threats of pain and ruin to despise,
To scatter plenty o'er a smiling land,
And read their history in a nation's eyes,

Their lot forbade; nor circumscribed alone
Their growing virtues, but their crimes confined;
Forbade to wade thro' slaughter to a throne,
And shut the gates of mercy on mankind.

The struggling pangs of conscious truth to hide,
To quench the blushes of ingenuous shame,
And crown the shrine of Luxury and Pride
With incense kindled at the Muse's flame.

Far from the madding crowd's ignoble strife,
Their sober wishes never knew to stray;
Along the cool sequester'd vale of life
They kept the noiseless tenor of their way.
        From 'Elegy Written in a Country Churchyard'

420

*The portent of the falling star explained in the words of a
soldier.*

RELIEVING GUARD

FRANCIS BRET HARTE

Came the relief. 'What, sentry, ho!
How passed the night through thy long waking?'
'Cold, cheerless, dark—as may befit
The hour before the dawn is breaking.'

'No sight? no sound?' 'No, nothing save
The plover from the marshes calling,
And in yon Western sky, about
An hour ago, a star was falling.'

'A star? There's nothing strange in that.'
'No, nothing; but, above the thicket,
Somehow it seemed to me that God
Somewhere had just relieved a picket.'

295

Our grandfathers directed their lives by the promptings of their consciences and the teaching of the Bible.

THOSE OLDER MEN
HARRY WAINE

Theirs was another world, those older men,
Our sires and grandsires—yesteryear
Of less mechanic age. No motors then,
No cinema, nor wireless, and the air
As yet unconquered, while, dread spawn of war,
The atom bomb's stark portent lay unborn.
Their simple living asked of life no more
Than daily routine, then calm rest till dawn.
Hard work and frugal fare, their earnings small,
Scant leisure, pastimes few—of such their lot,
With many mouths to feed. Stern duty's call
Guided them like a clarion few forgot.
Austerely noble, simply great, they wrought
As conscience bade them and their Bible taught.

Verses written by a wanderer who travelled far in search of better health. He was very ill at the time after a rough voyage across the Atlantic.

REQUIEM
ROBERT LOUIS STEVENSON

Under the wide and starry sky,
Dig the grave and let me lie
Glad did I live and gladly I die,
    And I laid me down with a will.

This be the verse you grave for me:
Here he lies where he longed to be;
Home is the sailor, home from sea,
    And the hunter home from the hill.

CONTENTMENT

423. Verses
424. The Shepherd Boy's Song . . *John Bunyan*
425. 'My mind to me a kingdom is' *Sir Edward Dyer*
426. Contentment . . . *Marjorie R. Walland*
427. Leisure . . . . . *W. H. Davies*
428. The Miller of the Dee . . *Charles Mackay*
429. The Enchanted Shirt . . *John Hay*
430. Idleness . . . . . *Andrew Young*

423

VERSES

I have learned,
In whatsoever state I am,
Therewith to be content.　　*Philippians* IV. 11

Godliness with contentment is great gain.
And having food and raiment let us be therewith content.
　　　　　　　　Timothy VI. 6, 8

Let your conversation be without covetousness;
And be content with such things as ye have.
　　　　　　　　Hebrews XIII. 5

The work of righteousness shall be peace;
And the effect of righteousness quietness and assurance
　　for ever.　　　　*Isaiah* XXXII. 17

The world is so full of a number of things,
I'm sure we should all be as happy as kings.
　　　　　　　　'*Happy Thought*'
　　　　　　　　Robert Louis Stevenson

　　O grant me, Heaven, a middle state,
　　Neither too humble nor too great:
　　More than enough for nature's ends,
　　With something left to treat my friends.
　　　　　　　　David Mallet

A song of contentment.

THE SHEPHERD BOY'S SONG
JOHN BUNYAN

He that is down needs fear no fall,
   He that is low, no pride;
He that is humble, ever shall
   Have God to be his Guide.

I am content with what I have,
   Little be it, or much:
And Lord, contentment still I crave,
   Because Thou savest such.

Fullness to such a burden is
   That go on pilgrimage;
Here little, and hereafter Bliss,
   Is best from age to age.

425

*Those who rise in the world maintain their positions only with
difficulty. Happiness comes from good health, an untroubled
mind, a clear conscience over one's treatment of one's fellows,
and no desire for more worldly goods.*

'MY MIND TO ME A KINGDOM IS'
SIR EDWARD DYER

My mind to me a kingdom is,
   Such present joys therein I find,
That it excels all other bliss
   That earth affords or grows by kind.
Though much I want which most would have,
Yet still my mind forbids to crave.

No princely pomp, no wealthy store,
   No force to win the victory,
No wily wit to salve a sore,
   No shape to feed a loving eye;
To none of these I yield as thrall,
For why? My mind doth serve for all.

I see how plenty suffers oft,
  And hasty climbers soon do fall;
I see that those which are aloft
  Mishap doth threaten most of all;
They get with toil, they keep with fear:
Such cares my mind could never bear.

Content I live, this is my stay,
  I seek no more than may suffice;
I press to bear no haughty sway;
  Look, what I lack my mind supplies.
Lo! thus I triumph like a king,
Content with that my mind doth bring.

Some have too much, yet still do crave;
  I little have, and seek no more.
They are but poor, though much they have,
  And I am rich with little store.
They poor, I rich; they beg, I give;
They lack, I leave; they pine, I live.

I laugh not at another's loss;
  I grudge not at another's gain;
No worldly waves my mind can toss;
  My state at one doth still remain.
I fear no foe, I fawn no friend;
I loathe not life, nor dread my end.

Some weigh their pleasure by their lust,
  Their wisdom by their rage of will;
Their treasure is their only trust,
  A cloaked craft their store of skill:
But all the pleasure that I find
Is to maintain a quiet mind.

My wealth is health and perfect ease,
  My conscience clear my chief defence;
I neither seek by bribes to please,
  Nor by deceit to breed offence.
Thus do I live; thus will I die;
Would all did so as well as I!

Trivialities of smell, sound and touch mean far more to the blind than to the sighted.

CONTENTMENT
MARJORIE R. WALLAND

The perfume of a summer rose,
The humming of a bee,
The gentle touch a soft wind brings,
These things mean much to me.
The handclasp of a steadfast friend,
The sun's rays warm and kind,
To me, these things are life itself,
Perhaps, because I'm blind.

427

In praise of the enjoyment of standing and staring......

LEISURE
W. H. DAVIES

What is this life if, full of care,
We have no time to stand and stare.

No time to stand beneath the boughs
And stare as long as sheep or cows.

No time to see, when woods we pass,
Where squirrels hide their nuts in grass.

No time to see, in broad daylight,
Streams full of stars like skies at night.

No time to turn at Beauty's glance,
And watch her feet, how they can dance.

No time to wait till her mouth can
Enrich that smile her eyes began.

A poor life this if, full of care,
We have no time to stand and stare.

*King Hal, impressed by the miller's contentedness, would
gladly have changed places with him in order to shed his many
cares.*

THE MILLER OF THE DEE

CHARLES MACKAY

There dwelt a miller hale and bold,
    Beside the river Dee;
He wrought and sang from morn to night,
    No lark more blithe than he;
And this the burden of his song
    For ever used to be—
'I envy nobody, no, not I,
    And nobody envies me!'

'Thou'rt wrong, my friend!' said old King Hal,
    'Thou'rt wrong as wrong can be;
For could my heart be light as thine,
    I'd gladly change with thee.
And tell me now what makes thee sing
    With voice so loud and free,
While I am sad, though I'm the king,
    Beside the river Dee?'

The miller smiled and doff'd his cap:
    'I earn my bread,' quoth he;
'I love my wife, I love my friends,
    I love my children three;
I owe no penny I cannot pay;
    I thank the river Dee,
That turns the mill that grinds the corn,
    To feed my babes and me.'

'Good friend,' said Hal, and sigh'd the while,
    'Farewell! and happy be;
But say no more, if thou'dst be true,
    That no one envies thee.
Thy mealy cap is worth my crown—
    Thy mill my kingdom's fee!—
Such men as thou are England's boast,
    O miller of the Dee!'

*A story of the happiness to be gained from doing one's
appointed work and so having no time to think about fancied
difficulties.*

THE ENCHANTED SHIRT

JOHN HAY

The King was sick. His cheek was red
  And his eye was clear and bright;
He ate and drank with a kingly zest,
  And peacefully snored at night.

But he said he was sick, and a king should know,
  And doctors came by the score.
They did not cure him. He cut off their heads
  And sent to the schools for more.

At last two famous doctors came,
  And one was as poor as a rat—
He had passed his life in studious toil,
  And never found time to grow fat.

The other had never looked in a book;
  His patients gave him no trouble—
If they recovered they paid him well,
  If they died their heirs paid double.

Together they looked at the royal tongue,
  As the King on his couch reclined;
In succession they thumped his august chest,
  But no trace of disease could find.

The old sage said, 'You're as sound as a nut.'
  'Hang him up!' roared the King in a gale—
In a ten-knot gale of royal rage;
  The other leech grew a shade pale;

But he pensively rubbed his sagacious nose,
  And thus his prescription ran—
The King will be well, if he sleeps one night
  In the Shirt of a Happy Man.

Wide o'er the realm the couriers rode,
  And fast their horses ran,
And many they saw, and to many they spoke,
  But they found no Happy Man.

They found poor men who would fain be rich,
  And rich who thought they were poor;
And men who twisted their waists in stays,
  And women that shorthose wore.

They saw two men by the roadside sit,
  And both bemoaned their lot;
For one had buried his wife, he said,
  And the other one had not.

At last they came to a village gate,
  A beggar lay whistling there;
He whistled and sang and laughed and rolled
  On the grass in the soft June air.

The weary couriers paused and looked
  At the scamp so blithe and gay;
And one of them said, 'Heaven save you, friend!
  You seem to be happy to-day!'

'O yes, fair Sirs!' the rascal laughed,
  And his voice rang free and glad,
'An idle man has so much to do
  That he never has time to be sad.'

'This is our man,' the courier said;
  'Our luck has led us aright.
I will give you a hundred ducats, friend,
  For the loan of your shirt to-night.'

The merry blackguard lay back on the grass,
  And laughed till his face was black;
'I would do it, God wot,' and he roared with the fun,
  'But I haven't a shirt to my back.'

Each day to the King the reports came in
  Of his unsuccessful spies,
And the sad panorama of human woes
  Passed daily under his eyes.

And he grew ashamed of his useless life,
  And his maladies hatched in gloom;
He opened his windows and let the air
  Of the free heaven into his room.

And out he went in the world and toiled
  In his own appointed way;
And the people blessed him, the land was glad,
  And the King was well and gay.

This is, perhaps, an excuse for doing nothing else but enjoying one's surroundings.

IDLENESS

ANDREW YOUNG

God, you've so much to do,
To think of, watch and listen to,
That I will let all else go by,
And lending ear and eye
Help you to watch how in the combe
Winds sweep dead leaves without a broom;
And rooks in the spring-reddened trees
Restore their villages,
Nest by dark nest
Swaying at rest on trees' frail unrest;
Or on this limestone wall,
Listening at ease, with you recall
How once these heavy stones
Swam in the sea as shells and bones;
And hear that owl snore in a tree
Till it grows dark enough for him to see;
In fact, will learn to shirk
No idleness that I may share your work.

CONCLUDING VERSES

Bless all who worship Thee
From the rising of the sun
Unto the going down of the same.
Of Thy goodness, give us;
With Thy love, inspire us;
By Thy spirit, guide us;
By Thy power, protect us;
In Thy mercy, receive us,
Now and always. Amen.

Fifth Century Collect

Blessed be the Lord God, the God of Israel,
   who only doeth wondrous things.
And blessed be his glorious name for ever:
And let the whole earth be filled with his glory;
Amen, and Amen.

Psalm LXXII. 18, 19

All that we ought to have thought and have not thought,
All that we ought to have said and have not said,
All that we ought to have done and have not done,
All that we ought not to have thought and yet have
   thought,
All that we ought not to have spoken yet have spoken,
All that we ought not to have done and yet have done,
For thought, words and works, pray we, O God, for
   forgiveness,
And repeat with penance. Amen.

From 'The Zendavesta'
Ascribed to Zoroaster

God be in my head,
And in my understanding;
God be in mine eyes,
And in my looking;
God be in my mouth,
And in my speaking;
God be in my heart,
And in my thinking;
God be at my end and at my departing.

Sixteenth Century Prayer

Finally, brethren, farewell.
Be perfect,
Be of good comfort,
Be of one mind,
Live in peace:
And the God of love and peace shall be with you.

2 *Corinthians* XIII. 11

NOTES ON AUTHORS

ADAM of St. Victor, 1130–1180: French monk, writer of hymns in Latin.

ADAMS, Sarah Flower, 1805–1848: wrote numerous hymns.

ADDISON, Joseph, 1672–1719: essayist, politician, eminent classical scholar; helped to establish *The Spectator*; wrote *The de Coverley Papers*.

ALDRICH, Thomas Bailey, 1836–1907: American, friend of Longfellow, Whittier, Lowell; enjoyed leisurely travel in Europe; wrote polished poems on slight themes.

ALEXANDER, Cecil Frances, 1828–1895: Irish hymn-writer, wife of a clergyman (later Archbishop of Armagh). *The Breastplate of St. Patrick*—perhaps entirely her own composition—was written for St. Patrick's Day, 1889. Also wrote: 'There is a green hill', 'Once in Royal David's city', 'All things bright and beautiful'.

ALLEN, Elizabeth Akers, 1832–1911: literary editor of an American newspaper.

AMBROSE, St., 340–379: greatest bishop of his time; courageous and wise in the religious disputes of the fourth century; exerted great influence on church music and wrote words for the services.

ARMSTRONG, Robert, b. 1901: poet and translator.

ARNOLD, George, 1834–1865: American humorous poet.

AUSTIN, Henry: seventeenth-century poet.

BAILEY, Philip James, 1816–1902: a barrister who devoted his whole life to poetry.

BARING-GOULD, Sabine, 1834–1924: Devonshire clergyman; keen antiquarian; collector of folk-songs and information on strange events; wrote novels and 'Onward, Christian soldiers'.

BARNFIELD, Richard, 1574–1627: country gentleman of the Midlands.

BARTLETT, R. N.: contemporary writer.

BARTLETT, Wilfred H.: contemporary writer.

BAX, Clifford, 1886–1962: studied art but abandoned it for literature; music plays an important part in some of his plays, especially *Midsummer Madness*; brother of Sir Arnold Bax, the musician.

BEECHING, Henry Charles, 1859–1919: a country clergyman; wrote, with great sincerity and simplicity, poems of religion and nature.

BELL, John Joy, 1871–1934: Scottish novelist, author of the well-known 'Wee MacGreegor' stories, descriptive books of Scotland and his reminiscences.

BELLOC, Joseph Hilaire Pierre, 1870–1953: essayist, poet, historian; fond of travel, though a lover of his native Sussex; a very sociable man who produced humorous verse.

BETJEMAN, John, b. 1906: critic, essayist, poet, editor and author of guide books, broadcaster; keenly interested in architecture; finds material for his poems in the everyday busy-ness of the modern world.

BINYON, Laurence, 1869–1943: playwright, poet, writer on the fine arts; ardent opponent of cruelty and injustice.

BLACKIE, John Stuart, 1809–1895: Scottish classical scholar, for thirty years Professor of Greek at Edinburgh University; keen nationalist.

BLAKE, William, 1757–1827: mystical poet of great imagination; made engravings to illustrate his books.

BLANCHARD, Sheila: contemporary poet.

BLUNDEN, Edmund, b. 1896: critic, lecturer in Hong Kong University, poet of the English countryside responsible for rescuing from obscurity the poems of John Clare.

BONAR, Horatius, 1808–1889: energetic and versatile Scottish minister and poet; wrote a great number of hymns for his congregation and Sunday School; one of the last to conduct open-air services.

BOWRING, Sir John, 1792–1872: great traveller, linguist, hymn-writer and translator of European folk-songs; M.P. who in 1835 procured the issue of the florin as a step towards decimal coinage.

BRETON, Nicholas, 1545–1626: a prolific, versatile writer of prose and poetry.

BRIDGES, Robert, 1844–1930: Poet Laureate, gifted scholar, musician; led life of culture, finding pleasure in beauty, rarely allowing sadness to appear in his poetry.

BRIGGS, George Wallace, 1875–1960: naval chaplain; rector of Loughborough College for which 'For the brave of every race' was written.

BROOKE, Rupert, 1887–1915: born at the Vicarage, Grantchester, Cambs.; wrote the poem whilst recuperating from illness; died in the First World War from fever in the Dardanelles; buried on the island of Scyros.

BROWN, Alfred J.: modern Yorkshire author.

BROWNING, Robert, 1812–1889: lived many years in Italy, where 'Pippa Passes' was written; much of his vast output of poetry states his belief that man should be judged by character and effort, rather than by his success.

BULLETT, Gerald, 1893–1958: writer; keen country-lover; ardent believer in freedom of thought.

BUNYAN, John, 1628–1688: a humble writer of vivid imagination; preaching gave him freedom from religious terrors, but led to imprisonment; wrote *The Pilgrim's Progress*, containing 'The Shepherd Boy's Song' and 'The Pilgrim's Valour', whilst in prison.

BURNS, Robert, 1759–1796: the Scottish national poet; a humble farmer with a vast output of songs in dialect.

CAMPBELL, Joseph, 1879–1944: Irish poet, playwright.

CANTON, William, 1845–1926: journalist, wrote stories and poetry for his daughter who died when eleven; in grief, turned to historical research.

CARLYLE, Thomas, 1795–1881: famous Victorian writer of history, politics, biography; an indefatigable worker, thorough, persistent, sincere.

CARRUTH, William Herbert, 1859–1924: American editor, teacher, poet.

CHALMERS, Stephen, 1880–1935: Scottish-born American poet.

CHAPMAN, John Jay, 1862–1933: American critic, essayist, translator, playwright; held strong views on individualism.

CIBBER, Colley, 1671–1757: Poet Laureate, dramatist.

CLARE, John, 1793–1864: Northamptonshire rural poet; almost uneducated, yet wrote prolifically and with ease.

CLOUGH, Arthur Hugh, 1819–1861: a scholarly intellectual; travelled widely, partly in search of health.

COATSWORTH, Elizabeth, b. 1893: travelled widely, then settled on a farm to enjoy outdoor life.

COLERIDGE, Hartley, 1796–1849: a Lake poet, had difficulty in gaining a livelihood; failed as Head of a school; suffered from depression.

COLERIDGE, Samuel Taylor, 1772–1834: Lake poet, philosopher, critic; friend of Wordsworth, Southey, Lamb; author of *The Ancient Mariner*, from which this extract is taken.

COLUM, Padraic, b. 1881: Irish poet and playwright; his father being governor of a workhouse inspired this poem; particularly fond of re-telling stories told by his grandmother.

CONDER, Josiah, 1789–1855: author, editor, prolific hymn-writer; compiled the first Congregational Hymn-book.

CONE, Helen Gray, 1859–1934: American poet.

COOLIDGE, Susan, 1835–1905: American author of the 'What Katy Did' stories.

CORBET, Richard, 1582–1635: Bishop of Oxford renowned for his wit, vivacity and jovial nature; favourite of James I; Vincent, aged three when the poem was written, did not fulfil his father's hopes.

CORNFORD, Frances, 1886–1960: well-known poet, member of a scholarly family.

COTTON, George Edward Lynch, 1813–1866: figured as a master in *Tom Brown's Schooldays*; Head of Marlborough College; much of his poetry inspired by the surroundings of Marlborough, which he left reluctantly to become Bishop of Calcutta; drowned in the Ganges.

COWPER, William, 1731–1800: forced to abandon a legal career owing to ill-health, and lead a quiet country life; wrote 'John Gilpin' and 'God moves in a mysterious way'.

CRABBE, George, 1754–1832: a clergyman; *The Library*, his first important composition, is his wise reflections on books and life generally; a friend of Sir Walter Scott.

DAVIES, William Henry, 1871–1940: lived the life of a tramp, to whom everything was of interest; wrote many poems and *The Autobiography of a Super-tramp*; was helped by G. B. Shaw.

DEARMER, Geoffrey, b. 1893: playwright, novelist, formerly editor of B.B.C. Children's Hour.

DEARMER, Dr. Percy, 1867—? clergyman, professor, writer; editor of *Songs of Praise*.

DE LA MARE, Walter, 1873–1956: wrote many poems specially for children, often inspired by the fantastic.

DOBSON, Henry Austin, 1840–1921: critic, biographer, writer of light verse; for forty years travelled daily from Ealing to his office in the City, so 'July' was probably closely personal.

DONNE, John, 1572–1631: Dean of Westminster, popular preacher; his poetry is remarkable for wit and learning. This extract is the beginning of a long poem on the marriage of James I's daughter, Elizabeth, on February 14th, 1613.

DOTEN, Elizabeth, 1829—? American poetess.

DRINKWATER, John, 1882–1937: playwright, writer of essays and much poetry for children.

DYER, Sir Edward, 1545–1607; a court official and friend of Sir Philip Sidney; sometimes in favour with Queen Elizabeth and sometimes not, he refused to cringe at court.

EBERHART, Richard, b. 1904: American; professor of English in American universities.

ELIOT, George, 1819–1880: novelist, author of *The Mill on the Floss*, *Silas Marner*; brought up in strictly religious circles; inclined to melancholy.

ELLERTON, John, 1826–1893: clergyman, prolific hymn-writer; wrote 'The day thou gavest'; the hymn included here was specially produced for a mid-day service in a city church.

EMERSON, Ralph Waldo, 1803–1882: American clergyman, philosopher, essayist, poet; popular in England and America.

311

FARJEON, Eleanor, b. 1881: has lived most of her life in the country writing happy verses for children.

FARRAR, Frederick William, 1831–1903: clergyman, headmaster at Marlborough, Dean of Canterbury.

FICKE, Arthur Davison, 1883–1945: American novelist and poet.

Foss, Sam Walter, 1858–1911: American journalist, humorist, public librarian; farmer's son.

FRANCIS, St., 1181–1226: after a gay youth, devoted himself to solitude, prayer and care of the poor; aimed at imitating the life of Christ in poverty and regarding all things as brothers.

FREEMAN, Robert, 1878–1940: American clergyman and writer.

GALE, Norman, 1862–1942: schoolmaster, critic, journalist; poet of the countryside and of cricket.

GALSWORTHY, John, 1867–1933: dramatist, novelist, author of *The Forsyte Saga*; had great compassion for all less fortunate than himself; lover of animals, led the movement for humane slaughtering; refused to follow the hounds.

GAY, John, 1685–1732: dramatist, poet; not a wealthy man, lost everything in the South Sea Bubble.

GIBBONS, Thomas, 1720–1785: Dissenting minister, hymn-writer.

GIBBS, Beatrice Ruth, b. 1894: co-principal of a school; takes a prominent part in public affairs.

GIBSON, Wilfrid Wilson, 1878–1962: devoted his life to poetry; favourite subjects were his fellow-creatures.

GILBERT, Sir William Schwenk, 1836–1911: wrote the operas with Sir Arthur Sullivan as musician; poked good-natured fun at people and customs.

GORDON, Adam Lindsey, 1833–1870: lived the latter part of his life in Australia in the mounted police; horses were his passion.

GORE-BOOTH, Eva, 1870–1926: Irish poet very sympathetic to the peasants; keenly felt the sufferings of the world; devoted to beauty.

GORELL, Lord, b. 1885: lawyer, editor, publisher, poet.

GOSSE, Sir Edmund, 1849–1928: critic, historian, university lecturer, librarian to the House of Lords; helper of many writers; brought up in a gloomy, sternly religious atmosphere.

GRAVES, Robert, b. 1895: historical novelist and poet.

GRAY, Thomas, 1716–1771: scholar, historian; lived a life of seclusion, reading in the British Museum, when a Cambridge professor.

GRUN, Anastasius, 1806–1876: pseudonym of an aristocratic Austrian poet.

GUEST, Edgar Albert, b. 1881: English poet popular in America; wrote daily poem in an American newspaper.

GUINNESS, Bryan Walter (Lord Moyne), b. 1906: Irish barrister and business man; his poems portray simply country scenes and family life.

HALLACK, Cecily R.: contemporary poet.

HARDY, Thomas, 1840–1928: novelist and poet, devoted to his native Dorset countryside; gained knowledge of London when an architect there, in early life.

HARTE, Francis Bret, 1836–1902: American writer famous for 'westerns'.

HARTNOLL, Phyllis: contemporary writer and translator.

HARVEY, Frederick William, b. 1888: wrote poems of home when in the trenches of the First World War.

HAY, John Milton, 1838–1905: American statesman; Ambassador in Britain for President Lincoln.

HEBER, Reginald, 1783–1826: Bishop, hymn-writer; many works include 'Brightest and best' and 'When spring unlocks the flowers'.

HERBERT, George, 1593–1633: of an aristocratic family, but after a life as scholar, courtier and favourite of James I, became a pious, hard-working, country clergyman.

HERRICK, Robert, 1591–1674: reluctantly became a country clergyman after a gay London life; his poems show both thought and humour.

HESKETH, Phoebe, b. 1909: writer, critic, editress, broadcaster; fond of quiet walks on the Lancashire fells.

HODGSON, Ralph, 1871–1962: poet, great animal-lover; strongly opposed to hunting and killing.

HOLLAND, Josiah Gilbert, 1819–1881: American teacher, novelist and poet.

HOOD, Thomas, 1799–1845: editor, poet; suffered ill-health and misfortune; had much sympathy with fellow-sufferers, and humour even in distress.

HOPKINS, Gerard Manley, 1844–1889: priest, poet, talented painter.

HOUSMAN, Alfred Edward, 1859–1936: scholar; wrote many poems of Shropshire.

HOUSMAN, Laurence, 1865–1959: novelist, dramatist; famous for his plays on Victoria and St. Francis.

HOWITT, Mary, 1799–1888: wrote novels, essays, children's books.

HUGO, Victor, 1802–1885: French novelist, poet.

HUNT, James Henry Leigh, 1784–1859: essayist, poet, newspaper-proprietor; made Shelley and Keats known to the public; imprisoned for criticizing the Prince Regent.

HUXLEY, Sir Julian Sorrell, b. 1887: lecturer, writer, professor of zoology; formerly Director-General of Unesco.

JENNER, Edward, 1749–1823: doctor who discovered the vaccine which prevents smallpox; keenly interested in fossil-hunting, perhaps the purpose of the walk in this poem.

JONSON, Ben, 1572–1637: actor, poet, dramatist, friend of Shakespeare.

KEATS, John, 1795–1821: abandoned a medical career to devote himself to poetry and the continual search for beauty; an intense admirer of Shakespeare's works, the beauty of which filled him with despair.

KEBLE, John, 1792–1866: brilliant scholar, clergyman, poet; held that the ideal life was that of a country parson; saintly and unselfish, exerted great influence; Keble College, Oxford, founded in his memory.

KEN, Thomas, Bishop, 1637–1711: courageous, strong-willed chaplain to Charles II; sang and played hymns of his own composing, every day.

KINGSLEY, Charles, 1819–1875: clergyman, historian, novelist; keenly interested in the social problems of his day; devoted himself to teaching his illiterate parishioners; wrote *The Water Babies, Westward Ho!*

KIPLING, Rudyard, 1865–1936: story-writer, poet, journalist; intensely patriotic; a fervent Imperialist.

LAMB, Charles, 1775–1834: critic, essayist, poet; devoted his life to his ailing sister, Mary, with whom he collaborated in poems and *Lamb's Tales from Shakespeare.*

LEATHAM, Edith Rutter, 1870—? poet whose work was popular in its day.

LEE, Laurie: contemporary writer.

LEWIS, Eiluned: modern Welsh poet and essayist; has written weekly magazine articles on rural topics.

LEVY, Amy, 1861–1889: a poet who responded more to melancholy surroundings than cheerful ones.

LONGFELLOW, Henry Wadsworth, 1807–1882: America's most popular poet; professor at Harvard; influenced by Charles Dickens, he became strongly opposed to slavery.

LOWELL, James Russell, 1819–1891: American poet, critic, Ambassador in London and Madrid; succeeded Longfellow at Harvard; opponent of slavery, fervent patriot, lover of out-of-doors.

LOYOLA, St. Ignatius, 1491–1556: Spanish nobleman, became austerely religious; founded the Society of the Jesuits—to be a spiritual army.

LOWRY, Somerset Corry, 1855–1932: clergyman, writer of hymns and theological books.

LYNCH, Thomas Toke, 1818–1871: a Free Church minister; a lover of nature, which was regarded as profane.

LYND, Sylvia: contemporary writer.

MACGILL, Patrick, b. 1891: at Glenties in Donegal; left home when twelve for casual work—farming and navvying in Scotland; wrote numerous homely poems.

MACKAY, Charles, 1814–1889: popular and successful song-writer, journalist, historian, novelist.

MAGEE, John Gillespie: a young airman killed in the Second World War.

MALLET, David, 1703–1765: Scottish farmer's son; became secretary to the Prince of Wales.

MALLOCH, Douglas, 1877–1938: American poet.

MARKHAM, Edwin, 1852–1940: American schoolmaster; liked to sleep on his verandah at night.

MARSTON, Philip Bourke, 1850–1887: a blind poet, friend of Swinburne and Rossetti.

MASEFIELD, John, b. 1878: Poet Laureate; novelist, dramatist; sailed in a windjammer in his youth.

McDOUGALL, Joseph Easton, b. 1901: Canadian journalist, founder-editor of a humorous magazine.

MEADE, Walter: contemporary writer.

MEW, Charlotte, 1869–1928: poet and prose-writer; lived a life of poverty and despondency caring for invalid mother and sister.

MILLER, Cincinnatus Heine (Joaquin), 1839–1913: American poet and prose-writer, journalist; eccentric, wandering adventurer.

MILTON, John, 1608–1674: an ardent Puritan, with a vast output of poetry; became blind in middle age.

MONSELL, John Samuel Bewley, 1811–1875: Irish clergyman, hymn-writer; author of 'Fight the good fight'.

MONTGOMERY, James, 1771–1854: Scottish poet, editor; strongly opposed to slavery and boys being chimney-sweeps; wrote many hymns for the Sunday Schools.

MOORE, Thomas, 1779–1852: Irish song-writer: *Lalla Rookh*, a collection of Eastern tales in verse, brought him much renown.

MOORE, Thomas Sturge, 1870–1944: poet, author, wood-engraver and designer; *Beautiful Meals* was written at the request of a schoolmistress, for her children.

MOULT, Thomas: modern poet, novelist, lecturer, critic.

MUIR, Edwin, 1887–1959: widely travelled novelist, poet, critic, translator, journalist; son of a poor Orkney farmer.

NEALE, John Mason, 1818–1866: clergyman; translated Greek and Latin hymns; author of 'The day is past and over', 'Happy band of pilgrims'.

315

Noel, Thomas, 1799–1861.

Noyes, Alfred, 1880–1958: playwright, critic, professor, poet; very fond of nature and much influenced by religion.

O'Sullivan, Seumas, b. 1879: Irish poet, dramatist; devoted to Celtic culture; his poems deal mostly with the smaller, homely items of life.

Oxenham, John, 1852–1941: a popular, prolific novelist and poet.

Pain, Godfrey S.: twentieth-century writer and editor, keenly interested in youth work.

Palmer, Herbert Edward, b. 1881: critic, journalist, teacher; has written a number of poems for public occasions.

Patmore, Coventry, 1823–1896: mathematician, astronomer, assistant librarian in the British Museum.

Patrick, St., 385–461: responsible for bringing Christianity to Ireland; this extract is, therefore, from the earliest Gaelic hymn.

Peacock, Thomas Love, 1785–1866: scholar, novelist, humorist; poked fun at good company and good eating; named 'The Laughing Philosopher'; this poem is a song at a party in his novel, *Crochet Castle*.

Pepler, Hilary Douglas C.: modern English writer.

Phillpotts, Eden, 1862–1960: popular novelist, playwright; many works have a Devonshire setting.

Pitter, Ruth, b. 1897: poet, broadcaster, keen gardener.

Pushkin, Alexander, 1799–1837: Russian poet famous for folk-tales in verse; although a courtier, hated the life; more interested in the peasants; killed in a duel.

Ratcliffe, Dorothy Una, b. 1894: Yorkshire poet, playwright, essayist; well-known public figure, ex-Mayoress of Leeds.

Richard, St., 1197–1253: Chancellor of Canterbury Cathedral; strict disciplinarian, keen on church privileges; hence suffered Henry III's displeasure.

Reeves, James, b. 1909: literary critic, broadcaster, poet; widely travelled; has written much poetry for children, having three of his own.

Rose, Margaret: twentieth-century writer.

Ross, Sir Ronald, 1857–1932: physician, bacteriologist; largely responsible for discovering that mosquitoes spread malaria.

Rossetti, Christina Georgina, 1830–1894: of a gifted, artistic family; deeply religious.

Sassoon, Siegfried, b. 1886: poet, novelist; spent a happy, active youth; gained a decoration in the First World War, but became an intense believer in pacifism; had one son only.

Sayers, Dorothy Leigh, 1893–1957: novelist, playwright; wrote religious drama for broadcasting.

Scott, Sir Walter, 1771–1832: wrote novels and poems based on Border country traditions; ill-health forced him to travel, but he insisted on returning in order to die in his native surroundings. This extract introduced a collection of Border ballads which established his reputation.

Shakespeare, William, 1564–1616.

Sharp, William, 1855–1905: Scottish poet and prose-writer.

Sherman, Frank Dempster, 1860–1916: American professor of architecture; wrote witty poems for children.

Smart, Christopher, 1722–1771: poet, journalist. This extract is from 'A Song to David', his best work.

Shuttleworth, Henry Cary, 1850–1900: clergyman, university professor; very interested in church music.

Smith, Horace, 1779–1849: poet, novelist; friend of Keats and Shelley.

Spenser, Edmund, 1552–1599: most famous poet immediately prior to Shakespeare; achieved fame with *The Faerie Queen*. The sonnet is from 'Amoretti', written to commemorate his marriage. He himself suffered pain and poverty.

Stephens, James, 1882–1950: self-educated Irish poet, story-writer; expert in Celtic lore; his poetry is almost monosyllabic.

Stevenson, Robert Louis, 1850–1894: Scottish poet, novelist, essayist; forced to travel widely for his health. 'Requiem' was written in 1880; died in Samoa, and was buried on a cliff overlooking the Pacific.

Story, William Wetmore, 1819–1895: American poet, sculptor; settled in Italy where he became a friend of the Brownings.

Struther, Jan, 1901–1953: a skilful, prolific writer; both these poems were written specially for *Songs of Praise*.

Swinburne, Algernon Charles, 1837–1909: poet, dramatist, critic; friend of the Rossettis. This extract is from a play written in the classical Greek style, which first gave him fame.

Tennyson, Lord Alfred, 1809–1892: Poet-Laureate; the most popular Victorian poet; lived in a country rectory when young; held strong religious and ethical convictions. 'In Memoriam', written at the death of his friend, Arthur Hallam, helped to revive the nation's dwindling faith in God and immortality.

Thomas, Edward, 1878–1917: Welsh essayist, poet.

Thomson, James, 1700–1748: Scottish poet of the countryside; first aroused attention through the unconventionality of 'The Seasons'.

Towne, Charles Hanson, 1877–1949: American editor, poet.

Twells, Henry, 1823–1900: rector, headmaster; helped to compile *Hymns Ancient and Modern*; by enthusiasm and hard work established two new churches.

317

VAN DYKE, Henry, 1852–1933: American clergyman, story-writer, essayist, poet; chaplain in the First World War, during which his sermons brought him fame; as a keen fisherman, enjoyed life in the Canadian wilds.

VEDDER, David, 1790–1854: Scottish poet.

WAINE, Harry: contemporary writer.

WALTER, Howard Arnold, 1883–1918: American clergyman, missionary.

WANLEY, Nathaniel, 1634–1680: clergyman, poet, historian.

WATTS, Isaac, 1674–1748: one of the greatest hymn-writers, producing over six hundred; wrote when the Puritan ban was being relaxed; as his congregation was illiterate, he dictated his words—written to fit existing tunes.

WESLEY, John, 1703–1791: clergyman, founder of Methodism; collaborated with his brother Charles in writing many hymns.

WHITMAN, Walt, 1819–1892: American teacher, editor, poet; in youth, enjoyed city life in Long Island; intensely opposed to slavery, he voluntarily tended the wounded in the Civil War; most benevolent and sympathetic to fellow-men and animals.

WHITTIER, John Greenleaf, 1807–1892: American Quaker poet, journalist; ardent believer in anti-slavery; inspired by Robert Burns; popular and respected.

WICKHAM, Anna, 1884–1947: poet, strong individualist.

WILCOX, Ella Wheeler, 1850–1919: American novelist, poet; very popular in her day.

WILLIS, Love Maria, 1824– ? American hymn-writer.

WILLIAMSON, Kennedy: contemporary poet.

WOODS, Margaret, 1856–1945: novelist, poet.

WORDSWORTH, William, 1770–1850: nature poet, lived most of his life in the Lake District.

YEATS, William Butler, 1865–1939: Ireland's greatest poet; keen patriot; when abroad, always longed to return.

YOUNG, Andrew, b. 1885: Scottish clergyman, poet; as a boy, played truant, thereby acquiring a lasting love of wild flowers.

YOUNG, Geoffrey Winthrop: contemporary poet and well-known mountaineer.

YOUNG, Francis Brett, 1884–1954: novelist, poet; writings set in his native Worcestershire.

INDEX OF FIRST LINES

	Poem No.
A cottage garden, speck'd with London pride . . .	307
A fire-mist and a planet	39
A flock of sheep that leisurely pass by . . .	152
A missel-thrush, I heard proclaim	92
A piper in the streets to-day	409
A pure white mantle blotted out	186
A robin redbreast in a cage	83
A thing of beauty is a joy for ever . . .	55
A truth that's told	238
Abou Ben Adhem (may his tribe increase) . .	261
After a day of cloud and wind	115
Again the summer comes	165
All honour to him who shall win the prize . .	383
All night the waves of darkness broke . . .	136
All that we ought to have thought . . .	431
All the world's a stage	325
All things are full of God	130
An emerald is as green as grass	381
And I, too, sing the song of all creation . .	322
And see—the Sun himself!—on wings . . .	144
And this for comfort thou must know . . .	392
Anger in its time and place	247
As a white candle	410
As Joseph was a-walking	211
As mountain peaks that tower above the plain . .	390
As the slow Evening gather'd in her grey . .	147
As Thou, Lord, hast lived for others . . .	247
Be not afraid to pray	12
Be useful where thou livest	372
Beauty remains but we are transitory . . .	52
Beauty—what is it?	52
Before the beginning of years	321
Before the paling of the stars	209
Behind the cloud the starlight lurks . . .	392
Behold us, Lord, a little space	354
Behold, we live through all things . . .	380
Beneath thy all-directing rod	43
Bless all who worship Thee	431
Blow, blow, thou winter wind	185
Born of a Monday, fair in the face . . .	333
Bread is a lovely thing to eat	4
Breathes there the man with soul so dead . .	306
Bursting on the suburbs	110

By the faith that the flowers show 20
By Will, Man dared in den and heath 382
Came the relief. 'What, sentry, ho!' 420
Carefully now Spring puts her stitches 164
Cat, if you go outdoors you must walk in the snow . . 80
Christ be with me, Christ within me 28
Christmas Eve, and twelve of the clock 206
Cold is the winter day, misty and dark. . . . 188
Come, let us remember the joys of the town . . . 292
Creator of the earth and sky 155
Cure me with quietness 156
Day by day, Dear Lord 23
Day by day the sun's broad beam 178
Days present, days to come 71
Dear Lord and Father of mankind 32
Did you hear of the curate who mounted his mare . . 268
Do all the good you can 247
Does the road wind uphill all the way? 385
Earth has not anything to show more fair . . . 291
England with mucky arms, and cheer, and spanner . . 308
Enrich, Lord, heart, mouth, hands in me . . . 32
Every branch big with it 293
Every friend that flatters thee 274
Every night and every morn 394
Fame is a food that dead men eat 273
Faster and more fast 141
Father, hear the prayer we offer 243
Father of men, in whom are one 272
Father, we praise thee, now the night is over . . . 136
February Fill-dyke 191
First, April, she with mellow showers 196
Flower in the crannied wall 67
For all skilled hands, both delicate and strong . . 11
For faith and works and gentle charity 6
For flowers that bloom about our feet 160
For friends to stand beside, for foes to fight . . . 5
For songbirds answering song on topmost bough . . 90
For the brave of every race 315
For the comforting warmth of the sun 303
For the strength of His body 30
For the want of a nail, the shoe was lost. . . . 351
For wild anemones star-shining in the little wood . . 161
Four things a man must learn to do 215
Friend, I have lost the way 396
From all that dwell below the skies 311
From quiet homes and first beginning 269
Gardeners are good 359

	Poem No.
Give me a good digestion, Lord	234
Give to me the life I love	300
Glorious the sun in mid career	132
Glory be to God for dappled things	58
Go, and be gay	336
God be in my head	431
God bless the field and bless the furrow	8
God give us men	375
God had filled the mountains with metals hard and bright	370
God! I will pack, and take a train	281
God keep my fingers clean and white	147
God of the granite and the rose	43
God who created me	324
God, you've so much to do	430
God's gifts so many a pleasure bring	338
God's might to direct me	32
Good name in man and woman	235
Good night! Good night!	147
Good-bye to the Town!—good-bye!	197
Great is the sun, and wide he goes	166
Great Lord and King of Earth	48
Green is the plane tree in the square	73
Grow old along with me	410
Hail, Bishop Valentine, whose day this is	190
Hail, universal Lord, be bounteous still	136
Happy is he who, in this Robot Age	369
He comes on chosen evenings	91
He doeth well who doeth good	247
He has no enemy, you say	265
He, of His gentleness	212
He prayeth well who loveth well	12
He sendeth sun, He sendeth shower	392
He that is down needs fear no fall	424
He was as old as old could be	413
Here in a crumbled corner of the wall	87
Here in the country's heart	296
Here lies an old woman who always was tired	416
Here they went with smock and crook	417
Hi! handsome hunting man	81
High o'er the lonely hills	140
His praise, ye Winds, that from four Quarters blow	47
Holy, holy, holy, Lord God Almighty	136
How nice it is to eat	61
How still the day! No branches stir at all	172
I am only one	372
I bind unto myself to-day	237
I have a Guide, and in His steps	27

	Poem No.
I have to live with myself	232
I hold with none who think not work a boon	367
I know the pools where the grayling rise	301
I look on nature less with critic's eyes	51
I love the fitful gust that shakes	174
I remember, I remember	280
I saw the moon, so broad and bright	135
I sing of a maid that is matchless	207
I sing the hymn of the conquered	374
I think I could turn and live with animals	84
I was angry with my friend	247
I will arise and go now, and go to Innisfree	284
I will have few cooking-pots	356
I wish for him strength	337
I would be true, for there are those who trust me	219
I'd liefer be nothing	395
I'm going back to Glenties	283
I've brought you nuts and hops	199
I've never travelled for more'n a day	121
If I should die, think only this of me	310
If radio's slim fingers can pluck a melody	18
If thou shouldst never see my face again	21
If when I come to Paradise	120
In books, or works, or healthful play	335
In this, O Nature, yield, I pray, to me	379
In time the whole of things shall alter	38
Into the sunshine	124
Is it not fine to walk in spring	181
Is there anything in Spring so fair	60
It is my joy in life to find	275
It is not growing like a tree	240
Jog on, jog on, the footpath way	398
Joy and temperance and repose	226
Laugh and be merry, remember	403
Laugh, and the world laughs with you	264
Let me go where'er I will	404
Let me to-day do something that shall take	266
Let praise devote thy work	366
Let the lowliest task be mine	378
Let us, with a gladsome mind	170
Like as the waves make towards the pebbled shore	278
Listen! I will be honest with you	384
Little things, that run, and quail	75
Live for to-day	147
Lord, I my vows to Thee renew	139
Lord, make us strong, for Thou alone dost know	386
Lord of the loving heart	26

Lord of the pots and pipkins 357
Lord, Thou hast given me a cell 285
Lord, though among this city's press 294
Lord, we hold in veneration 391
Lord, when I look at lovely things which pass . . 54
Loveliest of trees, the cherry now 162
Make haste, good Master Carpenter 360
Make sure of truth 222
Man putteth the world to scale 233
Man's life is but vain; for 'tis subject to pain . . . 408
March, blow by 192
Mary, young but very wise 31
Men! whose boast it is that ye 316
Month of leaves 195
Much can they praise the trees so straight and high . 70
My fairest child, I have no song to give you . . 340
My heart leaps up when I behold 326
My little Son, who look'd from thoughtful eyes . . 330
My mind lets go a thousand things 56
My mind to me a kingdom is 425
My mother bore me in the southern wild . . . 317
My New Year's wish shall be 187
My soul, thou shouldst to thy knees 12
Night is the time for rest 154
No, Bob; I will not go a walk— 86
No pitted toad behind a stone 53
No sun—no moon! 202
Nor love, nor honour, wealth nor power . . . 226
Not for a single day 136
Not on the vulgar mass 225
November is a spinner 200
Now praised be God for all these unfamiliar faces . . 314
Now pray we for our country 304
Now simmer blinks on flowery braes 165
Now that the daylight fills the sky 142
Now that the sun is gleaming bright 136
O Father, hear my morning prayer 143
O God, make it rain 113
O grant me, Heaven, a middle state 423
O little self, within whose smallness lies . . . 42
O Man, forgive thy mortal foe 246
O Most High Almighty Good Lord God . . . 1
O say! what is that Thing called Light 334
O summer sun, O moving trees 165
O Thou whose feet have climbed life's hill . . . 349
O you gotta get a Glory in the work you do . . . 364
Oft have I seen at some cathedral door . . . 16

Often with heavy burdens freighted	415
Oh, I have slipped the surly bonds of Earth . . .	134
Oh may I join the choir invisible	389
Oh, the wild joys of living	343
Oh, to have a little house	286
Oh, who can witness with a careless eye . . .	133
Old Ben Bailey	82
Old Winter, sad, in snow yclad	182
One man in a thousand, Solomon says	276
One road leads to London	123
Out of the house I saunter into sun	62
Out of the night to my leafy porch they came . .	99
Out of the scabbard of the night	136
Perhaps in this neglected spot is laid	419
Power from the sun	41
Praise God! Praise God! Give me my tools again . .	368
Praise the Lord for all the seasons	158
Praise ye and bless ye the Lord	1
Prayer is the soul's sincere desire	17
Question not, but live and labour	263
Read in old books, and you shall find	398
Remember us poor Mayers all	194
Ring out, wild bells, to the wild sky	204
Said an ancient hermit, bending	22
Said Day to Night	147
Say not the struggle nought availeth	393
Season of mists and mellow fruitfulness	173
She goes but softly, but she goeth sure	97
Silent at Joseph's side He stood	371
Sing a song of hollow logs	167
Sing to the Lord a joyful song	398
Slow moves the acid breath of noon	177
Snow-waxen point of life	68
Snug in my easy chair	358
So here hath been dawning	146
So nigh is grandeur to our dust	335
Some have much, and some have more	398
Sometimes we see a cloud that's dragonish . . .	114
Someone had asked a poet how to live	267
Souls are built as temples are	221
Spring goeth all in white	157
Sweet day, so cool, so calm, so bright . . .	239
Sweet is the breath of morn	151
Sweet is the Rose, but grows upon a brere . . .	397
Take up your glove again, I shall not fight . . .	244
Talk not of temples, there is one	43
Teach me, my God and King	355

Teach us, good Lord, to serve Thee as Thou deservest .	372
Tell me of Progress if you will	299
Thank God for sleep in the long quiet night . . .	145
Thank you for the world so sweet	2
That man may last, but never lives	372
The bells of waiting Advent ring	205
The buttercups in May	203
The cock is crowing	159
The common street climbed up against the sky . .	289
The farmer, in the pride of sea-won acres . . .	101
The friends thou hast, and their adoption tried . .	236
The frost is here	180
The gentle Twilight Lady	148
The hollow winds begin to blow	108
The King was sick. His cheek was red . . .	429
The law the lawyers know about	46
The loaded bee the lowest flies	242
The Lord is King! Lift up thy voice	1
The man that hath no music in himself	402
The men who work in wood	361
The off'rings of the Eastern Kings of old . . .	210
The perfume of a summer rose	426
The poetry of earth is never dead	100
The poor man's farthing is worth more . . .	247
The quality of mercy is not strain'd . . .	245
The robin on my lawn	189
The rounded buses loom through softest blue . .	288
The sailor plucked an apple from an orchard . .	279
The skylark's nest among the grass . . .	93
The spacious firmament on high	131
The storke she rose on Christmas eve . . .	331
The storm is laid, the winds retire . . .	116
The sun descending in the west	147
The trivial round, the common task . . .	351
The vast cathedral, now sublimely wrought . .	363
The wind cries and the shadow	150
The winds of heaven bare their teeth again . .	175
The Wise Ass turned from the hay. . . .	78
The world is so full of a number of things . .	423
The world itself keeps Easter Day	214
The year's at the spring	163
Theirs was another world, those older men . .	421
Then as Now; and Now as Then	313
There are hermit souls that live withdrawn . .	262
There are twelve months throughout the year . .	198
There are two kinds of people on earth to-day . .	377
There dwelt a miller hale and bold . . .	428

There is a flower, a little flower	69
There is a valued though a stubborn weed . . .	241
There is sweet music here that softer falls . . .	405
There lived a King, as I've been told	407
There lives and works a soul in all things . . .	50
These I have loved:	57
They rise like sudden fiery flowers	201
They told us how they walked	29
They who tread the path of labour	365
This boat of mine, oh Lord	111
This, book can do—nor this alone	348
This is our Lord and Elder Brother	342
This is the weather the cuckoo likes	107
This royal throne of kings, this sceptered isle . . .	305
This symphony of stillness is composed	168
This wind brings all dead things to life	109
Thou comest plainly, Lord of All	40
Thou must be true thyself	223
Though I do my best shall I scarce succeed . . .	380
Through the hushed air the whitening shower descends .	184
Time to go home!	153
To all the humble beasts there be	79
To see a World in a grain of sand	52
To spend the long warm days	49
To-day I broke a lovelier thing	59
To-day I think	176
Toil away and set the stone	362
'Twas a jolly old pedagogue, long ago . . .	406
'Twixt failure and success the point's so fine . .	380
'Twould ring the bells of Heaven	85
Tyger, tyger, burning bright	76
Under the storm and cloud to-day	392
Under the wide and starry sky	422
Up to the bed by the window, where I be lyin' . .	414
Upon the sky	149
We all are blind until we see	220
We are getting to the short night	193
We live in deeds, not years; in thoughts, not breaths .	372
We thank Thee, Lord, for quiet upland lawns . .	10
We thank Thee, Lord, for this fair earth . . .	7
We thank Thee, loving Father	2
We thank you, Lord of Heaven	9
We who were born	298
Welcome, wild North-easter	112
Were I, O God, in churchless lands remaining . .	63
Were I so tall to reach the pole	215
What are they thinking, the people in churches . .	297

	Poem No.
What asks our Father of His children save	224
What I shall leave thee, none can tell	341
What is this life if, full of care	427
When all the world is young, lad	418
When as a child, I laughed and wept	320
When Duty comes a-knocking at your gate	372
When God had finished the stars	89
When I catch myself agape	77
When I consider how my Light is spent	376
When the herds were watching	208
When to the sessions of sweet silent thought	277
When we are young, we are so clever	323
When you have gone from school into the world	332
Wherever smoke wreaths Heavenward curl	282
Where lies the land to which the ship would go?	122
Where the ripe pears droop heavily	98
While walking through the trams and cars	290
White Captain of my soul, lead on	19
Who believes that equal grace	74
Who can live in heart so glad	302
Who knows not, and knows not that he knows not, is foolish	350
Who would true valour see	387
Why, who makes much of a miracle?	3
Winter creeps	183
Winter is cold-hearted	169
Winter Willow is ruddy red	72
With proud thanksgiving, a mother for her children	309
Within a thick and spreading hawthorn bush	94
Yet if his majesty our sovereign Lord	213
Youth that goes wool-gathering	339

INDEX OF SUBJECTS

Numbers refer to poems

Advent, 140, 205

Adventure, 134, 300, 315, 337, 390, 418

Adversity, 239, 274, 276, 277, 394–397

Ages of Man, 278, 318–326, 415

Ambition, 407, 425

Anger, 244, 251

Animals, 31, 74–87, 206, 297, 302, 338, 342

April, 192, 193

Atomic power, 233, 421

Authority, 407, 425

Autumn, 39, 98, 101, 172–178

Beauty, 39, 50, 52–62, 67, 99, 145, 160, 161, 181, 184, 186, 189, 281, 289, 290, 291, 293, 367, 427

Birds, 8, 31, 47, 88–94, 107, 145, 150, 167, 169, 190, 193, 195, 297, 331, 430

Blindness, 62, 334, 376, 426

Brotherhood, 6, 204, 234, 251, 261, 267, 271, 276, 403

Chances and Changes, 392–397

Cheerfulness, 29, 51, 121, 234, 243, 261, 264, 282, 337, 342, 398–409, 413, 428, 429

Children, 280, 283, 302, 314, 325, 327–336, 341, 413

Christian Year, 205–214

Christmas, 78, 205–209, 211, 213, 331

Cleanliness, 36, 286

Colour problem, 313, 314, 317

Compassion, 31, 85, 251, 314, 316, 331, 382

Consideration for others, 185, 219, 224, 234, 245, 246, 250, 261, 263, 266, 267, 314, 316, 382

Contentment, 84, 124, 143, 279, 300–303, 371, 423–430

Countryside, 49, 51, 54, 58, 93, 94, 100, 107–109, 112, 148, 150, 153, 159–161, 163, 164, 167, 169, 183, 294–303, 338

Courage, 19, 27, 68, 69, 219, 236, 243, 263, 265, 300, 308, 309, 316, 334, 336, 337, 364, 371–374, 386, 387, 389, 393, 397, 403

Craftsmanship, 59, 66, 70, 76, 93, 164, 352, 359, 360–362, 364–371

Creation, 39, 45, 76, 89, 99, 127, 130, 131, 133, 137, 144, 164, 321

Creator, The, 43–51

Criticism, 77, 236, 254, 316, 369, 384

Daily needs, 4, 5, 61, 71, 145, 237, 300, 416, 417, 421, 425, 426

Dawn, 140, 141, 144

Dependence on others, 25, 262, 272, 275, 317, 358, 377

Determination, 27, 97, 219, 243, 349, 378, 381–383, 385–387, 390, 397

Devotion, 39, 86, 94, 139, 212, 271, 276, 382, 383, 393, 421

Difficulty, 396, 243

Disappointment, 225

Discipline, 33, 233, 268, 330

Duty, 216, 375, 376, 421

Easter, 78, 92, 162, 211, 214
Education, 348, 349
Endeavour, 143, 146, 156, 243, 263, 265, 322, 323, 343, 355, 362, 377, 380–387, 389–391, 397
Endurance, 39, 69, 239, 263–265, 322, 323, 334, 337, 390
Epiphany, 210
Evening, 80, 91, 92, 99, 115, 133, 135, 142, 147–156, 178, 289, 290

Facing odds, 122, 265, 309, 374, 384
Failure, 225, 283
Faith, 18, 20, 21, 27, 37, 46, 122, 296, 387, 421
Fallen, The, 309, 310
Family, 205, 211, 283, 330, 333, 341, 357
February, 189, 191
Fellowship, 187, 234, 261–264, 272, 275, 313, 314, 317
Fellow-workers, 308, 247–268
Fireside, 180, 182, 282, 286, 358
Fishermen, 111
Flowers, 50, 63, 67–69, 161, 164, 195, 196, 198, 203, 397
Fog, 48
Food, 4, 61, 101, 145, 234, 285
Forbears, 313, 315, 367, 380, 417, 421
Forgiveness, 15, 34, 38, 75, 246, 253, 255, 330
Freedom, 300, 301, 304, 316
Friends, 5, 6, 10, 21, 185, 187, 236, 244, 262–269, 271, 273, 274, 277, 278, 426
Frost, 103, 180, 182, 185, 189

Gardens, 91, 145, 166, 176, 195, 277, 278, 280, 359
Gentleness, 6, 26, 79, 317, 359
Giving, 14, 205, 219, 258, 267, 356, 374, 383, 387, 393
God and Man, 32–42
God's Presence, 40, 51

God's Power, 104, 128, 130
Good fight, The, 5, 19, 27, 35, 122, 143, 265, 309, 322–324
Goodwill, 38, 204, 244, 245
Graces, 61, 143, 219
Great men, 315, 375, 383, 384, 389, 391, 421

Happiness, 29, 38, 91, 124, 302, 314, 337, 338, 394, 409, 429
Harvest, 10, 98, 101, 106, 170, 171, 175, 198, 199, 283, 296
Health, 5, 234, 337, 341, 343, 379, 425, 429
Heavens, 125–135, 290
Helpfulness, 263, 274, 275, 377, 378
Holidays, 167, 197
Home, 9, 10, 57, 61, 66, 71, 80, 86, 91, 93, 107, 150, 153, 174, 182, 199, 213, 279–286, 304, 322, 338, 357, 358, 361, 414, 416
Honesty, 241, 425
Hope, 27, 38, 46, 68, 180, 183, 204, 219, 393
Hospitality, 213, 285
Humility, 42, 62, 67, 111, 142, 212, 224, 242, 273, 285, 329, 366, 371, 374, 378, 419, 424
Humour, 406, 407, 416
Husbandry, 96, 101, 285, 359, 373

Industry, 354, 358, 369, 370
Industry, Personal, 25, 93, 96, 228, 373
Influence, 223, 224, 231, 308, 350, 391, 402, 409, 419
Innocence, 20, 328
Insects, 168, 169

January, 188
Joy of living, 3, 4, 9, 94, 121, 124, 134, 159, 162, 163, 167, 169, 197, 199, 288, 292, 322, 324, 337, 338, 343, 364, 367, 368, 403, 406, 408, 409, 413, 418

July, 196, 197
June, 108, 195
Justice, 224, 245

Kindness, 14, 31, 48, 75, 77, 79, 83, 85, 204, 212, 218, 250, 263, 266, 267, 317, 328, 337, 425
Knowledge, 42, 67, 130, 337, 350, 382

Labour, 11, 96, 228, 263, 337, 354–357, 359, 360, 362, 364–371, 382, 383, 385, 387, 391, 403, 414, 416, 417, 429
Laughter, 29, 89, 264, 314, 403
Law, 46, 216
Leadership, 231, 378, 384
Learning, 46, 344–350
Leisure, 121, 167, 302, 427, 430
Lent, 212
Life's Journey, 122, 123, 415, 420, 421
Light, 140, 141
Loneliness, 262, 286
Love, 24, 38, 41, 187, 248, 249, 261, 271, 317
Loyalty, 185, 274, 276, 278

Manliness, 215–237, 321, 337, 368
March, 110, 159, 192
May, 194
Meekness, 16, 267
Mercy, 224, 245
Moon, 48, 131, 135
Morning, 47, 92, 151, 177, 266, 291, 136–146
Music, 18, 90–92, 168, 399, 400, 402, 404, 405, 408, 409

Nations, 311–317
Native Land, 270, 284, 304–310, 375
Nativity, The, 205–209, 211
Nature, 7–9, 39, 46, 48
Neighbours, 197, 262, 263, 266, 283

New Year, 204
November, 174, 200–203

Obedience, 33, 412, 421
October, 199
Old people, 11, 121, 286, 325, 410–422
Ordinary Things, 3, 4, 5, 8, 9, 40, 56, 57, 61, 145

Parents, 270, 283, 330, 338, 341, 412
Patience, 94, 97, 359, 376, 379
Peace, 6, 20, 38, 55, 155, 156, 304, 312
Perfection, 26, 38, 204, 240, 356, 382
Perseverance, 97, 220, 221, 225, 228, 360, 364, 373, 374, 377, 382, 385, 393
Pilgrims, 27, 387
Pioneers, 27, 262, 315, 337, 377, 384, 388–391
Praise, 1–11, 39, 44, 45, 47, 58, 87, 92, 129, 131, 132, 139, 158, 161, 188, 214, 315, 366–368, 370, 374, 400, 401, 414
Prayer, 12–22, 26, 28, 111, 113, 139, 143, 154–156, 210, 243, 272, 286, 294, 354, 367, 414
Pride, 305, 424
Progress, 299, 396
Providence, 22, 101, 113, 171, 237, 285
Purity, 19, 36, 64, 219, 224, 234, 342

Quarrels, 38, 236, 244
Quietness, 16, 49, 51, 97, 154

Rain, 105–108, 110, 113, 115, 171, 191, 289, 296
Reconciliation, 38, 251
Refugees, 314
Repentance, 34, 75, 194, 210
Reputation, 228, 232, 235, 273

Rest, 49, 150, 152–155, 172, 183, 286, 310, 416, 418, 421
Reverence, 7, 16, 30, 51, 131, 133, 135, 206, 209, 224, 297, 354, 355, 360, 391, 400
Rulers, 382, 407, 419, 425, 428, 429

Sailors, 119, 122, 123
Science, 18, 130, 133, 233, 370, 379, 421
Sea, 111, 119–123
Self-control, 217, 219, 223, 224, 233, 244, 268, 336, 375
Self-denial, 217, 267
Self-knowledge, 62, 232, 233, 350
Self-respect, 77, 84, 219, 220, 227, 232, 233, 236, 266, 356, 428
Self-sufficiency, 122, 262, 368, 384, 390, 425, 429
September, 198
Service, 24, 262, 315, 316, 324, 358, 361, 366, 367, 369, 372–379
Simplicity, 8, 20, 69, 121, 217, 285, 286, 300, 301, 371, 414, 417, 419, 421
Sincerity, 13, 204, 219, 223, 236, 239, 241, 316, 375
Small Creatures, 95–101, 212
Snow, 80, 112, 181, 182, 184, 186, 293
Son of God, The, 23–31
Sorrow, 264, 314, 394, 395
Spring, 54, 56, 60, 93, 157–164, 189, 191–193, 214, 288
Statesmen, 41, 375, 384, 407, 419, 425, 428, 429
Stewardship, 124, 367, 373, 407, 417
Storm, 110, 111, 117–119, 182
Strength, 35, 237, 243, 264, 308, 336, 337, 375, 381, 386, 387, 390, 393
Summer, 54, 94, 99, 100, 107, 108, 165–169, 195

Sun, 48, 126, 131, 166, 289
Sympathy, 251, 266, 267

Temptation, 19, 386
Thanksgiving, 1–11, 30, 48, 90, 127, 135, 142, 145, 155, 160, 285, 292, 303, 324, 338, 368, 370, 391, 400
Thoughtlessness, 81–83, 85
Thunderstorm, 110
Time, 240, 320, 325, 415
Tolerance, 38, 77, 245, 246, 254–256
Tongue, Control of, 142, 236, 244, 257, 266–268
Town, 73, 91, 110, 197, 202, 205, 287–294
Tranquillity, 6, 55, 140, 148, 168, 172, 177, 281, 291, 297, 307, 376, 378, 405, 419, 421, 425, 427
Travel, 121–123, 281, 283, 284, 300, 301
Trees, 60, 64–66, 70–73, 162, 181, 361
Troubles, 140, 156, 193, 239, 264, 276, 283, 314, 394, 397, 408, 415
Trust, 22, 27, 35, 37, 122, 276, 296, 387, 393, 402, 421
Truth, 222, 223, 241, 252, 256, 265, 340, 375

Understanding, 38, 77, 276, 316
Unity, 40, 53, 310, 317
Universe, 126, 129, 130, 131, 132, 144, 233
Unselfishness, 26, 234, 266, 267, 378, 380

Virtues, 40, 218, 219, 238–246

Waters, The, 48, 116–124
Weather, 9, 102–115, 159, 178, 202, 289, 293
Wind, 47, 48, 60, 109–112, 150, 174, 175, 178, 185

331

Winter, 68, 80, 100, 109, 105,
    112, 175, 179–186, 189, 192,
    203, 204, 208, 293, 294
Wisdom, 22, 95, 130, 133, 193,
    244, 336, 337, 344–350, 407
Workers, 11, 93, 111, 243, 292,
    313, 315, 351–363, 365,
    375, 377, 428

Worship, 16, 87, 92, 132, 135,
    142, 206, 209, 261, 303,
    354, 355, 360, 364

Year's Round, The, 50, 158,
    187–204
Youth, 162, 332, 335–343, 418